Canadian Literature in English

VOLUME TWO

W. J. Keith

Canadian Literature in English

REVISED AND EXPANDED EDITION

Volume Two

The Porcupine's Quill

Library and Archives Canada Cataloguing in Publication

Keith, W. J. (William John), 1934–
Canadian literature in English / W. J. Keith. – Rev. ed.

Includes bibliographies and index.
ISBN-13: 978-0-88984-283-0 (v. 1)
ISBN-13: 978-0-88984-285-4 (v. 2)

1. Canadian literature (English) – History and criticism.
I. Title.

PS8071.K45 2006 C810'.9 C2006-904471-6

1 2 3 4 • 08 07 06

Published by The Porcupine's Quill, 68 Main St, Erin, Ontario N0B 1T0.
http://www.sentex.net/~pql

Readied for the press by John Metcalf.
Copy edited by Doris Cowan.

Represented in Canada by the Literary Press Group.
Trade orders are available from University of Toronto Press.

We acknowledge the support of the Ontario Arts Council and the Canada Council for the Arts for our publishing program. The financial support of the Government of Canada through the Book Publishing Industry Development Program is also gratefully acknowledged. Thanks, also, to the Government of Ontario through the Ontario Media Development Corporation's OMDC Book Fund.

Canada Council for the Arts — Conseil des Arts du Canada

Canada

ONTARIO ARTS COUNCIL
CONSEIL DES ARTS DE L'ONTARIO

The formation of a canon ... is the key element in the self-understanding of any literary culture.

– Philip Marchand

Americans and Canadians are not the same ... Put simply, south of you you have Mexico and south of us we have you.

– Margaret Atwood
(speaking on 'Canadian American Relations' at Harvard)

If contemporary Canadian writers were less hasty to capitulate to what the international market appears to want, they might eventually create novels sufficiently committed to local detail to achieve universal resonance.

– Stephen Henighan

Table of Contents

References

To avoid excessive footnoting, references have been incorporated into the text. Details for shortened entries will be found readily enough in 'Further Reading' under the individual author discussed, the author of the quotation (if a notable Canadian writer), or the appropriate subsections ('Interviews', 'Fiction', etc.).

Abbreviations

ABCMA: *Annotated Bibliography of Canada's Major Authors.* For details, see 'Further Reading: Reference Books'.

CEECT: Centre for Editing Early Canadian Texts (Ottawa: Carleton University Press).

CCP: Canadian Poetry Press (London, Ontario).

CWTW: *Canadian Writers and Their Works.* For details, see 'Further Reading: Reference Books'.

DLB: *Dictionary of Literary Biography.* For details, see 'Further Reading: Reference Books'.

ECW: Either *Essays on Canadian Writing*, an academic journal, or ECW Press, a publishing company which grew out of the journal.

LHC: *Literary History of Canada.* For details, see 'Further Reading: Reference Books'.

M&S: McClelland and Stewart, 'the Canadian Publishers' (Toronto).

MQUP: McGill-Queens University Press (Montréal).

NCL: New Canadian Library (M&S).

OUP: Oxford University Press (Toronto branch).

PCL: *Profiles in Canadian Literature.* For details, see 'Further Reading: Reference Books'.

UTP: University of Toronto Press.

UTQ: *University of Toronto Quarterly.*

Introductory Note to Volume Two

Volume One consists of three parts: the first covers what I call the Early Stages – the beginnings of Canadian literature in Prose, Poetry, and Fiction; the second part is devoted to Poetry; the third, to Drama and Prose.

The present volume covers Fiction. Then follows 'Twenty Years After', an update referring to all genres and including a brief discussion of those whom I consider to be the most impressive writers to have appeared in the intervening years since 1985. Also included is a new 'Polemical Conclusion' and a brief appendix entitled 'A Note on "Postmodernism", Jargon, etc.' The volume concludes with a detailed Further Reading section, which lists works on individual genres, the main titles by individual authors, the most accurate and accessible editions of their work, and recommended biographical and literary-critical books. This section, at the time of printing, is the most up-to-date bibliography on the subject, and the most convenient guide for further exploration of Canadian Literature.

Part Four

Fiction

Chapter 9

Laying the Foundations

Fiction in Canada, as we have seen, endured a long and uncomfortable gestation. No novelists of unquestioned importance emerged in the early years, though individual works of fiction survive as successful but isolated attempts to come to grips with the country and its people in imaginative terms. But there were no masterpieces. To attain any commercial success Canadian writers were forced to adapt their attitudes and methods for readers abroad. Many proved remarkably successful in demonstrating that Canadian writing could gain a hearing, if only at a fairly low cultural level, but their achievements merely drew attention to the need for work of higher literary quality. The popularity of most of these writers can be explained by their shrewd but often crude blend of romance and realism. Their plots were generally melodramatic and contrived, but the settings seemed both authentic and excitingly different. The majority of these stories, indeed, involved settlement, the important national subject ultimately to be explored with impressive if earnest thoroughness by the first significant Canadian novelist, Frederick Philip Grove.

Gilbert Parker began his career with a series of stories about the northwest (which he had not at that time visited) and went on to write a number of historical romances set in French Canada. The best known of these is *The Seats of the Mighty* (1896), which purports to tell the story of the man who led Wolfe's troops up the cliffs to the Plains of Abraham in 1759. Although it is based on an actual memoir, Parker transforms his material into the stuff of soap-opera romance, filling his scenes with suspense (duels, battles), romantic attachments (full of erotic mystery), and what used to be called derring-do. The book inevitably recalls – and, since Parker much admired it, was probably intended to recall – Kirby's *The Golden Dog*, but here the romantic conventions are not rooted in saving historical detail. Parker lived most of his life in London, and his work was doubtless popular with English schoolboys, but it has no place in the history of the novel as a serious art form.

Much the same must be said of the Rev. Charles Gordon, who wrote his enormously popular novels under the pseudonym of Ralph Connor. Gordon was a Presbyterian minister who found in fiction of adventure a means of inculcating what he considered desirable virtues in sugared-pill guise. In *Black Rock* (1898) and *The Sky Pilot* (1899) he wrote of missionary activity in the west (with which he was familiar), but is best known for *The Man from Glengarry* (1901), which celebrates the past history of his native Ontario county. Connor's moralism is dazzlingly simplistic: his heroes always overcome their wicked adversaries, preferably by moral force but if necessary – and it generally is necessary – by physical prowess. His Christianity seems not so much muscular as pugnacious; in *The Man from Glengarry* any amount of violence (but not, of course, sex) is permissible so long as it leads ultimately to the greater glory of God. But Connor wrote his violently didactic romantic fiction within the regional local-colour tradition. This novel (along with a related volume of short stories, *Glengarry Schooldays,* 1902) retains an interest by virtue of its striking if somewhat idealized genre pictures of life in eastern Ontario in the last half of the nineteenth century. But it is cliché-ridden, predictable stuff, demonstrating all too clearly that Connor's devotees (in Britain and the United States as well as in Canada) were ill-equipped to respond to the challenges of complex, probing fiction.

Robert Stead was first inspired to write by Connor's example, and his early novels, though offering convincing accounts of prairie life, set against that background sensational stories that veer between melodrama and western romance. *The Homesteaders* (1916) has been justly characterized as 'the central romance of western settlement' (Harrison 90), but his work shows an increasing interest in the potentialities of realism, and in *Grain* (1926), the story of a clumsy, stubborn farm boy, he produced – almost in spite of himself – a novel of considerable subtlety that provides a worthy prelude to the more sustained work of Grove. It is a book that challenges some of the basic clichés of its kind: Gander Stake refuses to enlist, in part for selfish reasons, but is presented as a non-romantic hero who knows instinctively that 'the war must be won by wheat' (Ch. 14); he is a timid, inarticulate lover who fails; above all, he is attached to the land but comes to accept the world of the machine. As novelist Stead shares with his chief character a combination of clumsiness and solidity. Opening self-consciously, as if undecided about the proper narrative tone, Stead seems to grow into an understanding of his character's true worth. Had he lived in a country with an established cultural tradition and firm critical standards, he might have been spurred to produce fiction of unquestionable merit. As it is, *Grain* is frustrating because it never quite achieves its potential; for that very reason, however, it is an essential text for anyone seriously concerned with the evolution of the Canadian novel.

Stead's homesteaders are generally of English-Canadian origin, but settlers came to the prairies from all parts of Europe, and their struggles were duly chronicled in fiction. The novelists in question include not only Grove but Laura Salverson and Martha Ostenso in *The Viking Heart* and *Wild Geese* respectively. Neither can be considered a major writer, but these two books are important in adding a new dimension to our literary image of the prairies. Salverson was herself an Icelander, and her novel (1923) celebrates the Icelandic settlers who came to Gimli, Manitoba, in the last quarter of the nineteenth century. Influenced by the form of the Icelandic sagas, the book traces, through concentration on a single family, the progress of these settlers over several generations. This was Salverson's first book, and there is an amateurishness about it that is both awkward and engaging. It begins self-consciously and the opening pages are embarrassingly over-written, but Salverson learns as she proceeds, and, although we may suspect that her characters gain success rather too easily, we become involved in their fortunes. This is a sincere and unpretentious book – no masterpiece but solid and humane. *Wild Geese* (1925) is distinctly more professional in construction and tone but closer to the pattern of conventional novel-romance. Indeed, it contains all the standard ingredients of romantic regionalism: a stranger from outside to record events; an explosive family situation; a larger-than-life prairie patriarch; varied descriptions of work on the farm; an effort to root the characters physically and psychically in the land. Once again, realism and romance coexist rather uncomfortably. The book contains excellent pictures of a local community that contains Norwegians, Icelanders, Hungarians, and Indians, and Ostenso has a good ear for the speech-rhythms of immigrants for whom English is a second language. But the plot, though more skillfully controlled than those of Connor and Stead, is equally artificial. In some respects an audacious novel (parts of it read like D. H. Lawrence on an off-day), it fails to transcend its regional conventions.

Ostenso came into brief prominence when *Wild Geese* won a lucrative novel competition in 1925; the pattern was repeated, with more lasting effect, when a similar prize offered by the *Atlantic Monthly* was won by Mazo de la Roche's *Jalna* (1927). *Jalna* is a well-written and agreeable romance; the construction is skillful and the characters clearly differentiated (though they tend to go through their paces like comedy routines). Above all, it introduced an intriguing family, dominated by an irrepressible grandmother, whose fortunes could be extended almost interminably. And they were: between 1927 and 1960 de la Roche produced no less than sixteen novels devoted to the Whiteoaks clan, extending in time from the 1850s to the ageing novelist's present. Of Jalna itself (significantly named after an Anglo-Indian military station) we are told: 'A small army of men was employed to make the semblance of an English park in the forest' (Ch. 2). The writer has dreamed up an English landed family and settled them west of Toronto where they play out their lives and loves in an imaginary romance-world of graceful living and erotic temptation. It is often difficult to remember, in the process of reading these books, that they are set on the western side of the Atlantic. Whippoorwills replace nightingales as background for romantic love encounters, but that is about all the discernible difference.

The extent of Jalna's 'Englishness' has been hotly debated. Its significance resides perhaps in the fact that numerous readers of English extraction or allegiance (whether in England or elsewhere) wanted to believe that the books accurately portrayed a Canadian reality. The series reads like an enormous wish-fulfilment dream. It was doubtless popular because 'the clock seemed to stand still at Jalna' (Ch. 2); changes are always threatening but (comfortingly) they never prevail. Some have argued that the series chronicles the decline of British influence in Canada, but even if this is valid one doubts if de la Roche ever understood why or how it happened. *Jalna* itself – most commentators are agreed that the series quickly deteriorates in standard – is like a foreign shrub miraculously blooming in a far land; it is impressive (at the level of popular romance), but it does not belong.

Before we turn to the work of Grove, mention needs to be made of his almost exact contemporary, Frederick Niven. Niven made a minor reputation in Britain before coming to Canada in 1920, but he wrote his way into the literature of his adopted country with two remarkable historical-documentary novels, *The Flying Years* (1935) and *Mine Inheritance* (1940); a third, *The Transplanted,* published posthumously in 1944 and dealing with British Columbia in the early years of this century, is indisputably a lesser achievement. The first two use the imaginary biographies of representative observer figures to chronicle the rapid development of the west. *The Flying Years* traces the fortunes of Angus Munro from his eviction from Scotland in 1856 to the period immediately following the First World War; *Mine Inheritance,* through the invented diary of David Baxter, follows the Earl of Selkirk's Red River Settlement from its founding in 1812 through the Seven Oaks massacre to the combination of the Hudson's Bay and North West Companies in 1821. Both are notable for their convincing re-creation of history and their panoramic view of the changes in western settlement. Both are episodic in structure and might better be described as history popularized through fiction than historical fiction in the purest sense. Niven aims at what he calls, in the foreword to *Mine Inheritance,* 'essential truth', and this is one of the few novels accompanied by a substantial bibliography. But these are also books about the configurations of memory; Niven's is essentially *human* history that, in authenticity if not in artistry, anticipates the work of Rudy Wiebe. Moreover, Niven writes a graceful, appropriate prose that conveys effectively and effortlessly the elegiac quality of time passing, the 'flying years' of his title. All in all, these solid, unspectacular, but deeply moving books are among the most consistently underrated in Canadian fiction.

Frederick Philip Grove, born Felix Paul Greve, had established a modest literary reputation in Germany before arriving in Canada under dubious circumstances to begin a new life in 1912. There is something peculiarly appropriate about the fact that a European constantly preoccupied, in his own phrase, with 'a search for America' should become the first substantial Canadian novelist. Not only did his personal 'odyssey of an immigrant' resemble in general outline if not in particular detail the experience of many foreign settlers in a new land, but his almost schizophrenic vacillation between the virtues of Europe and America fitted well into a country attempting an always precarious balance between the historical and traditional pull of England and France and the geographical and technological challenge of the United States.

The two phrases quoted in the last paragraph constitute the title and subtitle respectively of an untypical but extremely important early novel. *A Search for America* (1927), which Grove allowed to be read as autobiographical fiction, purports to chronicle the adventures of a rich European, Phil Branden, who loses his fortune and is forced to rely upon his own abilities to survive in the New World. He begins work in a cheap restaurant in Toronto, becomes a book salesman in New York, but later deserts the city, which represents the false America of 'graft, "con", politics, and bossdom' (Book III, Ch. 4), for the country, where he hopes to discover 'the sanity, the good sense, and the good-will which are truly American' (Book I, Ch. 7). After an experience of 'the depths' and work as a hobo in the western farmlands, he decides to become a teacher of immigrants in Canada, where he finds some remaining traces of the ideal that has now been 'abandoned by the U.S.A.' (Book IV, Ch. 5). Although the first-person narrative gives the illusion of realism, the book is meticulously structured and, if examined with care, is found to be a triumph of symbolic artifice, filled with literary reference and philosophical implication. Basically, it presents a quest-journey in which the goal is not so much a country or continent as an attitude of mind.

In the course of the book Brandon is stripped of many European trappings – even his traditional education is found to be a liability in this new environment – but he never loses his Old-World ideals. At one point Branden persuades himself that 'Europe regards the past; America regards the future' (Book IV, Ch. 5), but elsewhere he seems to move from a false aristocracy in Europe only to encounter a false democracy in America. Indeed, his 'real America' (Book I, Ch. 7), we come to suspect, is no more than an ideal brought from Europe by the Pilgrim Fathers. In literary terms, New-World models – Lincoln, Twain, Thoreau – are balanced by equivalent Old-World mentors – Goethe, Tolstoy, the Classical and Judeo-Christian writers – and the book is dedicated to Meredith, Swinburne, and Hardy. *A Search for America* represents a desperate attempt on Grove's part to accept the American democratic dream while at the same time remaining true to his European faith in the superiority of 'the man with vision' (Book I, Ch. 5).

Phil Branden sees himself as 'a pioneer' (Book I, Ch. 3), and the main achievement of his equally pioneering creator was a series of novels beginning with *Settlers of the Marsh* (1925) that explores the situation of literal pioneers and early farmers in the Canadian west. Grove offers a classic presentation of such figures because, while he provides a convincing account of prairie life, his novels transcend the limitations of localized documentary. He is more interested in the psychology of his protagonists, in the always pathetic and often tragic condition that renders the man who is capable of creating a human settlement in virgin territory temperamentally unable to enjoy the fruits of his labour. Grove sees clearly, in a way that lesser writers like Stead and Ostenso did not, that the true pioneer must necessarily fail since his very achievement in humanizing wilderness negates his *raison d'être*. As he notes elsewhere, 'an ideal realized would be an ideal destroyed' (*It Needs to Be Said* 88). His characters are at odds with their families, their friends, even their deepest selves. If they are not defeated by the natural world they seek to dominate, they bring about their own destruction.

This basic pattern (though Grove rings many artistic changes on it) is to be found at its best in *Fruits of the Earth* (1933), which begins with Abe Spalding moving to his new territory and ploughing his first furrow. We see him emerging as the natural leader of the new settlers, but we also see him neglecting the emotional needs of his wife and family in his aggressive urge to power, an urge symbolized by the mechanism he employs to gain domination over the land. By the mid-point in the novel he has built the largest house in the district, but it gives him no satisfaction, and the rest of the book chronicles the decline of his home, his family, and his relationship with the developed community in which he is now superseded. But Abe grows as a human being in inverse relation to the decline in his power and influence. Like most of Grove's protagonists, he eventually asks himself about the ultimate meaning of life. The spiritual versus the material is always an issue in these novels. Despite their superficial connections with prairie realism, they consider the universal dilemma of men tempted to gain the world at the price of their own souls.

Settlers of the Marsh, Our Daily Bread (1928), and *The Yoke of Life* (1930) are all earnestly effective but often stiff and angular novels in which Grove presents variations on his basic theme. At times the general truth is imperfectly linked to the specific situation. In *Settlers of the Marsh* Ellen and Clara, the women in Lindstedt's life, too conveniently symbolize the spirit and the flesh; in *Our Daily Bread* the decline and fall of John Elliott Senior, 'Lear of the prairie' (Ch. 11), is deeply moving, but the members of his family are so numerous and so awkwardly differentiated that the effect is blurred; in *The Yoke of Life* the realistic and emblematic levels of the story are difficult to integrate. It is easy to criticize Grove's novels individually, and George Woodcock has noted how he 'never wrote a book that seemed completely to fulfil his possibilities' (*Odysseus* 149). Cumulatively, however, they are impressive in their solidity and intellectual coherence; the overall effect of his work is greater than the sum of its parts. One reason for Grove's pre-eminence as an early Canadian novelist is that his novels, instead of existing as a mere conglomeration of stories, constitute a clear and recognizable *oeuvre* with a discernible progression from the beginning of his career to the end.

For Grove, what he had to say took precedence over how he said it. Consequently, until the close of his life, he was no startling innovator in the art of fiction. Indeed, the early novels can easily be undervalued because they seem so naively conventional in form. In *The Master of the Mill* (1944), however, Grove extended his subject matter and found it necessary at the same time to extend his technique. His thematic emphasis moves from the producers of wheat to its processors; his protagonists here are not agriculturists but modern-day industrial capitalists. The novel becomes a searching analysis of human power and the capacity of men to enslave both themselves and others, and it is told in a complicated series of time shifts as Sam Clark, an old man verging on senility, relives the past in attempting to make sense of his life as he approaches death. Grove's old preoccupations here take on a new complexity. The book fluctuates violently between the two. Grove employs – somewhat clumsily, to be sure – a battery of modernist devices to catch the sense of linear and psychological time. Above all, the book is dominated by the haunting image of the mill itself, a Frankenstein's monster that man has created but cannot control: 'it seemed as if no human will could stop it, as if, even though the whole population of the earth perished, it would go on producing flour till it had smothered the globe' (Ch. 16). In this late novel Grove offers his most probing critique of human society, and an example to later Canadian novelists of how the novel form can be developed for the discussion of pressing contemporary issues.

Grove is pre-eminent among early Canadian novelists for many reasons. His creation of an extended body of work, involving a systematic examination of human nature in creative terms, has already been mentioned. This enabled him to attain a standard of artistic seriousness unparalleled by any of his predecessors. Only perhaps in Duncan's *The Imperialist* do we find within earlier Canadian tradition a novel clearly based on a firm grasp of the backgrounds of human behaviour, but Duncan was unable to sustain this level of achievement in other work. Grove's position as an immigrant gave him certain advantages here. He came to Canada with experience of other artistic traditions and measured himself against achievements in other literatures. His ambitions were large and his horizons broad. Indeed, his calamitous failure in Germany, partly artistic but primarily moral (he spent a year in jail for fraud), seems to have spurred him to extended creative efforts in Canada. In some respects, his work may be seen as a gigantic exercise in self-justification. He has often been censured for excessive didacticism, but this is more a criticism of the artistic presentation of his moral vision than of the vision itself. He is often unsubtle in driving home his points, in insisting upon the representative significance of a particular action, but this should not blind us to the importance of the deeply considered criticism of life that underlies and buttresses his major fiction.

On other matters, Grove could offer little help. There were many aspects of Canadian experience that, as an immigrant, he could witness from the outside – and this has its own value – but could never fully comprehend. He bore witness in himself to the diverse origins of the Canadian people, but his particular position in a nation twice at war with the country of his origins was inevitably off-centre. Above all, his command of English, though considerable, lacked the stylistic clarity and flexibility necessary to express the finer nuances of his thought. Grove was never quite able to realize his vast ambitions in English. He had a remarkable structural imagination, and was able to create situations within his novels that carried intrinsic emotional and intellectual impact, but they were never fully established through verbal precision and subtlety. Here was a writer and thinker who demonstrated that it was possible to produce serious and compelling fiction in Canada, but for a sense of style Canadian novelists and readers had to look elsewhere.

Morley Callaghan was all that Grove was not. He had no need to search for America since he lived and worked totally within the American grain, his early work appearing in the United States alongside Hemingway, Sherwood Anderson, and Sinclair Lewis. Indeed, his was the first sustained body of fiction in Canada that deliberately associated itself with American rather than European assumptions and traditions. Moreover, it was with very few exceptions a fiction of the city, of urban problems and urban mores. Callaghan caught the experience of life in a North American city – and, if we are in a position to pick up his references, the specific sense of particular Canadian cities – for the first time in our literature. Above all, from a purely artistic standpoint, he is known for the simple – some would say simplistic – directness of his style, for plain language without frills or snags. He displays, in short, a technical professionalism far removed from Grove's lumbering authenticity, but between them (though neither, quite naturally, showed any interest in the other's work) they were able, within the decade of the 1920s, to open up manifold possibilities for serious Canadian fiction.

The strengths and problems surrounding Callaghan's fiction are well illustrated by his first novel, *Strange Fugitive* (1928). The plot is straightforward. Harry Trotter loses his lumber-yard job, deserts his wife, mooches around with friends and other women, becomes a bootlegger, and gets involved in a life of sensual living and violent crime until gunned down by revengeful bootlegging rivals. The book fits smoothly into the context of contemporaneous popular American writing and film, but it is a refreshing new subject for Canadian fiction. What is more, it is told ostensibly in the language of its protagonist, though reflecting a conscious artistic (and moral) decision on Callaghan's part. This prose deliberately eschews metaphor or any elaborate literary effect, emphasizing the raw directness and immediacy of the objects and actions themselves. Once again, this simplicity can be refreshing after the rather heavy, portentous prose favoured by writers not yet emancipated from British (even Victorian) influence. But this effectiveness is bought at a price. While Callaghan wrote here and almost everywhere else as an omniscient narrator, he generally confined himself not only to the language but to the intellectual level of his characters. Trotter is presented in his own terms and, because he is slow and relatively inarticulate, it was difficult for Callaghan to raise the story above the literal level of sordid reality. Trotter's world is one of economic drives, cut-throat competition, and exploitation of all kinds. Callaghan, a thinking but liberal and worldly Catholic, had wider perceptions but could express them only clumsily within his narrative. Trotter's wife considers turning Catholic, and there is some desultory discussion about belief in God, but such references remain intrusive and unintegrated. As a result, *Strange Fugitive* is absorbing but limited.

Callaghan continually had to wrestle with this problem of egalitarian realism – how to create a medium for thought while presenting characters who rarely think. As early as *It's Never Over* (1930), for instance, he includes secondary and clearly representative figures of priest and communist to embody and articulate alternative glosses on his protagonist's dilemma, and this effect is repeated – extended, indeed, as formal debate within the narrative – in several later books. More particularly, under the influence of the Catholic thinker Jacques Maritain, he evolved a fiction that drew elements not only from the conventional novel but from older religious traditions of parable and *exemplum*. It is not accidental that Callaghan's cluster of fictions appearing in the mid-1930s – *Such Is My Beloved* (1934), *They Shall Inherit the Earth* (1935), and *More Joy in Heaven* (1937) – have biblical titles that invite or insist upon extrapolated moral and religious meanings. These are comparatively short books lacking the detailed descriptions of most novels, and might be better categorized as novellas. In *Such Is My Beloved,* Callaghan presents a Catholic priest (in the terminology Robertson Davies later made popular, a fool-saint) who befriends two street girls and tries to save them from a life of prostitution. The extremes of Christian idealism and hard-nosed practicalities clash head-on. Sacred and profane love are found to contain startling interconnections, and Callaghan is more interested in the profound implications of his theme than in establishing the surface plausibility of his story. But he pares down the story so rigorously to its essentials that we can accept it without difficulty on the level of fable. There is no question of oversimplification because the normal realistic criteria no longer apply. Moreover, the trained intelligence of the priest provides Callaghan with an excuse to introduce clear hints of the larger, more general issues implied in the narrative. The Christ-like Father Dowling becomes the centre of his own parable. Similarly, in *More Joy in Heaven* Kip Caley (criminal-innocent rather than fool-saint) re-enacts in his contemporary Toronto a version of the prodigal son story with a sour ending that challenges its readers to rethink some of their basic social assumptions. By forcing it to recognize its origins in parable, Callaghan teases us into thought.

Callaghan was virtually silent throughout the 1940s, but embarked on a new phase of fictional activity with *The Loved and the Lost* in 1951. In these later novels we detect a resolute determination on Callaghan's part to write ambitious, profound fiction. His style remains simple – at its worst it can be decidedly slack – but he has learned the disadvantages of avoiding metaphor or literary complexity. In many respects, *The Loved and the Lost* recalls the pre-war fables. Peggy Sanderson, the white girl who tries to break down colour and class divisions in Montréal single-handedly by associating with poor black musicians, functions as a parable-innocent like Father Dowling and Kip Caley. But if she inhabits the ambiguous centre of this impressive but elusive novel, Callaghan is careful to present her from the viewpoint of Jim McAlpine, an intellectual who, though ultimately found wanting, nevertheless provides the thinking consciousness guiding our response. The whole effect is much more elaborate (though not necessarily more successful) than the earlier work, and is achieved through a deliberate artistry. Peggy herself is made to turn Montréal objects into resonant symbols in the frequently quoted scene where she takes McAlpine to see a leopard wood-carving and an ancient church (Ch. 5). Throughout the book words like 'black' and 'white' and allied words like 'dark', 'night', 'light', and 'snow' accumulate complex associations, and Callaghan employs a host of imagistic, symbolic, and even mythic devices to create an intricate, highly literary texture which is notable without being rich.

Similarly, the titles of *The Many Colored Coat* (1960), with its conspicuous allusion to the Old Testament story of Joseph, and *A Passion in Rome* (1961), with its punning insistence on both the amatory and religious senses of 'passion', signal a self-conscious concern with image and symbol, and force the stories above the literal level. These novels get increasingly longer and more prolix without becoming more subtle or probing; the relatively commonplace characters are hardly more rounded than in the fables, and tend to collapse under a weight of words. And Callaghan's later books, though shorter, display a distinct falling off in fictional power and intellectual interest. The old Callaghan worlds are revisited – that of gangsters in *Close to the Sun Again* (1977), that of hookers in *The Enchanted Pimp* (1978, revised as *Our Lady of the Snows*, 1990). It is all rather coarse, tired – and dated. Late Callaghan comes dangerously close to self-parody. An impression of great talent dissipated is unavoidable, and *A Fine and Private Place* (1975), where the central figure is a neglected author of asserted but never demonstrated eminence, living in Toronto and writing books that sound remarkably like Callaghan's, only confirms this. When a writer is reduced to putting on scanty disguise to lecture his readers on the importance of his work, the effect is embarrassing.

The discussion of length in Callaghan's later novels reminds us that he has a further reputation as a short-story writer. Indeed, it has sometimes been argued that this represents his finest achievement. There can be no doubt that his example helped to establish the short story as an important genre within modern Canadian literature. His virtues of directness, clarity, and (when at his best) economy all show themselves to advantage in this concentrated form. Callaghan is a master at creating small situations that generate profound meanings: a plain woman is caught stealing a dress in which to get married; a priest gives absolution to a dying woman against the wishes of her husband; a woman is both distressed and ecstatic when her sister's fiancé displays his covert feelings for her. These are simple situations, but they are intensely human, and Callaghan tells them cleanly, without pretentiousness or sentimentality or any attempt to exalt them into a weakening generality. Story by story, they are effective; yet if we read them in bulk a certain monotony becomes evident. Callaghan's consistent skill suggests a formula. We know a story will end appropriately but without undue sensationalism; we know that, perfect in itself, it will stay within the bounds of its expectations. All this suggests that the novella was Callaghan's ideal form – one that offered him sufficient amplitude but without the sustained challenge of the full-length novel. His best work, then, is found in those middle-length fictions in which he gives us enough but not too much.

The appearance of both Grove and Callaghan in the 1920s promised an imminent flowering of serious Canadian fiction. Unfortunately, this did not materialize. No novelists of major importance came into prominence in the 1930s, perhaps because of the economic consequences of the Depression. At any rate, Canadians with an interest in fiction had to wait until 1941, and the publication of important first works by Hugh MacLennan and Sinclair Ross, for significant developments. Nevertheless a number of novels and short stories of individual merit were published in the interim, and they deserve brief treatment here.

Had Raymond Knister lived, he might well have developed into a distinguished writer of fiction. He completed two promising though imperfect novels, but his best prose work is undoubtedly to be found in his short stories and sketches, some of which appeared in the Parisian *This Quarter* along with early work by Callaghan. This is somewhat surprising, since his subject matter, generally set in rural Ontario, is closer to Grove's. His fiction is full of lovingly detailed accounts of farm work – picking and packing peaches, raking, ploughing, tending horses, etc. Nothing much happens in these stories; the mood is all. He is a master of indirection – the main point is generally left unspoken but recognized beneath the surface of events. Because these stories were not collected in volume form until the 1970s, it is difficult to assess the extent of their possible influence as a result merely of magazine publication. They are contemporary with early Grove (the two were acquainted), but look forward in some respects to the short stories of Ross, and even of Ernest Buckler. They are often marred by pompous phrasing, but Knister's ability to communicate the monotonous but oddly satisfying texture of rural life was considerable. There is enough in these stories, together with his poetry already discussed, to guarantee him a distinct if minor place in Canadian literature, but one continually gets an impression while reading him of extreme promise rather than assured achievement.

The decade that witnessed the lengthening, ever more threatening shadows of the Second World War also saw the publication of two novels portraying Canadian experience in the First. The little-known *Generals Die in Bed* (1930), by Charles Yale Harrison, occupies the extreme verge of fiction as it adjoins documentary. Intended to offer a representative account of an ordinary soldier in the ranks, it presents a determinedly unheroic perspective. 'It's beer we want. To hell with glory' (Ch. 6) sums up the whole. We never know even the name of the narrator, and learn nothing about who he is or where he comes from, save that he is Canadian. The characteristic pattern of such narratives – from embarkation through initiation into the trenches, attacks 'over the top', bayonet warfare, to wounding near Amiens – apparently coincides for the most part with the author's own experience. Harrison can hardly be designated a novelist (he wrote nothing else even remotely approaching the standard of this first book), but *Generals Die in Bed* is nevertheless a minor masterpiece. It is told in the present tense, in short unadorned sentences;

often a single sentence is set apart as a paragraph, producing a jumpy, disturbing but ultimately deadening effect as one event harshly and remorselessly succeeds another. There is a starkness, almost a nakedness, about the whole that is awesomely impressive. A scene of looting at Arras, when army discipline breaks down completely, is especially vivid; here and elsewhere Harrison is not afraid to show basically decent men (Canadians) behaving badly under appalling conditions. A resolutely honest book, it stands up well among other books of its kind – and in the inter-war years its kind was legion.

In approach it offers a total contrast to Philip Child's *God's Sparrows* (1937). Child's liberal humanism belongs to the pre-1914 years, and the effectiveness of his book derives in part from the forthrightness with which he chronicles the descent of an optimistic but naive society into the hell of modern war. Unlike Harrison's book, this novel portrays the family and social background of its protagonist in detail and depth. It is a comfortable middle-class world (one can imagine its members rubbing shoulders with the inhabitants of Jalna); in the early sections Child seems to be presenting the subject matter of Galsworthy with a technique suggesting though never equalling the approach of Forster or Woolf. But the second half, though containing a number of memorable and worthy scenes, reveals the limitations of Child's approach. The realities of the trenches were beyond the range of his quiet, smooth-flowing, reasonable style, and any radical stylistic change would have split the novel apart. We come to detect a stilted artifice in his principal characters; the procedures of the conventional novel prove inadequate for the presentation of this new, barely imaginable world. Child can reproduce the intellectual shock of Dan Thatcher as he moves from southern Ontario to the trenches, but he lacks the artistic and intellectual resources to paint a convincing picture of men fighting, in Yeats's phrase, like weasels in a hole. It is both possible and proper to respect his intentions, but in this novel his reach ultimately exceeds his grasp.

Child's novels are invariably intelligent and skillful, though he always found it difficult to reconcile a traditional plot interest (often contrived to the point of melodrama) with his sober humanist didacticism. Moreover, he inhibited readers from discovering a unified approach to his work by attempting a number of different kinds of fiction. These include a historical novel, *The Village of Souls* (1933), and what might be called a psychological spy thriller, *Mr. Ames against Time* (1949), but in my view the generally neglected *Day of Wrath* (1945) is the most consistently satisfying of his books. A story of Jewish persecution in Nazi Germany, it has been criticized for its type-characters and lapses in realistic credibility. But if we approach it as a moral fable comparable with the work of Callaghan's middle period or with Douglas LePan's *The Deserter* (1964), it reveals itself as a stylized and profound meditation on human evil confronted by a doomed but obstinately positive human dignity. The limited and simply differentiated cast of characters and the obviously non-realistic symbolic patterns that they form make up a novel with the structural artifice of a morality play. The book pursues its philosophical and often dream-like course to a relentless but intellectually satisfying conclusion, and it stands not unworthily alongside later and more daring fictional explorations of Nazi atrocity, MacLennan's *Voices in Time* (1980) and Hugh Hood's *Black and White Keys* (1982).

A writer with very different talents, who just made his début in the 1930s, also deserves consideration here. Thomas H. Raddall brought out a volume of short stories in 1939, but his most characteristic work as a writer of historical romance began in 1942 with *His Majesty's Yankees.* Raddall came as a child from England to Nova Scotia and steeped himself in Maritime history. Becoming a professional writer, he managed to establish a working compromise between his interest in the past and the need to satisfy public taste as a means of earning his daily bread. In terms of plot, *His Majesty's Yankees* is hardly less artificial than Kirby's *Golden Dog* or Parker's *Seats of the Mighty,* but in concerning himself with the evolution of dissident Nova Scotians into uneasy Loyalists during the 1770s Raddall explores a serious theme conscientiously and responsibly. What ultimately makes the difference is his scrupulous historical accuracy (transcending the mere creation of convincing genre pictures) and his style which, though unostentatious, is always appropriate and often quietly and movingly eloquent.

But the temptation for Raddall was to subordinate the less dramatic and exciting virtues of historical authenticity to the claims of swashbuckling heroism and romance. *The Governor's Lady* (1960), a late book also set during the American War of Independence, maintains a fine balance, but a novel like *Pride's Fancy* (1946), with its emphasis, to quote the blurb of a paperback reprint, on 'a Negro uprising, a search for missing treasure on the Spanish main, hotly contested sea-fights, sword-play, and suspense', becomes no more than a thrilling yarn. In his short stories, however, especially those chronicling incidents in the history of 'our town' (= 'Oldport', = Liverpool, Nova Scotia) and gathered together in *The Wedding Gift and Other Stories* (1947), Raddall impressively re-creates a community deriving strength and sustenance from its regional roots. And in *The Nymph and the Lamp* (1950) he was able to produce a twentieth-century romance which is nevertheless, in his own words, 'a story of real people in real Canadian scenes' (*In My Time* 195), thereby producing a poignant story both human and timeless. Raddall was an unpretentious novelist content to be first and foremost a storyteller, but, although the proportions are different, he shares the basic ingredients of romance and realism with his probing and ambitious Maritime contemporary, Hugh MacLennan.

'There is as yet no tradition of Canadian literature.' MacLennan made this observation in the foreword to his first published novel, *Barometer Rising* (1941), and we can now see that, if Grove is the first important Canadian novelist, MacLennan became the first to articulate a Canadian tradition in fictional terms, virtually creating it by prodding his readers into becoming aware of themselves and of their country. The means by which he achieved this goal were twofold. First, he realized that a Canadian fiction, to be recognized as such, must be firmly rooted in Canadian soil, that a novelist must provide real places for his settings and describe them in terms verging, if necessary, on the documentary. As a result, in Robert Kroetsch's phrasing, he 'dared to name the names of my world' (Cameron ed., *Hugh MacLennan 1982* 136). *Barometer Rising*, for instance, begins with the naming of Halifax and goes on to offer a minute description of 'the details of Halifax' as seen from Citadel Hill. That this seems an unremarkable procedure to us is a tribute to MacLennan's success and to his influence. George Woodcock has called the book 'the first novel about a *specifically* Canadian city' (*Hugh MacLennan*, 1969, 46), and if that praise technically belongs to Callaghan it belongs morally to MacLennan, since *Barometer Rising* could only have taken place in Canada while most of Callaghan's novels might have been set in a number of North American cities.

MacLennan's second way of establishing the foundations of an unequivocally Canadian fiction was by deliberately concerning himself with matters of immediate importance to Canada and its inhabitants. *Barometer Rising*, set in the First World War but published during the Second, explains the way in which wartime conditions, in taking men away from their country, led them to experience on their own pulses the complex fate of being a Canadian. Moreover, the Halifax explosion of 1917, the climactic event in the novel, dramatically initiated Canada into the technological dangers of the twentieth century. *Two Solitudes* (1945), this time looking at the beginning of one war from the end of another, tackles the central Canadian political and cultural problem: the uneasy coexistence of English- and French-Canadians. *The Precipice* (1948) examines the relations between Canada and the United States; *Each Man's Son* (1951) explores the sombre legacy of puritanism, and so on. Like Grove, MacLennan is a didactic novelist, a teacher or nothing, and his didacticism has an unabashedly nationalistic flavour.

While this didacticism need not detract from his success as a writer, it does mean, as in the case of Grove, that content takes precedence over artistry. MacLennan's situation, however, forced him to pay special attention to the latter. First, he needed to find the best means of expressing what he wanted to say in fictional terms; at the same time, he had to produce work that would gain him a hearing not only in Canada but, for economic reasons, in the United States, where his Canadian subject matter was likely to be a liability rather than an asset. In the event, he evolved his own unique version of the 'romance and realism' formula that had been the mainstay of so many earlier novelists. He took over the sanctioned recipe of the traditional popular novel – generally, of course, a love story – and used it as a vehicle to contain his own by no means conventional (because assertively nationalistic) way of looking at the world. Oddly enough, his Classical training (he had gained a Ph.D in Classics from Princeton) unexpectedly – and, be it noted, unconsciously – stood him in good stead. The 'Odysseus ever returning' pattern, MacLennan's preoccupation with a hero's quest for his lost homeland, which George Woodcock has traced as a recurring motif throughout his work, is basically a structure of universal appeal that enables him to maintain interest at the level of plot while at the same time leaving him free to create a realistic setting into which to insert local (i.e., Canadian) significance.

Sometimes, however, plot and meaning remain in an uneasy tension, and this results in the stiff, angular quality in MacLennan's fiction that so many commentators have recognized. In *Barometer Rising*, for instance, the Halifax explosion of 1917 provides him with an opportunity for some brilliant documentary writing, but it is also an intrusive *deus ex machina* device that conveniently kills off certain characters in a highly artificial resolution of the plot. Grove (who recognized a significant fellow artist by writing a letter of appreciation to MacLennan as soon as the novel appeared) voiced a related criticism when he judiciously observed that 'the problem of the book is brushed aside by a calamity' (*Letters* 414). Similarly, the marriage between French-Canadian Paul and English-Canadian Heather at the close of *Two Solitudes* is a neat plot conclusion that proves woefully inadequate at the level of socio-political ideas. And in *Each Man's Son*, where the Odysseus myth is most conspicuous (though in MacLennan's version wife is killed as well as suitor), the violence is again too pat in the way it rewards Dr Ainslie with a surrogate son.

The tyrannical demands of conventional plot, we can now see, often tend to overwhelm the subtler requirements of thematic propriety. Or, to put it another way, MacLennan found difficulty in reconciling the urge to instruct with the need to entertain. In *The Watch That Ends the Night* (1959), however, he achieved an extraordinary artistic breakthrough. He still adapts his central situation from a romance plot – the Odysseus story now combines with Tennyson's in 'Enoch Arden', the return of a wanderer presumed dead to discover that, unlike Penelope, his wife has married again – but this time the story is infused with a moving personal urgency. The book was written after the death of MacLennan's first wife, who had always been an invalid, and he draws upon their poignant but gruelling shared experience when they both lived, as it were, under the shadow of death. This is a profoundly religious book. While a religious element has always been strong in MacLennan's fiction – one could argue, for example, that the Christian pattern of death and rebirth is just as significant as Woodcock's Odysseus myth in *Barometer Rising* – here it becomes the main concern of the fiction. This is, quite literally, a novel about death and coming to terms with the fact of death; out of death's threat, however, comes a broadening awareness of the wonder of life. The book is quintessentially Canadian in its details (Montréal during the 1930s is unforgettably evoked, and most of the Canadian themes that had preoccupied earlier novels recur here); yet in offering an impressive portrayal of a non-sectarian religious experience, MacLennan produces one of the most ambitious works in Canadian fiction by tackling a subject of universal concern.

But this new expansion of vision is matched by a similar development in technique. *The Watch That Ends the Night* is MacLennan's first published novel to be narrated in the first person, and the personal cadences that come through the writing help to break down the stiffness evident in his earlier work. George Stewart, the narrator, is a passive figure – the action and physical suffering in the novel are shared by Jerome Martell (a socialistically committed doctor cast in the conventional heroic mould) and Catherine, the woman whom they both love. But Stewart is the ideal narrator for this particular novel. Like MacLennan, he is a university lecturer and also a writer and broadcaster on socio-political topics. MacLennan has thus created a didactic protagonist as much a teacher as himself, one who can communicate his own sentiments and experience with a minimum of strain. Moreover, as a basically decent man struggling desperately to come to terms with decades of depression, social inequality, and the threat of Fascism, he is a modern, thoughtful Everyman, and we respond sympathetically to his sometimes unremarkable ideas and attitudes because we share with him the intensely realized human and social situation that provokes them. This is a novel that stoutly asserts the importance of the individual (MacLennan implies that the George Stewarts of this world are at least as worthy of respect as the Jerome Martells) in a threatening period of conflicting political ideologies. Ultimately, however, the characters pass through their respective dark nights of the soul to some form of religious transcendence; the novel is refreshingly old-fashioned enough to celebrate the strength and resilience of the human spirit.

Return of the Sphinx (1967) may be considered characteristic of MacLennan's work because (as usual, a little ahead of his times) he finds his subject in the almost universal social and political unrest that dominated the late 1960s. For his particular example he returns once more to English-French tensions in Canada. It is as if, with the advent of the Québec 'quiet revolution' that was threatening to become not-so-quiet (though the novel appeared three years before the Montréal kidnappings of 1970), MacLennan felt the need to reconsider the subject he had already treated, somewhat over-confidently, in *Two Solitudes.* Although he makes one fictive experiment – Alan Ainslie, who had appeared as a boy in *Each Man's Son,* is introduced as an adult here – the book returns to the standard omniscient-author tradition, and seems a much more conventional novel than its immediate predecessor. It lacks the depth of *The Watch That Ends the Night,* and the reader can be forgiven for wondering if MacLennan understands the younger generation, which naturally plays a large part here, as thoroughly as he understands his own.

But in *Voices in Time* (1981) MacLennan makes a daring new departure. The novel is set some fifty years in the future, after a nuclear devastation triggered by computer error – an event that suggests the Halifax explosion of *Barometer Rising* amplified to world-wide scale. Civilization as we know it has collapsed, and one of the handful of survivors, interpreting records preserved through sheer chance, tries to re-create events in what for him is the distant past – North America in 1970, Europe in the 1930s and early 1940s. He does so by arranging diary entries, playing over tapes, transcribing fragments of autobiography, thus creating a coherent account with the help of his own memories.

As in *The Watch That Ends the Night,* MacLennan moves back from a particular point in time further and further into the past in an attempt to reveal the causes of the current situation. The technique, which displays him at his boldest, creaks somewhat at the beginning, but as he finds his main subject in the story of Conrad Dehmel involved against his will in the horrors of Hitler's Germany, the novel gains momentum and ultimately takes fire. Dehmel's story, central to twentieth-century experience, is offered as a modern tragedy at a time when we were beginning to think that the larger tragic sense was no longer possible in our world. Once again the basic plot – Dehmel, a gentile, ostensibly joining the Nazis in the hope of saving the Jewish girl he loves – belongs to romance, but upon this foundation MacLennan has built a remarkable structure which (to change metaphors) takes the pulse of modern civilization. The novel begins in Montréal – or, rather, the ruins of Montréal – but it is a Canadian book that speaks to the world. In some respects it recalls Grove's *The Master of the Mill* in its scope and range as well as in its somewhat cumbersome presentation. But it is a novel that unquestionably achieves amplitude and impresses as a remarkable act of imaginative courage, especially from a writer in his seventies. *The Watch That Ends the Night* and *Voices in Time* are the high points in a consistently solid and engaged artistic career that reveals MacLennan as one of the founding fathers of serious Canadian fiction.

Chapter 10

Establishing a Tradition of Fiction

MacLennan, as we have seen, not only demonstrated in his early work that a Canadian fictional tradition was possible, but laid solid foundations for its building. Yet it is doubtful if, in his later life, he could have produced *The Watch That Ends the Night* or *Voices in Time* had he not profited from the technical experiments undertaken by many of his contemporaries. What surprises modern readers about Grove and the early MacLennan is their initial naivety about some of the basic techniques of their trade, their apparent ignorance concerning the modernist principles of fiction-writing that had been commonly preached in Britain and the United States since the beginning of the century. But the 1940s and 1950s saw the emergence of a number of writers who were not prepared to confine themselves to the older fictional methods. For the literary historian these are decades with little coherent shape so far as Canadian fiction is concerned. Certain common, albeit overlapping, thematic or generic strands – humour, satire, the Jewish dimension, and the experience of war and violence – can be isolated, and these provide some elements of continuity in the discussion to follow. But no easily discernible, cumulative pattern emerges. Instead, individual novelists are best seen as writing what they wanted to write, often influenced by Canadian predecessors but showing no conspicuous sense of belonging to a recognizable group or movement. Yet their combined efforts, achieved by boldness and determination, not only opened up the possibilities for fiction in Canada but produced numerous works of lasting merit.

One especially independent spirit was Howard O'Hagan, a law student turned wilderness guide, whose first and best book, *Tay John,* was published in England at the most unpromising time imaginable – the opening of the Second World War. Not surprisingly, despite its quality, it fell flat, and although an American reprint appeared in 1960 it was not generally discovered until it became available in the New Canadian Library in 1974. The book has not therefore been particularly influential, but it represents a radical break from the standard novelistic fare of its period. It is, in fact, the closest in style, technique, and attitude of any Canadian novel to the work of Joseph Conrad.

Tay John, a corrupt version of Tête Jaune, is a half-breed, the son of a Shuswap Indian woman who had been raped by a renegade white missionary. His life is doomed because he belongs neither to the Indian tribe nor to the white civilization currently intruding on Indian territory; inhabiting a mysterious borderland between the two, he is accepted by neither. But the distinction of the novel lies not so much in the story itself as in the way O'Hagan tells it. The first part, 'Legend', presents the early life of Tay John as an Indian myth complete with supernatural detail (and, indeed, O'Hagan draws on authentic Indian beliefs in this section). Later, when Tay John moves towards the world of the white man, omniscient narration is replaced by the voice of Jack Denham, a white wilderness man who tries to piece together the half-breed's story from 'Hearsay' (the title of Part 2) – from letters, interviews, occasional personal encounters, etc. Denham, in other words, plays Conrad's Marlow to Tay John's Lord Jim. And the resemblances to Conrad are not confined to fictional method. They involve the employment of exotic setting, a brooding meditation on the world of violent action, a basic philosophic attitude (uniting a hard practicality with an abiding sense of mystery), and a style that, though sometimes vague, can combine awesomeness with a rough eloquence.

I do not mean to imply, however, that O'Hagan is derivative – merely that he learned from Conrad as genuine artists habitually learn from each other; Conrad's technical audacity was something which Canadian fiction had hitherto lacked. The novel is important for its serious integration of Indian material into English-Canadian fiction, and above all for its extraordinary evocation of wilderness. Denham at one point describes his story as 'An adventure. A real one. Blood in it' (Ch. 5). That is accurate enough, but it also involves an elaborately symbolic drama that renounces contemporary realism to attain a complex fictional mode in which elements of moral allegory, dream-vision, and psychological insight are welded into a perplexing but weirdly satisfying union.

O'Hagan also wrote a volume of short stories, *The Woman Who Got On at Jasper Station* (1963), and another novel, *The School-Marm Tree,* written in the 1950s but not published until 1977. These reinforce his standing as a powerful writer with unusual gifts (the novel is an extended fable, elemental and almost Lawrentian in tone, about what can happen when men and mountains meet). It is, however, for *Tay John* that he will be remembered.

Sinclair Ross's *As For Me and My House* appeared in 1941, and when Roy Daniells came to write an introduction for the New Canadian Library edition of 1957 he could still describe it as 'a book so unfamiliar to the Canadian public'. That it is now one of the most widely read Canadian novels gives some indication of the burgeoning interest in our literature in recent decades, but its general neglect in the 1940s and 1950s does not mean that it was unknown to younger novelists. Margaret Laurence, for instance, has acknowledged that it had 'an enormous impact' upon her when she read it within a few years of its publication (Introduction to Ross's *The Lamp At Noon* 7). *As For Me and My House* can reasonably be described, indeed, as a seminal work in Canadian fiction.

The story of the Bentleys, reluctant minister and frustrated minister's wife, with its forbidding portrait of the narrow-minded and false-fronted town of Horizon, its evocation of dust-bowl farming and the depressed 1930s, has established itself as the quintessential prairie novel. But artistically the plot is nothing, the telling everything. The story is narrated by Mrs Bentley in diary form; through the day-to-day accounts of her husband's unhappiness as it leads from religious hypocrisy to apparent sexual infidelity, accounts that reveal her own character as much as his, we experience a claustrophobic sense of emotional and spiritual deprivation. Ross achieves this through a simple use of imagery that turns inexorably into symbol. The architectural false fronts of Horizon reflect the personal false fronts of its inhabitants (the Bentleys included); the dust that seeps into their houses becomes metaphorical and encrusts their souls; the drought develops into an emblem of inner dryness; its wind suggests a biblical whirlwind out of which the Lord who is *not* served ('as for me and my house we will serve the Lord', Joshua 24:15) is menacingly silent. The economic depression itself comes to stand for a general human malaise.

Ross was extraordinarily bold in choosing Mrs Bentley for his narrator, but she is as convincing a woman as any in our literature, and her cadences dominate the book. Her tired, resigned, repetitive monotone is both moving and pathetic. 'Because you're a hypocrite you lose your self-respect, because you lose your self-respect you lose your initiative and self-belief – it's the same vicious circle, every year closing a little tighter' (1957 ed. 85). Ross could suggest monotony without ever allowing his book to become monotonous. He also showed mastery in the use of a narrator who is by no means wholly reliable, though this technical experiment led to misreadings in the early years. Even as sophisticated a reader as Daniells could describe Mrs Bentley as 'pure gold' when the phrase fits Ross's technique but not his protagonist. We sympathize with Mrs Bentley, but we also watch her deceiving herself. She only partly realizes that, as she judges, so is she judged. Paranoia lingers threateningly at the back of her character, and she undoubtedly lacks 'charity'. The whole of the action is viewed through this exceedingly complex and deceptive figure, and as readers we participate in the exhilarating experience of picking our way through an interpretative minefield.

Not the least remarkable aspect of *As For Me and My House* is its unified design. The action involves a carefully limited number of characters confined to a single place and extends in time for little more than a year. This preoccupation is carried still further in Ross's last novel, *Sawbones Memorial* (1974), where the Classical unities of time and place are strictly observed; the action is confined to a party for a retiring prairie doctor and the time involved matches that required by readers to complete it at a single sitting. Told entirely in dialogue or monologue, with flashbacks of memory that reveal the whole story, it is a technical *tour de force* and a decidedly successful novel. Indeed, Ross apparently needed a technical challenge to stimulate his best work; his intermediate novels, *The Well* (1958) and *A Whir of Gold* (1970), were less ambitious and far less effective.

Ross was also accomplished as a short-story writer, his best stories being collected in *The Lamp at Noon* (1968). Most of them pre-date *As For Me and My House*, which they often resemble in their portrayal of unfulfilled female characters. Their stories recall Knister's, though they are generally more traditional in plot and stronger in tone. Like Knister's, Ross's narrators are often young, sensitive, and imaginative, a poignant contrast arising between their personalities and the nature of the relentless land against which they live their lives. As always, images of snow, dust, and storm recur. These stories sometimes tremble on the verge of melodrama, but when Ross writes at his best – in 'The Painted Door', for example – a simple tragedy archetypal in its pattern unfolds with claustrophobic intensity. Ross's output was small, and the amount of unquestionably fine work smaller, but he was a writer from whom many later Canadian novelists drew inspiration and technical awareness.

Perhaps the most radically original as well as the most unjustly neglected of Canadian novels, Elizabeth Smart's *By Grand Central Station I Sat Down and Wept,* first appeared in 1945. Though technically fiction, it is virtually a prose poem and at the same time an impassioned autobiography. It offers a searingly frank account of what it is like to be hopelessly and ecstatically in love. The writer-speaker tells a simple story of her love for a married man, their travelling across North America, her pregnancy, the break-up of their relationship, and her desolation which in a strange way is also a triumph. This plot, if plot it can be called, is unvarnished but nevertheless uncertain, since one can never be quite sure how much is to be accepted as fact, how much recognized as the protagonist's imagination or even hallucination; the language at one moment seems literal, at the next wildly metaphorical.

The book best defines itself by way of paradox. Totally original, it draws upon aeons of tradition from Classical mythology (via Virgil and Ovid) onwards. It tells a timeless story in surrealistic terms as it catches the symbolic pulse of twentieth-century America. A novel of extremes, it portrays intense happiness and utter depression, rural beauty and metropolitan squalor, bourgeois conventions and complete liberation. Stylistically it resembles nothing except, perhaps, the Song of Songs (King James version). Certainly it connects with nothing else in Canadian literature, though Canadian literature frequently shares aspects of its story. If Sheila Watson's *The Double Hook,* published fourteen years later, occasionally comes to mind (though their prose styles represent opposite poles), this is because both ring their own inimitable changes on similar basic patterns of human experience. An artful but nakedly direct book, it is an idiosyncratic masterpiece, incomparable and unrepeatable.

Another writer of the 1940s who extended the technical possibilities of the novel was the most brilliant of all the Canadian literary birds of passage, Malcolm Lowry. It is, of course, a moot question whether Lowry, who was born in England and died there, and whose greatest novel, *Under the Volcano* (1947), is set in Mexico, qualifies as a Canadian novelist just because much of his work was written in a squatter's shack near

Vancouver. Lowry certainly liked to think of himself as a Canadian writer, and it was strategically tempting to claim him as such when Canadian literature was less impressive in quality and quantity than it is today. But his art was nurtured and developed within a European context; he derived nothing from Canadian tradition and bequeathed little or nothing to it. I am inclined to agree with a recent commentator, Richard Hauer Costa, who describes him as 'a Canadian only by an accident of geography' (*Malcolm Lowry*, 1972, 127). Nevertheless, in view of his stature and the portrait of Canada he presents in one book and a handful of short stories, he deserves consideration here.

Under the Volcano is the only mature Lowry novel that can be considered complete, the rest being published posthumously after complex editing from manuscripts that lacked Lowry's final literary varnishing. But all present the inner life as it is being constantly interrupted and bombarded by images from the material – and materialistic – world. A character may be reliving his past in memory, his mind flitting from one association to another, but juxtaposed with these thoughts will be snatches of overheard conversation, music from another room, advertisements seen on billboards. Lowry gives us a cinematic, bewildering, deeply probing, and surrealistically convincing presentation of human experience. In addition, his protagonists (always aspects of Lowry himself), as students of ancient religion and philosophy, occultists, visionaries, and doomed alcoholics, view the world in apocalyptic terms. And for Lowry, if the Mexican Quauhnahuac (= Cuernavaca) of *Under the Volcano*, with its sinister *barranca* into which the body of its Faustian hero is thrown on the last page, represents Hell, a rural section of British Columbia (in the fictions, Eridanus) is the closest approximation to Paradise that he can imagine on earth. The scenes set in Canada are therefore among the most lyrical and positive in his work.

October Ferry to Gabriola (1970), the one novel set wholly in Canada, reproduces a day in the life of Ethan and Jacqueline Llewelyn as they travel by bus from Vancouver to Nanaimo and then, after various frustrations and misadventures, take the ferry to Gabriola Island. They are seeking refuge because they are threatened with eviction from their home on the shore near Vancouver (Eden is always precarious). Nothing much happens, but it is all part of what Lowry called 'the voyage that never ends' and, while physically travelling into the future, Llewelyn is emotionally and obsessively reliving his past. Although it lacks (because Lowry died before he had time to insert) the dense verbal texture of *Under the Volcano,* the book is notable for its fresh and vivid presentation of the British Columbia scenery through which they pass, and for Llewelyn/Lowry's fluctuating hopes and fears concerning the Eridanus that is Canada. At one moment he believes, though against his better judgment, that 'some final wisdom would arise out of Canada' (Ch. 26), at another that the beauty and stability of the country would be ruined by industry and the blight of so-called civilization. As always, it is an apocalyptic – and perhaps an outsider's – evaluation.

The Canadian short stories, 'The Bravest Boat', 'Gin and Goldenrod', and 'The Forest Path to the Spring', are all collected in *Hear Us O Lord from Heaven Thy Dwelling Place* (1961). Suggesting a serene morning after nightmare, they provide an Edenic frame to the other stories in the volume. 'The Forest Path to the Spring', more properly categorized as a novella, is a lyrical paean of praise for the simple beauty first recognized and appreciated among the squatters' shacks threatened by the prosperous and insensitive. It is permeated with a love for the wildlife of the area, the weather, the cloud formations. Civilization exists as a dark smudge on the horizon, but the path from the life-giving natural spring to the Lowrys' cottage-refuge becomes an emblem of peace, goodness, and continuity. The narrative is most Canadian, perhaps, in its documentary preoccupation – not so much fiction as patterned reminiscence. But it is in 'Gin and Goldenrod' that Lowry, under the guise of Sigbjørn Wilderness, most clearly expresses the Canadian paradox. Canada is 'a pretty large country to despoil', yet its history has been 'the history of spoliation in one form or another'. Man, because he is Man, must conquer wilderness (the speaker's own name) as 'part of his own process of self-determination'. Like Grove a generation before, Lowry is a European in search of a paradisal America that he sees as doomed by the very qualities that lured human pioneers into the wilderness in the first place. Lowry remained an outsider, but (unlike Grove) was able to articulate the paradox with subtlety and grace.

Other writers in this period, though not conspicuously experimental, developed their own unique gifts with a confident independence. One of these was Ethel Wilson, who had been born of English parents in South

Africa and came to British Columbia as an orphan at the age of ten. Brought up by a grandmother, grand-aunt, and aunt – the character of Rose in *The Innocent Traveller* (1949) parallels her creator's own experience – she inherited an English tradition of politeness and good manners, cultivating poise and a propriety that was firm without ever being stuffy. (Yet the mind boggles when one realizes that she could easily have passed a drunken Lowry on the Vancouver streets.) When she came to publish her first novel, *Hetty Dorval* (1947), at the advanced age of fifty-nine, Wilson brought to her art a polished mastery of the sanctioned conventions of the novel as well as a prose style of remarkable clarity and grace. The latter was of particular concern to her. 'If you ask me what I most like', she once wrote, 'I like the English sentence, clear, un-lush, and un-loaded', and of her favourite novelists she observed: 'They have *style*, each his own, and without style ... how dull' (qtd. in Desmond Pacey, *Ethel Wilson*, 1968, 179, 18).

Her novels are technically assured in that she can always achieve the literary effects she needs readily and without fuss. *Hetty Dorval* is the only full-length novel (really no more than a novella) that she wrote in the first person, and the interest of the book depends upon the way in which she communicates the enigmatic nature of Hetty's sophisticated experience through the eyes of the naively innocent Frankie Burnaby (Henry James's tour de force in *What Maisie Knew* may come to mind). And in *The Innocent Traveller* the opening scene of the dinner party in honour of Matthew Arnold is superbly rendered from the viewpoint of the three-year-old Topaz who has slid beneath the table where she observes the assembled company, Arnold included, at boot-level. But Wilson allows herself full range as an omniscient narrator and will move from limited viewpoint to quasi-divine omniscience at will. She is even prepared to intrude into her narrative in the often-criticized manner of the Victorian novelists, though she does so not with the distancing or cynical irony of Thackeray but with something closer to the passionate wisdom of George Eliot.

She has, then, an enviable technical versatility and this extends to her subject matter. While she usually confines her main characters to the articulate middle class (*The Equations of Love*, 1952, coming to the limits of her social range in its presentation of Mort and Myrt and the waitress Lilly), she can vary the tone of her work from the amusing social comedy of irrepressible Aunt Topaz in *The Innocent Traveller* to the deeper pathos and poignancy of *Swamp Angel* (1954) and the darker vision that becomes evident in her last novel, *Love and Salt Water* (1956). Moreover, despite the sense of decorum and high principles that we find throughout her work, she is in no way blind to the complex and morally blurred realities of life. Her characters are continually breaking moral conventions. (Lilly, in the second story in *The Equations of Love,* lies and deceives in her efforts to bring up her illegitimate daughter; Maggie in *Swamp Angel* deserts her husband, while Nell Severance never even went through the marriage ceremony.) Yet their actions are tacitly, sometimes even overtly, approved. Indeed, Wilson seems fascinated by the moral exception, the special circumstances under which personal integrity takes precedence over generally but by no means invariably valid standards of social behaviour. She is, then, a moral novelist of a particularly delicate and subtle kind.

In its exquisite control and serene wisdom, *Swamp Angel* takes pride of place in Wilson's consistently executed work. It is a profound novel about marriage, about time and the relationship between past and present, about the limits of both selfishness and selflessness, about a sense of sacred mystery within all life. But these themes are explored within the polarities represented by the lives of Maggie Lloyd and Nell Severance, opposites who are yet, in a curious way, complementary. Thus Maggie is invariably associated with the outdoors, while Nell confines herself inside, within a protective screen of cigarette smoke. Maggie finds a sense of purpose in nature while Nell stands by the art and artifice of which the 'swamp angel' revolver of her circus act is an emblem. Maggie acts; Nell theorizes. Maggie is young enough to build her own future; Nell can only look back to a probably tawdry but in retrospect exotic past. The book develops naturally enough out of this basic structure, but the literal narrative is always suggesting larger meanings. Maggie's flight through the appropriately named Hope includes a three-day retreat by the Similkameen River during which she lifts her heart 'in desolation and in prayer' (Ch. 6).* The swamp

---

* *Swamp Angel* exists in two different versions. Originally, the American edition contained two chapters not included in the Canadian text. The New Canadian Library initially reproduced the Canadian text but changed to the American, which Wilson apparently preferred, in 1990. In earlier editions the quotations here occurred in Chs. 6, 27, 17, and 20 respectively. For details, see Li-Ping Geng, 'The Rival Editions of Ethel Wilson's *Swamp Angel*', ECW 77 (Fall 2002), 63–89.

angel is described at one point as 'some kind of a symbol' (Ch. 28), but Wilson avoids the restrictive self-consciousness of symbolism, preferring the subtler power of indirect suggestion. 'All this nowadays of symbol symbol symbol', dreams Nell, 'destroying reality' (Ch. 18). But there are many levels of reality in the book, and whatever the scene, whether Maggie watching kitten and fawn in the clearing (Ch. 21) or disposing of the swamp angel in the final chapter, it takes place within a larger pattern. Indeed, Wilson's omniscient control, here and elsewhere, suggests an overall meaning and purpose in the universe. She works, without ever falling into a narrow dogmatism, within a deeply felt Christian scheme of things.

Poise, straightforwardness, profundity, exquisite control of tone, delicate human insight, and above all the compassion that becomes a redeeming feature of so many of her human and therefore imperfect characters: all these qualities are communicated through the delicate verbal texture of her novels, and are evident also in her short stories, most of which were gathered together in *Mrs. Golightly and Other Stories* (1961). Moreover, one of her supreme artistic qualities is that she never repeats herself. The books have a family resemblance, but each differs significantly from what has gone before and what is to come after. Deceptively simple – sometimes, indeed, deceptively artless – they reflect a Wordsworthian sense of the still sad music of humanity and an impression of sensitivity and sureness that we associate with the English tradition that includes Jane Austen and E. M. Forster but is rarely to be found in the Canadian novel.

W. O. Mitchell burst on to the literary stage with *Who Has Seen the Wind* (1947) and, for all his gifts, never quite succeeded in matching his early achievement. The story of Brian O'Connal contains all the ingredients of a popular as well as an artistic success. Technically a *Bildungsroman* or novel of development, it traces Brian's growth from four to twelve, his first encounters with the mysteries of birth and death, the frustrations of human institutions, his coming to terms with God and the land, and the growth towards adulthood that entails loss as well as gain. This is another novel set in the drought and depression of the 1930s, but the town (never formally named in *Who Has Seen the Wind* but apparently identical with the Crocus in *Jake and the Kid*) is presented far more warmly and positively than Ross's Horizon. Though there is a sombre side to Mitchell's version – one character towards the end of the novel observes that the town has revealed to her 'the heart of darkness' (Ch. 31) – the emphasis is upon humour, humanity, and energy.

But the novel is far more complex than its plot description suggests. The title derives from a poem by Christina Rossetti, and it refers not merely to the wind blowing across the prairie but to all the clustering and related meanings of 'wind', 'breath', and 'spirit' that come down to us in the Western Christian tradition from the Bible onwards. Moreover, the novel's recurrent imagery encourages us to consider its archetypal associations. Brian's puzzlement with the mystery of birth (his baby brother and pigeons in a nest) connects with the larger mystery of Incarnation; the pigeons themselves suggest the dove, symbol of the Holy Spirit, and the Lord speaks out of the whirlwind to Bent Candy. Like God the wind is palpable but invisible: it can be felt (compare Brian's 'feeling', his personal intimations of immortality) but not seen. As breath it associates with life yet (as in the scene with the grandmother at the end) can also bring death. In these senses it is an image of God. Mitchell only occasionally insists upon these connections, but they are integral to the novel's larger meaning. Characteristically, he is anything but solemn in the overall effect, and the same imagery and reference often work at a comic level. Brian's grandmother 'belshes' (Ch. 1) – i.e., she suffers from wind; then Ben introduces 'spirit' into the Presbyterian church with a vengeance (Ch. 14).

Naturally, but also symbolically, Mitchell sees the human community, where decency and warm-heartedness are always confronting narrowness and meanness, within the open prairie that can be harsh, even merciless, but contains within itself an impersonal, non-personal principle of justice. Brian's counterpart on the prairie is the Young Ben, tough and vital, and it is part of Brian's maturity that he develops some of the qualities of prairie and Young Ben alike. The human story, then, is framed by 'the least denominator of nature, the skeleton requirements simply, of land and sky – Saskatchewan prairie' (Ch. 1), and Mitchell draws upon his full resources to convey the complex interaction of delicacy and crudeness, beauty and ugliness, good and evil, that makes up the background to human life on earth. He has sometimes been accused of sentimentality, of looking through rose-coloured spectacles, but there is nothing soft about his accounts of the discrimination against the Wongs or the stuffiness of the town's respectable vested interests. The joyousness of Brian's childhood is continually punctuated by sorrow – each part ends with a death. Mitchell's humour has connections with Leacock, but it embraces the bitterness of *Arcadian Adventures* as well as the gentler mode of *Sunshine Sketches.* There is a satisfying wholeness about his vision.

Who Has Seen the Wind develops a succession of almost self-contained incidents, and thus betrays its origins in Mitchell's stories about the Kid and the hired man which began in *Maclean's* and later became popular as a radio and, later, television series. Thirteen of these stories were subsequently published as *Jake and the Kid* (1961), and if they show a tendency towards cuteness and whimsy they also reflect the western tradition of the tall tale to which they belong. This tradition is also visible in *The Kite* (1962) and *The Vanishing Point,* which followed after a long interval in 1973. Both are comic novels in which realism is stretched in the direction of hilarious and often biting fantasy. *The Kite* centres upon Daddy Sherry, the irrepressible oldest man in Canada, who blatantly uses his age and a deftly selective deafness to indulge his fancies and annoy those who oppose him. *The Vanishing Point,* the product of Mitchell's work in the Eden Valley Indian Reserve, is darker in tone; beneath the breathless pace and ebullient high spirits lies a sobering analysis of contemporary humanity's self-alienation (an earlier version of the novel was entitled *The Alien*). *How I Spent My Summer Holidays* (1981), darker still, tries to become an adolescent *Who Has Seen the Wind* but lacks the tonal balance of the earlier work. Here the comic blends into the macabre and the sordid, and Mitchell gets bogged down in an incredible plot that he never satisfactorily resolves. None the less, he has been underestimated by the critics – no full-length literary study has appeared to date – because any attempt to combine the commercially popular with the permanently serious is always viewed with suspicion, and because a basically comic vision is too often assumed to be less substantial than a more sober 'criticism of life'. But *Who Has Seen the Wind* has long since established itself as a Canadian classic, and Mitchell's exuberance and humanity will ultimately find their true level.

Ernest Buckler's finest achievement, *The Mountain and the Valley* (1952), contains an acknowledgment to Mitchell, and the book bears a decided if superficial resemblance to *Who Has Seen the Wind.* Another novel of development, it presents the life of its protagonist from eleven to thirty against the rural background of the Annapolis Valley. Like *Who*

Has Seen the Wind, the book is a patchwork of memorable scenes which Buckler evokes with poetic sensitivity: a funeral after a fishing mishap; David's first sexual experience and its tragic aftermath; his distressing row with his father; his accident at the pig-killing. In both books acute happiness blends with equally acute sorrow, and in both the authors maintain their admirable balance between pain and wonder through the force of their individual prose styles. And both struggle to universalize their intensely regional subject matter. But at this point resemblances cease. *The Mountain and the Valley* is a *Künstlerroman* (novel of an artist) as well as a *Bildungsroman*; it is the story of a writer with the over-insistently symbolic name of David Canaan who dies at the top of an equally symbolic mountain just as he has achieved his creative vision of human community in the valley of his childhood. There is an awkward tension between the literal narrative and its larger implications that Mitchell manages to avoid – perhaps because he makes Brian O'Connal imaginative without making him an embryo novelist.

Buckler developed out of the community he celebrates, and is obviously drawing upon his own experience for much of his material, as his memoir, *Ox Bells and Fireflies* (1968), makes clear. We come to realize, indeed, that Buckler is a David Canaan who survived to tell what he had seen. As a sophisticated writer portraying the lives of simple, down-to-earth, uncomplicated people, his authorial stance is inevitably a delicate one. This is evident in the rustic mask he assumed when interviewed by urban journalists or literary critics. Thus he once described himself as 'a farmer who writes, not a writer who farms' (Cook ed., 22) – but the farmer in question held a master's degree in philosophy from the University of Toronto! He could describe with extraordinary immediacy a way of life that few have experienced, one that has now passed away; but he could do so only by using artistic methods alien to the people about whom he wrote.

At the level of plot, there is none of the heightened exuberance and exaggeration that we find so refreshing in Mitchell. Buckler worked from a base in realism, but the ordinary lives of his characters are articulated, transformed, rendered extra-ordinary by what can only be called his stylistic pyrotechnics. As David ascends the mountain he makes a discovery which is really the secret of Buckler's style: 'Everything seemed to be an aspect of everything else. There seemed to be a thread of similarity running through the whole world' (Ch. 40). In stylistic terms, this implies a highly sophisticated approach to language. Images are evocative and close-packed. Moreover, throughout the book emphasis is always on words: the text of the school play that David and Effie rehearse ('The words were something no one else had', Ch. 7); the Christmas present of *Robinson Crusoe* with its 'wonderful waiting words' (Ch. 9); his first conscious awareness of the power of language ('having things stated exactly for the first time', Ch. 28). *The Mountain and the Valley* exists by virtue of its style, which has to be read slowly and savoured in the mouth like a liqueur. For some palates, this way of writing is too cloying, but its force can hardly be questioned. Its weakness is that it links Buckler too closely with his protagonist. When David begins to write within the book, his style is indistinguishable from the narrative that contains it. More conspicuous than Mitchell's in *Who Has Seen the Wind,* it calls undue attention to the artifice of *The Mountain and the Valley*. It is fair to suggest, indeed, that the style sets the book apart in a somewhat ambiguous way, rather like David's scar within the narrative itself.

Buckler is often regarded as a 'one-book man' but this is hardly fair. His second novel, *The Cruelest Month* (1963), though concerned among other things with the problem of the artist, disappointed many readers who wished for more of the nostalgic intensity that had characterized the first. This is a symposium-novel on the Peacock model, in which various human types – a local Nova Scotian, a successful novelist, a rich young woman, a spinster – gather in the house of a philosophical artist with the giveaway name of Paul Creed. The house is called Endlaw (a name symbolic in itself but also an anagram of Thoreau's Walden) and there they engage in a sort of intellectual group therapy. When stated baldly, the set-up sounds unpromising, to say the least, but Buckler's intelligence and piercing insight combine to create a wordy, didactic, sometimes exasperating but often strangely absorbing novel. Again, in his short stories, which have been gathered together in *Thanks for Listening: Stories and Short Fictions* (2004), one finds the same conscious blend of art, artfulness, and artificiality. A comparison with Mitchell again suggests itself, since Buckler too has a homely, folksy, cracker-barrel-rustic-philosopher side to his nature in which humanness can come close to sentimentality. Fortunately, however, the humanness predominates. These are *made* stories that draw attention to their making. Like the older David Canaan,

Buckler can never observe the world of nature without yielding to the impulse to turn it into a highly self-conscious art. All in all, Buckler gives the impression of being a potentially major figure who never quite disciplined his narrative and stylistic gifts.

With the exception of MacLennan and the influential *As For Me and My House,* the fiction of the 1940s and 1950s shows a remarkable leaning towards humour and satire. One of the earliest and clearest examples is Earle Birney's *Turvey: A Military Picaresque* (1949). A war book with a difference, it conforms to the sanctioned pattern established by writers who had exposed the horrors of the First World War – a pattern followed, as we have seen, by Harrison's *Generals Die in Bed* – but Birney's, which is more unusual in dealing with the Second World War, also differs from most accounts in that it displays amused contempt rather than bitter anger. Instead of being shifted up to the front with appalling speed, Private Turvey does not reach 'the Sharp End' until the seventeenth of the book's nineteen chapters. Instead of being a sensitive man disillusioned by experience, he is the quintessential innocent frustrated by his failure to get into the excitement of action. The satirical targets are military red tape, inefficiency, and the absurdities of psychological testing, rather than the evil of war itself. Birney has in fact borrowed ('stolen' might be a more appropriate word) the basic situation from Jaroslav Hašek's *The Good Soldier Schweik* and transformed it into a work that is both original and thoroughly Canadian.

Birney's main strengths, of course, lay in poetry, and *Turvey* is at its best when displaying the verbal high spirits that characterize his later vernacular poems. The book is filled with characters from all parts of Canada, and many parts of the world, whose dialects and idiolects are masterfully caught in a few sentences. There is even a South American colonel somewhat improbably in charge of an officer-selection camp whose impressionistic English anticipates speakers in poems like 'Sinaloa' and 'Cartagena de Indias'. Turvey himself (inevitably nicknamed Topsy) is a good-hearted, simple-minded, inarticulate *homme moyen sensuel* ('Well, like Sergeant Swingle always says, you gotta take the nishitive', Ch. 14), whose adventures – or, rather, misadventures – range in tone from the amusing-pathetic to the farcically hilarious, and whose character allows him to ride the military absurdity as well as come into recurrent conflict with it. *Turvey* is closer to Joseph Heller's *Catch-22* than to *Generals Die in Bed* (or to Colin McDougall's *Execution*, 1958, an effective documentary fiction of Canadians in the Italian campaign), but Birney keeps on the credible side of parody. Those totally unfamiliar with his subject matter are likely to find the book amusing but exaggerated; however, those who, like the present writer, have experience of military service will be impressed by its only slightly heightened realism.

Since Robertson Davies's fiction developed so remarkably in range and depth during the 1970s, I shall confine myself in this chapter to the satiric comedies of manners in the 'Salterton' trilogy: *Tempest-Tost* (1951), *Leaven of Malice* (1954), and *A Mixture of Frailties* (1958). Readers of these novels will not be surprised to learn that Davies was a great admirer of Leacock, since Salterton, a small city modelled to a considerable extent on Kingston, is treated with that mixture of loving amusement and cogent criticism that we find in Leacock's presentation of Mariposa. It was therefore appropriate that *Leaven of Malice* won the Leacock Award for Humour on its first publication. But unlike Leacock, Davies can control an extended narrative. These are novels of artifice since part of the pleasure derived from them consists in watching Davies juggle expertly with his themes and characters while bringing his work to a dramatic and satisfying conclusion. At this point, too, we may recall that Davies was a dramatist before he attempted fiction. These novels are decidedly theatrical in subject matter and structure. *Tempest-Tost* centres upon an amateur production of *The Tempest*, dramatic or musical performances appear throughout the trilogy, and in various ways this early fiction displays the characteristics of the well-made play. The denouement of *Leaven of Malice* ('"I don't intend to make a stage-play of this ..."', 'This, too, should have been a satisfactorily dramatic moment ...', Part 6) is a particularly clear example.

Davies is periodically criticized for his English emphasis, and it is certainly true that he owes more to British than to North American literary models. But his satire in the Salterton trilogy is directed against the pseudo-English Ontario of that time. Thus there is an early reference in *Tempest-Tost* to 'the eccentric Prebendary Bedlam, one of those Englishmen who sought to build a bigger and better England in the colonies' (Ch. 1), and Davies's satiric target is the society built on Bedlamite principles. The Salterton hierarchies certainly recall English class squabbles – a crisis arises when the director wants Caliban to be played by 'one of the stewards in the liquor store' who might not be 'acceptable to the rest of the cast', and a woman is recommended for (of all parts) Juno because 'she has been a very faithful worker in the Little Theatre since its foundation, and the head of the refreshment committee for the past seven years' (Ch. 3) – but this is precisely Davies's satiric point (one that is close to F. R. Scott's in 'The Canadian Authors Meet'). In *Leaven of Malice* Solly Bridgetower notes that so much was made in Canada of 'our British heritage', but that this always meant Chaucer and Shakespeare rather than the more representative Bevill Higgins, 'the little pipsqueak ... mooing Tennyson to all those old trouts in the drawing room' (Part 4). And in *A Mixture of Frailties,* where Monica Gall is sent to England to undertake musical studies, Davies creates a situation in which both Canadian and English manners can be compared, contrasted, and parodied.

Although it has been a preoccupation in all these books, it is in *A Mixture of Frailties* that Davies most clearly diagnoses the Canadian disease described by one of the English characters as 'cultural malnutrition' (Part 2, Ch. 8). The satiric tension in *Tempest-Tost* derives from the implicit contrast between the world of wonders contained in Shakespeare's play and the unimaginative approach to it on the part of the provincial Canadian cast. In *Leaven of Malice* Davies has great fun with the puritan cult of respectability that neglects the musical genius of Humphrey Cobbler because of his social nonconformism, and attacks the beginnings of Canadian nationalism for its overrating forgotten poets imitative of the English tradition, especially Charles Heavysege whom Davies (rightly) considered more heavy than sage. But in *A Mixture of Frailties,* where Monica may be read as a sheltered but highly talented Canadian exposed to universal standards of artistic achievement and imaginative creation and re-creation, Davies offers a full-scale cultural critique. Moreover, in Giles Revelstoke, the young, wayward, but brilliant English musician by whom Monica is intellectually and physically seduced, Davies created a complex and disruptive figure who, while threatening to burst the fabric of the novel in which he appears, looks forward to the deeper, more subtly drawn Faustian characters who appear in the later fiction.

All these novels are polished, witty, amusing, well structured; moreover, an artistic development is discernible within the trilogy.

Tempest-Tost displays a rich but not wholly disciplined satiric talent. Sentence by sentence it reads well; scene by scene it does not always flow smoothly. In *Leaven of Malice* the characterization is sharper, the form clearer; the concentrated time scheme (all takes place within a week) encourages a tightness of construction. *A Mixture of Frailties,* with its blend of comic and profound, now reads as a transitional novel, more serious and searching than its predecessors though not as artistically assured as the Deptford trilogy. Technically, the main difference between these novels and Davies's later work is that here he is the puppet-master of his theatrical effects, depending heavily on his role as omniscient narrator, whereas the later novels offer the immediacy of the personal voice. But in the Salterton trilogy Davies needs the detachment that omniscience provides; the traditional mode is appropriate for the traditional nature of his satiric attitude.

The fiction of Mordecai Richler bears little obvious resemblance to that of Davies, yet both are satirists, humorists, and moralists, and both showed remarkable artistic confidence from the start of their careers. Richler always paid keen attention to the tools of his trade, and seemed able to achieve any fictional effect he desired. At his best he displays a breath-taking exuberance, a fine and totally convincing command of dialogue, compulsive readability, and of course a broad range of humour. Always the professional, he was notorious for his determination to be judged in world rather than merely Canadian terms. He is at the opposite pole from Grove, who subordinated technique to content, and this explains why Richler dismisses Grove as overrated within the sheltered boundaries of Canadian letters. If pure skill were all that counted, Richler would be at the top of any list of major novelists; unfortunately for Richler, it is not all that counts, and, despite his formidable talents, he may be said to have produced only one early novel of unquestioned literary excellence.

His first book, *The Acrobats* (1954), sets the tone for much of his subsequent work. Richler once described himself as seeking in his writings for the values with which, in a doubt-ridden, directionless contemporary world, 'a man can live with honour' (qtd. in G. David Sheps ed., *Mordecai Richler,* 1971, 38). Here André Bennett, a Canadian expatriate, is searching (too late) in Franco's Spain of the early 1950s for the expatriate world of Hemingway and the possibility of moral commitment available to those who fought in the Spanish Civil War. Richler's novels are full of expatriates because the expatriate condition serves as an image of the quest for lost moral certainty. Related and recurrent themes like Jewish persecution and the Nazi menace, treated more subtly in *Son of a Smaller Hero* (1955) and *A Choice of Enemies* (1957), are subjected here to the first of many changes that Richler rings on the conflict between good and evil – or would ring if such simplistic absolutes existed on earth. And at this point we detect a moral ambivalence that crops up so often in discussions of Richler. Expressed sympathetically, he shows how the qualities of the 'villains' (preoccupied with power) blend surprisingly with those of the 'heroes' (in search of goodness and love); expressed more harshly, he presents the world of phoniness and corruption that is ultimately rejected with such verve and gusto that one suspects him of wanting to have his cake and eat it. This is a continual problem in satire, and becomes increasingly acute in Richler's later fiction.

The Apprenticeship of Duddy Kravitz (1959) is Richler's early masterpiece, partly because he uses the moral ambiguity of his chief characters to maximum advantage. Duddy is a young Jew from the Montréal 'ghetto' determined to find a place in the capitalist Canadian sun. He pursues property and power with a resourcefulness and ruthless energy which readers cannot help admiring, though, as the pace quickens and Duddy resorts to shaky deals and unscrupulous manipulations, sympathy gives way to appalled horror. The land he covets is a 'promised land' of real estate, and in his efforts to acquire it Duddy grows closer and closer to the stereotype of the Jewboy on the make, or, in Canadian terms, an ironic depraved embodiment of the pioneering paradox. The book ends pathetically but appropriately with Duddy's being offered credit at a restaurant; for one who was refused loans when he desperately needed them, this represents 'status', but here as elsewhere he fails to recognize the crassness and vulgarity of his newly won position. The novel is a bitterly harsh *Bildungsroman* in which brilliant descriptions of social conditions in the Jewish section of Montréal and the superbly economical reproduction of the local language and manners serve as a mere backdrop for a complex study of human greed and the reductive temptations of materialist success.

The Apprenticeship of Duddy Kravitz was both a commercial and an artistic triumph. Since then Richler has succeeded in repeating the former but not, I think, the latter. His next two novels, *The Incomparable Atuk* (1963) and *Cocksure* (1968), move in the direction of satiric fantasy. At the very time when Richler was being recognized as a popular literary figure, he became the relentless satirist and parodist of popular and fashionable attitudes – and was applauded by those he implicitly criticized. Moreover, this coincided with the period when book publishing entered the age of permissiveness, and Richler claimed all the new freedoms. As a result his language and effects became coarser; naturally he remained very funny, and often brashly clever, but there is a lessening of depth and subtlety even in the longer and more ambitious novels, *St. Urbain's Horseman* (1971) and *Joshua Then and Now* (1980). Both books are well controlled and excellently constructed, but the moral complexity that characterized his earlier work is absent. Neither Jake Hersh nor Joshua Shapiro seems to me a particularly sympathetic character, and I find few signs of their seeking the values by which 'a man can live with honour'. Jake is involved in a sordid and sensational sex scandal, and, although he is partly framed, one's sympathies are lessened because, throughout the novel, he responds to any sexual reference like one of Pavlov's dogs. Joshua is wrongly accused of homosexual connections (it is hardly Richler's fault that this dates it in the present politically correct climate), bringing the charge upon himself by helping to forge a sensational correspondence to sell to a university library, but the satire on academic greed hardly justifies the silliness. Both men are obsessed with the search for Nazi war criminals, but the moral credit that this assures them is doubtful. What was once a moral complexity has surely relapsed into formula. Moreover, the second of these books is so similar in basic plot to the first that one cannot but assume a decline in inventiveness on Richler's part.

Richler is especially important as a novelist of the modern city; we derive from his work an acute sense of people living close together, and the tensions that this creates. The city in question is generally London or Montréal, but even in London the characters are as often as not Canadians, and (like Davies in *A Mixture of Frailties*) he is fond of setting European customs and moral attitudes against North American ones. He frequently achieves memorable effects by means of vivid, detailed, but (in terms of overall plot) detachable set pieces. One thinks of the bar mitzvah film or Virgil's newsletter for epileptics in *Duddy Kravitz,* the baseball game on Hampstead Heath in *St. Urbain's Horseman*, the meetings of the Mackenzie King Memorial Society in *Joshua Then and Now*. Richler's was an art close to journalism, of which he wrote much, and his problem was to transcend the journalistic without sacrificing the vigour and colour of life in the raw. His achievement was substantial even if we question the extent to which it represents his full capacity as a creative artist.

Most of the other novelists who produced work of lasting interest in this period have either been underrated because their subject matter or approach went against current literary fashion or because they have produced only a small body of work – sometimes, indeed, no more than a single novel. A prominent exception was Brian Moore, another bird of passage, an Ulsterman who emigrated to the United States via Canada and picked up Canadian citizenship on the way. His novels are notable for convincing characterization, skillful construction, and effortlessly clear prose, but their relation to Canadian literature is for the most part questionable. The two that most obviously qualify are *The Luck of Ginger Coffey* (1960), about an Irish emigrant to Montréal, and *I Am Mary Dunne* (1968), about a Nova Scotian in New York. Moore was at his best with displaced persons, characters who in one way or another suffer loneliness or exile. He was a successful and admirable writer whose work maintained literary quality while conforming to commercial requirements, but in this context he is a peripheral figure.

Hugh Garner has been neglected because he was unable to maintain Moore's perilous balance. Several of his books are merely commercial pot-boilers, but his best achieve a literary realism that can stand alongside Callaghan's. He is best known, and properly so, for *Cabbagetown* (1950, complete text 1968), a documentary-type novel portraying a working-class district of Toronto in the 1930s. Valuable for its vivid re-creations of place and period in all their political and sociological complexity, it ranks as literature because the story of Ken Tilling, while representative, is also individual and well sustained by an art that inconspicuously conceals art. Garner was also a short-story writer who covered a wider range than Callaghan, and although his style is crisp and direct, we are never conscious, as we are with Callaghan, of a forced attempt to limit vocabulary to the capacity of the subject or deliberately to muffle literary effect. Garner was a simple, unostentatious writer offering little opportunity for critical exegesis. Inferior to Callaghan at his best, he nevertheless attained the art of lucid and competent narrative.

Like Garner, Fred Bodsworth has a greater following among non-specialist readers than among literary critics; unlike Garner, he is a novelist of countryside and wilderness whose favoured mode is moral fable rather than realistic narrative. His first book, *The Last of the Curlews* (1954), belongs to the animal-story tradition established by Roberts and Seton, but Bodsworth has a more deliberately scientific and conservationist purpose. He reconstructs the life of what could be the last surviving Eskimo curlew in the world, and this narrative, which scrupulously avoids anthropomorphism and explains the bird's instinctive impulse to migrate, establish a territory, and reproduce its kind, is interspersed with documentary sections giving factual information about the shocking story of the human lust to kill that has brought the species to almost certain extinction. It is a sad story economically, elegantly, and beautifully told.

With his next volume, *The Strange One* (1959), the career of a barnacle goose blown off-course from the Hebrides to northern Canada, where it proceeds to mate with a Canada goose, is juxtaposed with a human love story between a Scot and an Indian girl (both 'strange ones'). And in *The Atonement of Ashley Morden* (1964) a reluctant scientist is educated in the ways of the wild by a girl who recalls W. H. Hudson's Rima in *Green Mansions* or the heroine of Roberts's *The Heart of the Ancient Wood* (1900). The artifice here is obvious, but Bodsworth sets didacticism over verisimilitude, and his stories work smoothly on their own terms. His last novel, *The Sparrow's Fall* (1967), also belongs to fable in that its plot, a northern Indian's efforts by means of his skill as a hunter to survive the threat of starvation and the vengeance of his rival in love, is secondary to the philosophical issues lying behind it – the relation of humanity to the animals, the adequacy of Christian precept (as in the title) to the harsh realities of the wilderness. Bodsworth writes from a viewpoint unusual in Canadian or any fiction; above all, he is a genuine novelist in that his fiction forms a consistent *oeuvre*, each book, satisfying in itself, contributing to a larger pattern within the context of his whole work. It is unfortunate that, as a novelist, he has been silent since 1967.

In the work of Henry Kreisel the contrast between Europe and North America, a theme that has preoccupied Canadian novelists as diverse as

Grove, MacLennan, Davies, and Richler, is explored again from yet another angle. *The Rich Man* (1948) recounts the story of a Jewish-Canadian immigrant returning on a visit to his native Austria in 1935 just before the Nazi takeover. His personal story (a poor man, he allows his friends and relatives to believe him rich) is played out against a sober portrait of human prejudice and political manipulation. It is a thoughtful and moving book, but less distinguished than its successor, *The Betrayal* (1964), in which a victim of Nazi atrocity in Europe comes to Canada to revenge himself upon the man who betrayed his mother and other fugitives to the Fascists.

Like MacLennan in *The Watch That Ends the Night,* to which this novel bears some interesting resemblances, Kreisel here moves to a first-person narrative. The book is appropriately told from the sidelines – in 'an innocent country' (Ch. 3) and by a narrator who is intellectually uninvolved but becomes involved by the very condition of being human. He is a Jewish-Canadian professor of history, interested in discussing the moral complexity of situations safely ensconced in the past, now suddenly propelled into a profound moral dilemma in the immediate present. His symbolic name – he is a Mark Lerner who inwardly digests – indicates that *The Betrayal,* though plausible enough on a realistic level, belongs also to the mode of moral fable employed by Bodsworth. The story is itself gripping, but it is secondary to underlying philosophical problems including questions of responsibility, the limits of selflessness, the ethics of revenge and punishment. In an enthralling existential drama, Kreisel here as elsewhere explores 'how thin the veneer of civilization is even in the most civilized nations' (Ch. 13).

Kreisel was a slow and deliberate writer; his only other volume of fiction is *The Almost Meeting,* an impressive collection of short stories published in 1981. A small output for over thirty years of writing, it is a testament to his artistic integrity. Everything Kreisel published was well wrought and deeply considered. These short stories, like the novels, are centred upon moral and humanistic values, and, again like the novels, are written in a direct, spare prose that studiously avoids the rhetorically ornate. They have, too, a curiously delayed effect. Though likely to impress immediately, they go on to expand and develop within the mind. It is not merely his subject matter that reminds us without incongruity of the great Russian writers. Kreisel must be judged in qualitative rather than quantitative terms, and his quality is considerable.

Finally, there are three books excellent in their individual ways that fit into no obvious categories. A. M. Klein's *The Second Scroll* (1951) is the poet's fictional version of a visit he made to the newly established state of Israel. It takes the form of a fascinating, eccentric, wordy yet brilliant allegorical narrative that qualifies as fiction for want of any more suitable description. In five chapters which are assigned the names of the books comprising the Pentateuch, and to which are attached appropriate glosses in poetic, dramatic, essay, and even psalm-like form, it recounts a quest by a Canadian Jew for his uncle Melech (= king) which is also, as Malcolm Ross remarked in an early review, a search for Israel and for himself (Marshall ed. 90). All the verbal pyrotechnics of Klein's poetry are here brought together in a mannered but richly textured prose that communicates even when gentile readers may find the full meaning elusive. *The Second Scroll* is one of the supremely idiosyncratic books in the Canadian tradition.

By contrast, Charles Bruce's *The Channel Shore* (1954), a regional novel of Nova Scotia, employs a strangely flattened, almost monotonous style that nevertheless captures the slow rhythms of life in a remote but closely knit Maritime community. The novel chronicles life on 'the channel shore' between 1919 and 1946, from the end of one world war to the end of another, and follows the intricate interrelations between a series of local families – Gordons, McKees, Marshalls, etc. But what happens to individuals is ultimately less important than the larger patterns of communal tradition into which all fit. Bill Graham, who has escaped though he returns on a brief visit, discovers when far away that 'the Shore was part of him, a habit in the flesh, like breathing and sleep' (1945 Section). We see the community partly through his eyes, partly from the generalized viewpoint of those who have never left. On the one hand, it is loved; on the other, we receive a sense of 'the dullness of it' (I 1). The book offers a curiously haunting picture of 'past and present and future, eddying here in the flow of time' (Concluding Section). There is much that recalls Buckler's *The Mountain and the Valley*, but Bruce does not possess the stylistic power that explodes into conspicuous art. Yet *The Channel Shore* is a quiet minor masterpiece that would have been much more highly praised if its intensely regional subject and approach were not, almost by definition, so remote from the literary norms of urban Canada.

Equally remote from the metropolitan centres is the Cariboo district of British Columbia, setting for Sheila Watson's brilliant experimental novel, *The Double Hook* (1959). Watson wrote nothing more except a modest number of short stories and an early, less original novel, *Deep Hollow Creek*, not published until towards the end of her life in 1992. In *The Double Hook* she returned fiction to its prime elements: a death, a birth (for both of which the principal character is responsible), a suicide, a burning, a wounding, a theft, a flight, and a return. The imagery is archetypal (fire, water, fish, dust, storm, darkness, light), the background an external and internal waste land both regional and universal. There are no indications of time: the story exists within eternity. As the title suggests, it is a novel of polarities, the double hook symbolizing and embodying both glory and darkness, peace and serenity set against fear and violence. Clearly a modernist work, it is suffused with echoes of T. S. Eliot, and Northrop Frye's apocalyptic and demonic image-patterns are much in evidence. Though it is packed with biblical analogues and resonances, the Christian deity is less conspicuous than the Indian trickster-god, Coyote. A fruitful tension is established between subject matter and technique, between the primary feelings and responses of the characters and the sophisticated subtlety through which Watson communicates them. The novel is remarkable for its stylistic directness – we are offered no authorial commentary – and a hauntingly poetic spareness of phrase. An initially baffling but richly rewarding *tour de force*, the book has been well characterized by Rudy Wiebe as 'a beautifully structured ballad in prose' (Wiebe ed., *Stories from Western Canada*, 1972, 273). *The Double Hook*, then, is an astonishing achievement; unfortunately, however, its very nature precludes its usefulness as a direct model. Though the product of tradition, it is essentially one of a kind.

Chapter 11

Creating Fictional Worlds of Wonder

The Canadian writers who came to prominence in the 1960s and 1970s, though as varied as their immediate predecessors, are linked by a common energy, confidence, and sophistication. This is, I believe, indisputable, even if cultural historians comparing this fiction with the work produced at the same time in Britain and, especially, in the United States discern what might be regarded as a typically Canadian cautiousness. Although writers like Robert Kroetsch have explored the possibilities of 'postmodernism', 'deconstruction', and 'metafiction' (literature preoccupied with its own fictiveness), and others like Jack Hodgins have produced work allied to if not identifiable with the South American 'magic realists', most contemporary Canadian writers have found an abundance of promising material to be presented within technically complex but none the less traditional modes. This is a paradoxical result of the late development of the country's fictional potential. Some novelists, like the poets, have discovered a neglected past: Rudy Wiebe has written epic-like novels about the Indian and Métis rebellions of the nineteenth century, while Margaret Laurence and Alice Munro, among others, reconstruct the more recent past of their own childhoods. Similarly, Margaret Atwood has found a new way of exploring the brittle, oppressive, and emotionally deadening world of North American urban life by viewing it from an off-centre Canadian perspective, while Austin Clarke is in a position to exploit unique creative opportunities in fiction based on the uneasy multicultural and interracial complexity of contemporary Toronto. All these, and many others to be discussed in this chapter, have been able, thanks to the experiments and achievements of their immediate predecessors, to build out of their Canadian experience an exciting if sometimes disturbing variety of imaginative worlds of wonder.

One of the most noticeable features of recent Canadian fiction has been the number of accomplished women writers who have achieved distinction since the 1980s. Of these, though Canada has not recognized her eminence until very recently, Mavis Gallant is perhaps supreme. For various reasons, partly because she has generally lived abroad, partly because her favoured form is the short story or novella rather than the novel proper, but mostly because her qualities display themselves only gradually, she has not gained the popularity of Laurence, Munro, or Atwood. But the effectiveness of her fiction is cumulatively impressive. Although her world is not easy to get into, once entered it proves irresistible.

Gallant is less interested in plot than in mood and atmosphere. What goes on below the surface – or is said between the lines – is invariably more important than the narrative itself. Her work does not have any obvious thematic preoccupations; in retrospect, however, we come to realize that she continually concerns herself with human beings as they are affected by change and especially by war. She is, in consequence, an excellent analyst of mid-twentieth-century spiritual malaise. Though her fiction is not *about* international events, it unerringly sums up particular (political) times and places. In *From the Fifteenth District* (1979), for example, the stories focus either on the threat of war (as in 'The Four Seasons') or on its aftermath. Many of her characters lead shabby post-war lives and pathetically cherish pre-war memories. Thus the central, significantly unnamed figure in 'His Mother' 'had known what it was to take excellence for granted. That was the difference between [herself and her son]. Out of her youth she could not recall a door slammed or a voice raised except in laughter.' Similarly, the scars of war are visible throughout *The Pegnitz Junction* (1973), her most obviously unified volume of short stories dealing with Europeans attempting to come to terms with depressing post-war realities. The characters are uniformly conscious of 'a joint past that lay all around [them] in heaps of charred stone' ('An Alien Flower'). Most of them, here and elsewhere, are exiles, displaced persons in the broadest sense even if war is not directly responsible. Human relationships in Gallant are usually unsatisfactory. Children are separated from their also separated parents; individuals are forced to live alone, literally or metaphorically; some, like Flor in her short novel *Green Water, Green Sky* (1959), find the ultimate solitude in madness. The resultant mood is frequently dour – one did not think life had undone so many.

The artistry, by contrast, is exhilarating, and although Gallant never draws attention to it the reader is always aware of the sheer skill behind her narratives. She is remarkable alike for the sharpness of her perceptions and the cool restraint of her style. Her sentences possess a rhythmic clarity; every phrase counts. Sometimes she can be devastatingly witty, as in this dissection of Iris Cordier in 'The Moslem Wife': 'Tall, loud, in winter dully pale, she reminded Netta of a blond penguin. Her voice moved between a squeak and a moo' (*From the Fifteenth District*). Her capacity to catch a whole social ambience in a sentence is amazing, but her characters, though always presented clear-sightedly, are often viewed with a deep compassion. It is true, as several critics have noted, that she is not strictly speaking a psychological writer since her characters are never formally analyzed in depth. But the portraits that emerge imply considerable psychological insight on the novelist's part.

Gallant tells her stories straightforwardly; there are no frills and no short cuts. She is equally adept at omniscient and first-person narration, though the characters who tell their own stories invariably share their creator's keen eye for detail and her subtle sense of verbal texture. Thus Jean Price in 'Its Image on the Mirror' (*My Heart Is Broken,* 1964) has the same gift for recording imagistic minutiae that we find in the obviously autobiographical Linnet Muir stories in *Home Truths* (1981) and, indeed, throughout Gallant's work. By means of images repeated and interrelating with the individual narrative, she quietly imposes a containing structure upon what is often the fluid experience of her characters.

As a writer she exists within a broader tradition than that of Canadian literature. Although W. H. New may be justified in seeing Sara Jeannette Duncan and Ethel Wilson as her Canadian predecessors (LHC III 254), references within her texts to Edith Wharton and Katherine Mansfield place her in a larger, more appropriate cultural context. 'I'm a writer in the English language', she insisted in an interview (Hancock 119). There is, however, a recognizably Canadian detachment about her authorial stance, and her expatriate insights may be traced back to Canadian roots. Thus 'In Youth Is Pleasure' contains Linnet Muir's observation, 'I did not feel a scrap British or English, but I was not an American either' (*Home Truths*), and the remark can be applied to both Gallant and her work. She has brought an uncommon polish and sophistication into the literature of her native country and has also introduced an independent Canadian perspective to the literary world of both Europe and the United States.

Margaret Laurence also discovered her art outside Canada, though her travels took her to various so-called underdeveloped countries in Africa rather than to an established artistic centre like Paris. The result included a promising first novel, *This Side Jordan* (1960), and a book of remarkably accomplished short stories, *The Tomorrow-Tamer* (1963), both set in the Gold Coast just before its transformation into Ghana. But what Laurence gained most from her African experience was a sense of human tribalism – whether of families, clans, classes, nations, or ethnic groups within nations – that she was able to explore in artistic terms in her series of Manawaka novels. Set in a Manitoba prairie community based on her own Neepawa, this whole sequence is concerned with an ancestral past. All five heroines are of Scots descent, all at some time or another find themselves strangers in a strange land, and all eventually leave Manawaka physically though they acknowledge that they will never leave it emotionally. A culmination of sorts is reached in *The Diviners* when Morag Gunn, following in the footsteps of her creator, makes an ancestral pilgrimage to Scotland only to discover that her real roots exist on the prairies.

The Manawaka novels have been legitimately praised for many qualities: for the familial and regional interconnections between the stories that cumulatively reveal a unique sense of place; for an extended and coherent expression of women's attitudes and viewpoints; for the presentation of supposedly Canadian themes such as survival. But Laurence's main contribution is more explicitly literary and involves the control of voice that expresses a peculiar Canadian sensibility. The first three books in order of writing, *The Stone Angel* (1964), *A Jest of God* (1966), and *A Bird in the House* (1970), are all first-person narratives, and Laurence successfully reproduces the authentic voice of all three speakers. Hagar Shipley in *The Stone Angel*, a tough, obstinate, proud but impressively independent ninety-year-old 'rampant with memory' (Ch. 1), looks back over her life and comes to some understanding of herself. She belongs to the pioneering past, has comparatively little education, but possesses a sharpness of mind reflected in a sharp articulation of speech. The achievement of the novel resides principally in the superb fusion of form and content. Laurence's message *is* her medium; Hagar convinces because her speech is individually distinctive yet representative and wholly credible.

The thirty-four-year-old Rachel Cameron of *A Jest of God* belongs to a much later generation. An insecure, frustrated, socially gauche, highly self-critical schoolteacher, she is as sharp-minded and sharp-tongued as Hagar, though her qualities display themselves in a very different idiom. She tells her story in terse, clipped speech that necessitates extraordinary tonal control on Laurence's part. Vanessa MacLeod, in *A Bird in the House* (not strictly a novel but a collection of linked short stories with the effect of a novel), is a sensitive girl who wants to be a writer; Vanessa shares Laurence's poised clarity of mind and style, but the dominating figure in the book is her pioneer grandfather, a male Hagar, whom Vanessa fears, even hates, yet comes to respect as she recognizes some of his qualities within herself: 'I had feared and fought the old man, yet he proclaimed himself in my veins' ('Jericho's Brick Battlements'). She derives from him some of the determination that will make her a writer.

The two later novels, *The Fire-Dwellers* (1969) and *The Diviners* (1974) are, in my view, less successful because verbal decorum is imperfectly maintained. Neither Stacy MacAindra (Rachel's married sister) in the former nor Morag Gunn in the latter tells her story directly, though the narration confines itself in each case to the heroine's vocabulary and speech patterns. Stacey lives in a world of newspaper headlines, women's magazines, and television commercials, and her language cannot fully articulate the pathos of her situation. She is, as it were, a victim of a life-style she dislikes but cannot escape. Her story is never quite redeemed from cliché because she can only consider it in terms of cliché. In *The Diviners*, Laurence makes a bold attempt to round off the whole series, and to present a new kind of heroine originating from 'the wrong side of the tracks'. Morag is also a writer (two out of five is, one feels, a mistake) yet, although she is always discussing words and fiction, Laurence never manages to provide her with a convincing idiom. The muddled, indecisive, all-too-human Morag oddly lacks the mental and stylistic acuity so evident in Laurence herself. The book, though containing excellent scenes (the character – and speech – of her stepfather Christie Logan is original and a triumph), seems a willed conclusion that lacks the illusion of spontaneity so noteworthy in the early books.*

---

* I have argued this minority evaluation at greater length in the essay 'Margaret Laurence's *The Diviners*: The Problems of Close Reading' in *An Independent Stance* (1991), 200–220.

Laurence occupies a crucial transitional position in Canadian literature. She has herself built upon the country's literary past. Thus she acknowledges the 'enormous impact' that Ross's *As For Me and My House* had upon her because it 'seemed the only completely genuine [novel] I have ever read about my own people, my own place, my own time' (Introduction to Ross's *The Lamp at Noon* 3), and much the same might be said about her own work. Similarly, Hagar and Grandfather Connor represent Laurence's version of Grove-like superseded pioneers, and her coming to terms with her puritan past may be compared with MacLennan's, whose influence is fitfully discernible in *A Bird in the House*. We also see the beginnings of an essentially Canadian tradition passed on to numerous younger writers who have benefited from her example. Manawaka, like Leacock's Mariposa, has passed into the national consciousness. Most impressive of all is the extent to which she offers a broad panorama of twentieth-century Canadian experience.

The fiction of Alice Munro establishes connections with the work of both Gallant and Laurence. With Laurence she shares a concern for regional specificity; the area of southwestern Ontario that contains Jubilee and West Hanratty has become almost as distinctive as Manawaka. It is worth noting, moreover, that Laurence's Canadian series might aptly have borne the overall title 'Lives of Girls and Women'. But Munro has yet to demonstrate that she either can or wants to sustain a traditional full-length novel; the books frequently categorized as novels, *Lives of Girls and Women* (1971) and *Who Do You Think You Are?* (1978), resemble *A Bird in the House* in that the sections are printed as individual narratives rather than as chapters. In the latter case, indeed, most had appeared separately in magazines as short stories in their own right – an additional connection with Laurence's book. But Munro is closer to Gallant, of course, in her preference for the short fictional form. Both are realists and miniaturists preoccupied with literary texture. Munro tends, however, to be less detached from her main characters; while Gallant's 'Linnet Muir' sequence is an exception, and of special interest for that reason, Munro's stories based on her own experience (however transformed) are central – at least to her earlier work.

In her first volume of short stories, *Dance of the Happy Shades* (1968), Munro draws, especially in 'Images', 'Boys and Girls', and 'The Peace of Utrecht', on her own memories of childhood. This does not mean, of course, that the events are autobiographically accurate, but the atmosphere certainly is. It is not simply a matter of background, though the area is memorably evoked; rather, she preserves within the formaldehyde of her art the record of a whole way of life, an amalgam of relatives, friends, and bittersweet impressions. Indeed, her stories often seem to arise out of a context of local gossip. Thus the Munro-like narrator in 'Winter Wind' (*Something I've Been Meaning to Tell You,* 1974) remarks: 'I am only doing in a large and public way what has always been done … Even in that close-mouthed place, stories were being made.' In the prefatory note to *Lives of Girls and Women* Munro is careful to insist that the book 'is autobiographical in form but not in fact'; the story of Del Jordan is at one and the same time hyper-realistic in its immediacy yet representative in its presentation of a teenage girl's psychological – and sexual – initiation into the adult world. Munro is excellent at portraying the awkwardness of adolescence, the ignominy of girlhood (to adapt Yeats). A sense of 'shabby reality' (the phrase occurs in the 'Providence' section of *Who Do You Think You Are?*) is continually being transformed into the at-least-momentarily wonderful. 'People's lives in Jubilee, as elsewhere', Del realizes in the epilogue, 'were dull, simple, amazing and unfathomable.' 'As elsewhere' is an essential part of the insight; in Munro the universal is always incarnate in the local and particular.

Reference is frequently made in Munro's work to photographs and cameras (see, for instance, 'Winter Wind', 'The Ottawa Valley', and the epilogue to *Lives of Girls and Women*). Her photographic or documentary realism is an essential (though not exclusive) aspect of her art, but it raises corresponding problems since the camera records without judging, and Munro's life-is-like-that fidelity can easily be misrepresented and runs the risk of appearing reductive. Thus Del is interested in her own past, yet the past that predates her own consciousness as recorded by Uncle Craig is dismissed in the 'Heirs of the Living Body' section of *Lives of Girls and Women* as 'heavy and dull and useless'. The adolescent girl's exploration and eventual rejection of any transcendental religious belief is another example. Munro refrains from direct authorial comment, but most of the religious references in the book – and elsewhere in her work – are decidedly negative, although in an interview Munro herself has, rather reluctantly, described her own attitude as close to 'some kind of religious feeling about the world' (Cameron 241). It is doubtless ironically significant that Del meets her first lover at a revivalist meeting and that her sexual initiation is presented through the imagery of the section title, 'Baptizing'. There is, of course, nothing wrong with a committedly secular viewpoint, but it may be indicative of a certain narrowness of range. The immediacy and human resonance of her work is, however, supreme, and stylistically her insistence on the precise word and appropriate cadence set her in the forefront of the writers of her generation.

As a general rule, however, despite some splendid exceptions like 'Tell Me Yes or No' (*Something I've Been Meaning to Tell You*) and the name stories in her first two story collections), the fictions that do not draw upon her 'Jubilee' past lack the magic that associates with the realism in her best work. By the same token, *Who Do You Think You Are?* suffers by comparison with the earlier books since the pattern and attitudes are already familiar. West Hanratty is suspiciously similar to Jubilee, and Rose often seems no more than a coarsened reworking of Del. Munro's meticulous and creative brooding over her own experience has been inestimable but it exacts a price, and only time will tell whether she can attain to the expansiveness that would match her unquestioned stylistic and psychological powers.

Margaret Atwood belongs to a somewhat younger generation than the writers just discussed, and this is reflected in both the subject matter and tone of her fiction. She is preoccupied with minds at the end of their tether as a result of the threatening pressures of modern living. Though she can employ vividly realistic effects, her main concerns lie elsewhere; her principal modes include satire, parody, brittle comedy, and fable. Moreover, she brings to her gift for fiction the verbal and metaphorical sensitivity of a poet. The basic imagery so characteristic of her verse – water, mirrors, photographs, etc. – recurs throughout her prose narratives, and always her characteristic sharpness, even asperity, of mind is filtered through a flexible but tangy prose style.

The Edible Woman (1969) is a witty comedy of manners of the traditional kind, artfully transformed to become a medium for piercing insights into contemporary attitudes. On first publication it was easily assimilated into the literature of feminist protest, but this severely underestimates the extent of its relevance. Marian McAlpin's dilemma as a woman is only part of her larger dilemma as an individual within a prepackaged consumer society. Like all Atwood's books, it is profoundly deceptive. The extraordinary immediacy of its rendering of the Toronto scene suggests extreme realism but certain sequences (notably the chase in Ch. 9) deviate into a Gothicism which Atwood habitually exploits as a means of drawing attention to the horrendous absurdity of so much modern life; moreover, the whole conception of the cake, the edible woman, which she has herself described in terms of 'symbolic cannibalism' (*Second Words* 369), reveals a fabulous quality that derives from her earlier poetry and anticipates *Surfacing*. Though a youthful novel, it is technically assured: Atwood is artfully bold in switching from first- to third-person narrative and back again, thereby suggesting that Marian has lost control of her individuality in the central section. This is an extremely funny novel, even if its comedy is wickedly abrasive, but its basic concerns are deeply serious.

Surfacing (1972) is harsher in tone, but connections with *The Edible Woman* are clearly evident. The loss of individuality is here rendered ironically by the employment of a narrator whose character we come to know intimately but whose name we never discover. A novel about lying, madness, guilt, and the elusiveness of the past, it is also tantalizingly ambiguous. Within it a Swiftian trap is set against superficial present-day assumptions: the lies and madness belong as much to the generation of the late 1960s as to the society against which it rebelled; the deep-rooted psychological guilt emerges as the result of an abortion; the past can only be re-entered by giving up not merely what makes us modern but what makes us human. Atwood's icy dissection of contemporary clichés ('They all disowned their parents long ago, the way you are supposed to', Ch. 2) is consummately managed. The interrelation between her poetry and fiction is especially noticeable if we compare the novel with *The Journals of Susanna Moodie* published two years earlier; in both the present shares its neuroses with the past. Stylistically, the clipped, deadened sentences in *Surfacing* are also related to her verse. This is a novel in which one steps gingerly as into the dangerous modern world. If on one level it is a quest for identity, on another it virtually parodies the possibility of such a quest.

Atwood's novels develop out of each other in a remarkable way. *Lady Oracle* (1976) returns to the comic mode of *The Edible Woman*, even verging upon black farce, but it parodies almost anything (including the artist-novel, Atwood's own fascination with Gothicism, and attempts to discard or escape the past); moreover, the theme of lying in *Surfacing* is here developed in a novel where, as Robert Lecker has remarked, 'every "I" is a lie' (Davidson eds., 194). *Life Before Man* (1979) returns to the almost oppressive sombreness of tone that characterizes most of *Surfacing*, though its Torontonian setting recalls *The Edible Woman*. It extends its time span to embrace the prehistoric past and what may be the end of the world, concerns itself with the pathos of people living what seem to them meaningless lives, yet ultimately becomes Atwood's most compassionate and human book. Like all the others, however, it ends on an essentially ambiguous note in which there is 'room for hope but also for disaster' (penultimate section). *Bodily Harm* (1981), while revealing itself as more politically committed, seems less complex than its predecessors; Atwood's books, however, have a habit of revealing their subtleties only gradually. Her fiction as a whole is remarkable for its range of mood, its effortless combination of the bizarre, the hilarious, and the chilling. Our pleasure derives not merely from her cogent insights but from the poised artistry with which they are expressed.

If the basic realism of the conventional novel appears to split at the seams under the impact of Atwood's Gothicism, it meets an even greater challenge in the ambitious and startling work of Robert Kroetsch and Rudy Wiebe. Despite the fact that these two writers belong to (or, at least, began at) opposite ends of a fictional spectrum, they have much in common beyond their challenge to realism, and the qualities they share are important for the development of the contemporary Canadian novel. Both are prairie writers, but the essentially psychological view of the prairies that they offer differs dramatically from that of Ross or Laurence. This is partly because they both emerge, at different degrees of remove, from non-English-speaking backgrounds, and have no reason to follow the basically English fictional traditions that have so far dominated Canadian writing. In addition, both are profoundly suspicious of the literary traditions – as well as the literary centres – of eastern Canada. True to their own sense of place, they explore alternative approaches to fictional form and enrich the Canadian novel in the process.

Kroetsch, who comes from a family of German homesteaders, spent the 1960s and most of the 1970s in the United States. All his early novels were written during this period, and it seems clear that, despite his insistence that he remains Canadian in outlook and allegiance, this resulted in his coming under the influence of 'postmodernist' literary theories and techniques earlier than if he had remained in his native country. At the same time these methods fitted the particular kind of Canadian literary tradition that he wished to exploit, for in rejecting the traditions of eastern Canada Kroetsch was by no means rejecting tradition *per se*. But the tradition he found on the prairies was that of the tall tale, the Paul-Bunyan-type stories of the frontier, the conventions of the western. All these have links with the oral tradition that Kroetsch describes as 'the stuff of literature' (Cameron interview 85). Moreover, he detected a mythical quality in the prairie experience (coexisting with the apocalyptic tendency of prairie politics) that he has also exploited.

The result is a curious series of novels in which we can see the realistic elements of conventional narrative gradually but relentlessly giving way to other modes. In his first novel, *But We Are Exiles* (1965), he is closest to the norms of 'eastern' fiction. It owes much to Conrad and, through its deliberate naming of actual places on or near the Mackenzie River, to MacLennan, whom Kroetsch has praised for initiating this practice in Canada (see p. 31). This novel is built around the pattern of a voyage and also displays distinct traces of the bizarre and the mythical. But these elements are developed more confidently in *The Words of My Roaring* (1966), which provides perhaps the best – and certainly the easiest – introduction to Kroetsch's world. This is a social and political tall tale in which a provincial election between an undertaker and the doctor who assisted at his birth (omega and alpha) is fought in the wasteland of the depressed 1930s on a prophecy of rain. Clearly we are concerned here with concepts and patterns that take precedence over any claims for verisimilitude, though the novel remains poised between realism (nothing happens that is totally incredible) and the dynamics of an exaggerated yarn. It is unified, however, by the dominating and distinctive narrative voice of John Judas Backstrom (names always have meaning in Kroetsch), an exuberant larger-than-life figure who offers an authentic if idiosyncratic prairie voice.

But it is in *The Studhorse Man* (1969), *Gone Indian* (1973), and *Badlands* (1975) that Kroetsch develops the parody-picaresque form which has become his trademark and which he blends with all the technical tricks of deconstructionist theory. In *The Studhorse Man* an Odyssean stallion-owner wanders across the prairie in an endeavour to rent his horse for stud purposes and gets into numerous sexual scrapes himself; in *Gone Indian* an eastern, urban American graduate student travels to Alberta in search of the wilderness values he finds embodied in Grey Owl (who was, we remember, an English impersonator); in *Badlands* an eccentric archaeologist leads an expedition in search of dinosaur bones, the whole novel becoming a dissection of human obsession with the past and fascination with an all-pervasive death. And in each case Kroetsch uses different voices to tell the story indirectly, ambiguously – a mad biographer who writes, Diogenes-like, in a bath; a demented professor editing tapes; the archaeologist's daughter who deciphers (and deconstructs) his field notes and provides a feminist perspective on a male enterprise.

Here and throughout Kroetsch's work the serious games played with meaning, form, and language are conspicuous. He believes that traditional fiction limits the ways in which we view reality, and deliberately rejects the sanctioned conventions in order to build up new forms. The result is a curious combination of the gutsily vigorous (the energy in Kroetsch's work surely derives in some measure from Mitchell) and the self-consciously cerebral. Kroetsch's are unequivocally intellectual tall tales. In *What the Crow Said* (1978), indeed, he carries all these tendencies to an extreme. Realism is flouted by impossible and unexplained happenings (seasons interchange, time reverses), and narrative continuity is fractured to the extent that the book is always in danger of breaking down into smaller segments. Here is a paradoxical world in which, to quote Backstrom in *The Words of My Roaring*, 'you've got to be half-goofy – just to stay sane' ('Monday'). At the same time Kroetsch depends upon what he denies; his effects rely upon the shock to our sensibilities that would not work without our attachment to realistic conventions and a literary tradition implying continuity. By altering certain aspects of the logic and habitual procedures of the ordinary world Kroetsch, through his undoubted if peculiar talent, introduces us to an often puzzling, sometimes disorienting, but always exhilarating imaginative realm.

In terms of fictional theory and practice Kroetsch is at an opposite extreme from Grove (though he celebrates Grove's doubleness in a poem); for Rudy Wiebe, however, Grove is an important author. Wiebe was first attracted to Grove when he encountered *The Yoke of Life* and found there 'story-telling particular to my world', and although Grove is usually seen as a rather dour realist Wiebe praises him as 'a writer who wrote mythically and imagistically about the world I know' (Keith ed. 214, 216). This statement provides a clue to Wiebe's general fictional principles. Until recently a less radical innovator than Kroetsch, he extends the imaginative potential of realism from inside, discovering the mythical and imagistic within realistic conventions. Instead of deconstructing existing tradition, he develops and transforms it.

As a somewhat independent but thoroughly committed Mennonite, Wiebe brings to his fiction a moral seriousness, a didactic instinct, and a crusading zeal for raising religious issues. His first novel, *Peace Shall Destroy Many* (1962), is a technically stiff, occasionally over-earnest but often movingly effective account of a young Mennonite in 1944 split between the pacifist principles of his church and an uneasy conscience that insists on facing the fact of a world at war. This split is complicated by a realization that, despite all his convictions about peace, he harbours tendencies to violence within himself. It is a story, then, of a young man caught between traditions derived from the past and challenging contemporary realities. Set in an isolated Mennonite community in northern Saskatchewan, it also records the presence of local Indians whose land the Mennonites now own, and so introduces the Mennonite protagonist to native traditions of which he is ignorant. There are many rough edges, structurally and stylistically, to this book, but it involves a multiplicity of issues that Wiebe will explore and extend in later fiction.

After a transitional and technically experimental novel, *First and Vital Candle* (1966), Wiebe comes into his own with *The Blue Mountains of China* (1970). Here he is concerned with the recent history of his own Mennonite people, and he chooses to tell it in a complex and ambitious way that approaches the epic mode. Though not a long book, it gives the impression of length as well as breadth by the way in which it moves from Canada to Russia to Paraguay and involves a whole series of individuals and families whose stories ultimately cohere when representatives of the dispersed groups meet together on an Alberta highway in the Canadian centennial year. But what makes this novel such an advance for Wiebe, and indirectly connects him with Kroetsch's 'postmodernism', is his discovery and mastery of voice. The transposed Low-German idiom of Frieda Friesen's recurring reminiscences intersperses with third-person narrations, other voices, and transcribed conversations; within individual sections monologue often interrupts third-person narrative. By such means Wiebe creates remarkable complexity within his fiction. Both saga of endurance and religious odyssey, this novel about individuals also possesses the wider dimensions of a people's chronicle. Out of history, documents, and orally presented accounts Wiebe half extracts and half creates an imaginative vision that in no way dispenses with realism but certainly transcends it.

'Where Is the Voice Coming From?' is the title of a brilliant short story written at about this time, and henceforward voice will be a vital factor in all Wiebe's work. The voice in question is that of a Cree warrior slain by the North West Mounted Police in 1896, and the story, about the problem of making stories, leads smoothly towards Wiebe's major contributions to historical fiction, *The Temptations of Big Bear* (1973) and *The Scorched-Wood People* (1977). His subjects, naturally, belong to prairie history – the disturbances arising out of the Indian treaties and the Riel rebellions of 1869–70 and 1885 – and, again naturally, Wiebe offers a prairie viewpoint differing from the official account provided by historians of eastern Canada. Wiebe is scrupulous in his historical research, but he notes that the written records are invariably white records. Anxious to restore the balance, he gives centre stage in the earlier novel to Big Bear, the Plains Cree chief who withstood the reservation system and is presented as more imaginative, far-seeing, and essentially religious than most of the white Christian officials. And in *The Scorched-Wood People,* focusing on the perennially fascinating and ambiguous figure of Riel, Wiebe provides a Métis narrator to tell the story of the Métis leader and the rise and fall of his nation.

In these books Wiebe uses the full resources of his language to achieve an epic scope. Voice is violently juxtaposed with voice – Big Bear's emphatic dignity of speech against that of the materialistic whites who have no use (or need) for rhetoric, Riel's visionary eloquence against the foul-mouthed blather of Thomas Scott or the suave political double-talk of Sir John A. Macdonald. Above all, Wiebe presents here two ways of life in fatal conflict. Big Bear is a spiritual leader of his people who suffers for them both physically and emotionally, while Riel sees himself as a prophet of the Métis chosen to proclaim a new religion. Both attain tragic stature because in their failures we watch and partake in the failures of the people they represent. These books are extraordinary in the way they combine the qualities of tragedy, epic, history, and religious testimony within the novel form. In so doing Wiebe achieves an expansiveness unparalleled in contemporary Canadian writing through a unique blend of historical re-creation, vehement partisanship with the repressed, stylistic vigour, and a searing empathy in which protagonist and creator seem at one. He displays a creative audacity that is content with nothing less than total engagement, and ultimately demands comparison with the great Russian novelists, especially Tolstoy. There is the same combination of creativity and didacticism, the same presentation of individual lives within a context of historical crisis. Moreover, there is the same building upon the foundation of realism to achieve effects of high imaginative resonance, though in his experimental novel, *My Lovely Enemy* (1983), involving a radical examination of Christian and sexual love, the connection with realism is ultimately shattered. Wiebe makes greater demands upon his readers than almost all other Canadian novelists, but the rewards are equivalently substantial.

The 1960s and 1970s saw the appearance of a number of novelists of considerable stature, and these have inevitably established a sense of what is typical of Canadian writing of this period. Fortunately, however, the urge to follow personal and even idiosyncratic interests has continued, and these decades have produced a healthy crop of writers who, if not central to the Canadian fiction tradition, are nevertheless important presences.

Douglas LePan published his one novel, *The Deserter,* in 1964. The story of an English soldier who goes 'on the loose' just after the end of the Second World War, it belongs to the psychological world of LePan's poems about the Italian campaign in *The Net and the Sword.* But whereas in the poetry soldier and sensitive poet were united, here they are curiously divided between narrator and protagonist. Rusty (we never learn his real name) feels the urge to 'go down into the dark ... to find out where we are and what has gone wrong' (Ch. 7), though he is by no means clear about why he has to do this. In fact, the book offers a radical analysis of a sick world replete with recurrent imagery (emanating from LePan rather than Rusty) of wilderness, labyrinth, exotic but anarchic jungle, and apparently all-embracing darkness. The setting is London (though it is distanced for allegorical purposes and called merely 'the capital'), and the presentation of a shabby world of deserters, refugees, criminals, prostitutes, and the ubiquitous poor recalls the tone of Eliot's *Waste Land.* Yet the humanism integral to the writing forbids depression: 'There would always be the taste of perfection in his mouth' (Ch. 10). Not obviously Canadian, *The Deserter* nevertheless portrays post-war London from the objective sidelines, a perspective that no Englishman, or American, could have achieved. Above all, the book is memorable for the smooth dignity of its prose that makes no attempt to reproduce Rusty's idiom but mediates his responses as though he were totally eloquent and articulate.

Two years after *The Deserter,* a very different novel by a very different poet appeared: Leonard Cohen's *Beautiful Losers* (1966). A novel of extremes, it has received diametrically opposed responses. Some greeted it as a triumphant paean to liberation; others found it only a frustrating blend of *curiosa* and *kitsch,* the expense of genius in a waste of perversity. For Desmond Pacey it was 'the most intricate, erudite and fascinating Canadian novel ever written', while George Woodcock found it 'on the whole ... a tedious book' (Gnarowski ed., *Leonard Cohen* 74, 165). Despite its own excess the novel exists in an uneasy middle ground between two extremes: that all is holy and that nothing is sacred. In it Cohen rings all possible changes on sex, death, revolution, and religious mysticism – but especially the more bizarre varieties of sex. The novel is difficult to come to terms with since Cohen's characters (like Cohen himself) parody the modern world while remaining its willing victims. Stylistically, the almost shamanistic, repetitious, rhythmic lists are most conspicuous, and provide a connection with Cohen's poetry. Indeed, the brilliance of the style *almost* redeems the distastefulness of much of the subject matter, but on balance I find myself veering towards Woodcock's end of the spectrum. Sensational as it may have been in 1966, one reads it now with a curious detachment; when the four-letter words prove neither shocking nor liberating, when the attitudes of the 1960s seem, for the most part, either dated or pathetic, what then? Only an extremely gifted writer could have produced it; nevertheless, *Beautiful Losers* looks less odd but also distinctly less interesting in a milieu that has acclimatized itself to 'post-modernism' and magic realism.

Another poet's novel, Michael Ondaatje's *Coming Through Slaughter* (1976), employs many of Cohen's techniques to greater effect. A recognizable extension from *The Collected Works of Billy the Kid*, with the emphasis turned from narrative poetry to poetic fiction, this novel combines documentary and imaginative re-creation to produce a decidedly more satisfactory representation of the artist *in extremis*. Buddy Bolden was a jazz musician who went mad during a virtuoso performance and lapsed into over twenty years of silence. Like Billy, he was a man about whom more legends than facts have survived, and Ondaatje, exploiting once again his inclination for photography (Bellocq, a professional photographer, is a prominent character) and cinema (the fictional techniques clearly derive from film) builds up an unforgettably vivid word-portrait of the early jazz world of New Orleans. A deftly arranged collage of historical record, personal impressions, imagined dialogues, actual and imagined monologues, and sheer invention, it uses modern techniques so surely and consummately that they are immediately accepted as both natural and inevitable. Here, for once, popular culture is splendidly integrated into serious art. Yet although this is one of the most radically original of Canadian novels, the nurturing influence of tradition can readily be seen within it; Ondaatje has benefited not merely from Cohen but from Wiebe, whose *Temptations of Big Bear* surely lies somewhere behind the method and achievement of this book. A compelling technical and stylistic tour de force, *Coming Through Slaughter* is a novel that proves fascinating even for those (like the present writer) who have little or no interest in jazz as an art form.

If we are tempted to wonder whether *Coming Through Slaughter* deals with 'unCanadian' subject-matter, we should remember that the change in the ethnic proportions of the Canadian urban population in the last few decades has not hitherto been conspicuously reflected in fiction. A notable and (until recently) characteristically neglected exception is Austin Clarke's trilogy, comprising *The Meeting Point* (1967), *Storm of Fortune* (1973), and *The Bigger Light* (1975), which traces the fortunes of a closely knit group of Barbadian immigrants in Toronto. We get to know Bernice and Estella, Dots and Boysie, intimately; they are presented sympathetically but without sentimentality. Clarke shows them as employees confronting employers, in their relations with each other and with the neighbouring white poor; he is especially skillful in his subtle presentation of racial tension (including the tendency to anticipate prejudice on the part of those subject to it). Throughout the trilogy there is an admirable blend of humour, anger, and pathos.

Clarke's great virtue is his capacity to make his ordinary, often ignorant and foolish people both warmly and deeply human. He forces us to qualify any preconceived response to characters who lie, exaggerate, and fantasize, since the prejudice from which they suffer comes through so clearly. He places little emphasis upon plot, so nothing much happens in the course of the trilogy (though the characters gradually change class, finding security but not happiness – the third book is more a novel of loneliness than of race). But his dialogue, often violent, is superb; he can reproduce colloquial Barbadian speech rhythms without ever caricaturing his characters, save when in a spirit of prideful obstinacy they caricature themselves. He has a good eye for social gradations, which he can pinpoint with extraordinary economy, as when he divides Toronto apartments into 'urban, suburban, laboururban and snoburban' (*Storm of Fortune*, Part 2). While he is thoroughly committed to his exposure of racist bias, black and white skin colour is never translated into black and white moral evaluations. His general attitude seems neatly summed up by Boysie: 'All white people is bitches, if you ask me. And we, as black people, ain't much different, neither' (*Storm of Fortune*, Part 2). Clarke transcends the limitations of the 'black writer' category since his mixture of toughness and compassion knows no ethnic boundaries.

In total contrast to Clarke's realism is Timothy Findley's intellectual melodrama, though the society evoked in his first novel, *The Last of the Crazy People* (1967), is essentially that in which Bernice is employed as a maid in Clarke's *Meeting Point*. Here and in *The Butterfly Plague* (1969) Findley displays an ability to create compelling melodramatic worlds, the former a transformation of the Toronto Rosedale ethos of his own origins, the latter a fictional parallel to the fantastic never-never land of Hollywood he experienced as actor and scriptwriter. But it was in the work of his middle period that Findley unquestionably succeeded in raising melodrama to the level of art. In *The Wars* (1977), a formidable literary technique is welded to awesomely gripping subject matter. Findley combines documentary research with creative imagination to produce a profound analysis of the First World War that goes far beyond earlier Canadian treatments by Harrison and Child. Through the subtle interconnection and repetition of dominant images (fire, water, horses) Findley exposes the complex interactions of power, violence, and sexuality, as they manifest themselves under wartime conditions. This is developed in *Famous Last Words* (1981) to encapsulate the part-shameful, part-dazzling period that culminated in the Second World War. He takes certain historical events (the mystery surrounding Rudolf Hess's landing in Scotland, the Harry Oakes murder, some troubling incidents in the lives of the Duke and Duchess of Windsor) and creates a story that interlinks them and proves wholly convincing at the time of reading. As the narrator (Pound's Hugh Selwyn Mauberley) remarks, 'this is history as she is never writ' (Part 4). On later reflection acceptance may be difficult, but Findley as magical melodramatist provokes a willing suspension of disbelief while we are under his spell. (Moreover, a little historical research results in the scary realization that many of the incidents that might seem like Findley's 'conspiracy-theory' inventions have a sinister historical basis.) There is an almost paranoid intensity about all Findley's books which is both impressive and disturbing; he plays his own inimitable variation on the exploration of wonder that, as we shall see, preoccupied a number of our novelists in the 1970s.

At this point, however, it is important to remember once more that some of the most notable fiction in modern Canada has been written in the short-story form. Of course many novelists, including Laurence, Atwood, Wiebe, and Clarke, have produced distinguished shorter fiction, and most short-story writers have attempted full-length novels. I have already discussed the work of Gallant and Munro, and shall soon be considering Hugh Hood, who writes with equal ease in short and extended narratives. But some writers seem most successful, and most comfortable, when writing short stories. This is partly because the form allows an emphasis on the intricate texture of experience seen at close range and uncomplicated by the more artificial demands of an elaborate plot, partly (and this may be another way of saying the same thing) because the short story is a form of prose narrative that can aspire to the condition of poetry. A synchronic presentation is possible, a minute analysis of feelings and motivations that can hardly be offered in the larger diachronic sequences favoured by the traditional novel.

Norman Levine's stories, collected in *One Way Ticket* (1961), *I Don't Want to Know Anyone Too Well* (1972), and *Thin Ice* (1979), are for the most part told in the first person by a narrator whose life – Jewish origin, service in the air force during the war, years spent in England as an expatriate writer, etc. – reflects Levine's own. They are quiet stories that articulate a mood, catch a passing phase, express the subdued melancholy of ordinary experience. External details are rendered with a sharp impressionistic precision, but the stories are essentially introspective, preoccupied with the sensibility of the inner man. Accounts of outsiders, Canadians in England or expatriates returning briefly and painfully to Canada, are convincingly presented, yet one feels that Levine is more interested in their generalized condition as individuals never quite able to fit into their society. His stories can easily be underrated because their unobtrusive effectiveness seems simple, unremarkable, restrained. But they record a sense of Levine's particular angle on life, compassionate but at the same time resigned. A common greyness, an existential loneliness, silvers everything.

While Levine was a Canadian who lived much of his life abroad, several of the short-story writers have been born elsewhere and bring fresh perspectives on Canada from the outside. John Metcalf, for instance, has produced a number of stories in which inspiration comes from his English childhood. Retrospection is a predominant subject in his earlier work; the past seems a better because more human place, and he has a sharp eye for the absurdities, even obscenities, of modern living (Evelyn Waugh is one of his culture-heroes). But although his satiric streak finds ample material within Canadian life (notably in the savagely amusing novel *General Ludd,* 1980), the more deeply probing side of his creative consciousness did not acclimatize so quickly. His most serious and accomplished stories tended to be English in tradition and attitude as well as in subject and setting, and for all their delicacy and subtlety (or, perhaps because of them) seem off-centre in a Canadian context. The English child is as yet an uncertain father to the Canadian man, though in his more recent stories, especially the novella *Girl in Gingham* (1978), we can see him adapting his remarkable talents to the material around him. Like Levine, he often uses writers for his protagonists, the art of writing often serving as a way to comment indirectly on the art of living.

More complex, at least in terms of the way biography determines subject matter, is the fiction of Clark Blaise, born in the United States of French- and English-Canadian parents. His stories involve the continual rearranging of personal experience, an almost obsessive brooding over a haunting past. The same basic elements – life in Florida, a series of schools in which the protagonist is always an outsider, a child's less-than-innocent view of his parents' unstable marriage – recur again and again, and Blaise takes full advantage of his own variant on James's 'international theme'. In *A North American Education* (1973) the stories are divided among Norman Dyer, an American living in Canada; Paul Keeler, a Canadian who is seen travelling in Scandinavia and visiting India after his marriage with an Indian (thus duplicating his creator's experience); and Frankie Thibidault, a French-Canadian always an uncertain stranger in a shifting American locale. Each seems to represent an aspect of the others; as Robert Lecker comments, 'Frankie Thibidault is destined to become Norman Dyer' (*On the Line*, 1982, 29). And in *Tribal Justice* (1974), though the names and immediate details change from story to story, the protagonists share a basic sensibility and the same patterns of experience. Oddly enough, in Blaise this becomes a strength rather than a weakness. For him, as for Metcalf, the pain of growing up is an endlessly fruitful subject because it offers an available image of change and enforced adaptation. Blaise creates a world in which we can continually move deeper to discover the wellsprings of human behaviour. The polished lens of his clear and euphonious prose accentuates the familiar patterns of life, transforming the ordinary into the extraordinary, fictional story into symbolic quasi-biography. Though he lacks the impressive detachment of a Gallant or a Hood, Blaise creates super-realism out of an exquisite artifice.

All these writers share a lucid, even fastidious style, an emphasis on solid craftsmanship, an insistence on subtlety, aesthetic standards, and a consistently developing art. Others, notably Leon Rooke and Audrey Thomas, show a remarkable richness and inventiveness, their best stories impressing by their excitingly original qualities and, especially in Rooke's case, by a powerful if idiosyncratic style. As yet, however, they have failed to convey a coherent, unifying vision. Still other younger writers promise to develop in the years ahead. Special mention should perhaps be made of Alistair MacLeod's *The Lost Salt Gift of Blood* (1976), a series of stories concerning Cape Breton, all united by the theme of a sensitive consciousness brought up against the harsher realities of life, and by the quiet, slow dignity of a prose that expresses the essence of sadness. Thanks to Metcalf, whose numerous anthologies of short stories have been appearing regularly since the early 1970s, a whole generation of talented writers is emerging who find the short story a satisfying and infinitely varied form of expression.

Perhaps the most remarkable fictional development of the 1970s was the insistence on the part of a number of writers with very different interests and talents that contemporary fiction could partake of rich imaginative possibilities as yet unconsidered. This is not simply a matter of breaking the link that seemed to bind the novel to realistic conventions; rather, it acknowledges the presence of the marvellous and fantastic within the real. In so doing, it opens up an exciting new wing to the house of fiction.

The publication of Robertson Davies's *Fifth Business* in 1970, the first volume of his Deptford sequence of 'linked novels' (as he described them in a preliminary note to *World of Wonders*), was a remarkable literary event. Within the pattern of Davies's own development, it showed an extraordinary maturation; he was now sounding deeper notes than those he employed in the 'Salterton' trilogy (see pp. 52–54) without losing the polish and wit that had characterized his earlier work. But within the context of contemporary North American fiction, it signalled a revolt against the tyranny of the inarticulate 'Yahoo hero' (*A Voice from the Attic* 343), and the drab sordidities of flophouse and kitchen sink. Superficially, the idea of Dunstan Ramsay, an ageing, somewhat eccentric schoolteacher, telling the story of his life, both physical and psychological, in an incredibly long letter-report to his headmaster seems unpromising, doomed to banality. But Davies's emphasis on surprising events and urgencies that disturb the surface of seemingly ordinary lives proves refreshingly unusual. His lightly worn wisdom, his blending of the profoundly serious with the grotesquely comic, above all his elegant sense of style, combine to create a rich and original fictional experience.

Technically, Davies had moved from the convention of an omniscient narrator in the Salterton trilogy to first-person narration, but this represents a development within carefully designated limits. His protagonists – the schoolteacher, a lawyer, a magician-cum-actor, and in *The Rebel Angels* (1981) members of the university community – are invariably people who earn their living through speech. All possess the gift of the gab. This certainly restricts his range: if the average Canadian is tongue-tied and inarticulate, then he or she has no place in these novels, and it is also true that the narrators all tend to use the eloquently rounded periods of Davies himself. But the novelist establishes a coherent fictional world, a world that he moulds to his own intellectual interests. One of the most impressive features of Davies's work is the transformation of his diverse interests into viable fictional terms. In *Fifth Business* this includes the nature of religious belief and commitment, and the accompanying concepts of evil and sanctity; in *The Manticore* (1972) the focus is on Jungian psychology; in *World of Wonders* (1975) Davies spotlights the magical, theatrical world of illusion and make-believe that has always been one of his prime enthusiasms; and in *The Rebel Angels* he offers a shrewd, idiosyncratic, intellectually stimulating anatomy of a university. Davies's adventures are adventures of the mind, the romance of scholarship, the satisfactions of expertise; and he communicates a delight in all their related quirks and quiddities.

At the same time, if his interests have the attraction of the unusual, and occasionally the patina of the old-fashioned, some of his basic presuppositions are by no means out of line with contemporary trends. Ramsay is fascinated by the ways in which history verges upon myth, and *The Manticore,* which employs Jungian psychoanalysis as a framing device, explores the extent to which universal symbols establish their presence within the fabric of personal lives. Again, Davies's novels present sexual experience in a way that combines modern and traditional attitudes. He draws with equal ease upon Freud and (especially) Jung in the modern period, and Rabelais (who haunts *The Rebel Angels*) in the past. He portrays both the pleasures and the agonies of sex, and, while never underestimating its importance, neither divorces it from moral issues nor overlooks its humorous aspects. His novelistic technique similarly partakes of the old and the new. On the one hand, he acknowledged indebtedness for the trilogy form to Joyce Cary; on the other, he told the interrelating Deptford stories so that we see the same events from different perspectives and are sometimes forced to make radical readjustments of our earlier assumptions. This concern for the intricacies of fictional technique fits with surprising ease into 'postmodernist' theories of art necessarily preoccupied with art. Davies was never, indeed, afraid of artifice. Part of his legacy from the theatre was a delight in the joy of displaying skills, the creation of something out of nothing (the plot of the whole Deptford trilogy develops from a misdirected snowball). The image of the magician that pervades the series is an image of invention and mystery as well as of deceit and illusion.

Davies succeeded in tapping an imaginative spring in the human psyche that realism too often inhibits – especially in Canada. I have already discussed his satire on Canadian stuffiness in the Salterton novels. Here, as in other respects, his analysis goes deeper. Canadians, he insists, are not so dull and uninteresting as they are often painted; to understand them one must penetrate to the suppressed inner selves only occasionally manifest in a cold climate. Davies was no nationalist, but his view of Canadians as living 'bizarre and passionate' lives under a veil of moderation and respectability (Cameron interview 38) not only extended the line of Canadian comedy he derived from McCulloch, Haliburton, and Leacock, but used the national character as illustrative of a broader (Jungian) pattern of human behaviour. Davies thereby transcended the national to embrace the universal (in Smith's terms he is a cosmopolitan writer) and so enlarged the Canadian literary tradition.

At first sight, Hugh Hood's novels are far removed in tone and effect from Davies's, yet the two shared many characteristics in common. Both were conscious of inhabiting a world of wonders that ultimately makes sense, though Hood's partook of the divine wonder and purpose sanctioned by traditional Catholicism. Again, Hood noted that his early fiction tempered a basic moral realism with 'an inclination to show ... credible and unpredictable, and often melodramatic, things' (*Governor's* 127); both, then, recognized an elusive but essential connection between the imaginative and the down-to-earth, the eternal and the ephemeral. Hood described painting as 'an art that exhibits the transcendental element dwelling in living things' (ibid 130), and the remark could well be applied to his own work. Hood's range, however, is wider than Davies's. There was less of the satirist in his make-up, little that he rejected because virtually everything is redeemable. Thus an extraordinary feature of his fiction is Hood's interest in, and knowledge of, the things of this world (in *Reservoir Ravine*, for instance, he even writes authoritatively about the evolving designs of brassieres in years before his own birth).

Because he was seldom conspicuously innovative in technique, Hood's firm control of his material can easily pass unnoticed. He was, however, preoccupied with formal matters, believing that artistic design is analogous to the design he recognized in the world about him.

Superficially, this fictional organization is revealed in symmetrical chapter- and part-divisions (the four elemental sections of *A New Athens*, for instance) or the balance and arrangement of his volumes of short stories. A good example of the latter is *Around the Mountain* (1967), a collection of twelve stories centred thematically and geographically on Montréal and arranged in a seasonal cycle that reflects the city's changing moods. But this formal concern becomes more subtle when his characters play out patterns already prefigured in sacred story. Thus in *You Cant Get There From Here* (1972), a political novel set in an imaginary African state, the prime minister presides over a cabinet of twelve, one of whom betrays him. At the same time the country in question is split between two tribes with different languages and customs, both mistrustful of the other, and Hood therefore invites us to read the book with English and French Canada in mind. He has spoken generally of his work as 'an essay in the mode of Christian allegory' (Struthers ed., 102) and even suggests that the Dantesque fourfold levels of interpretation could be applied to his own writings.

Hood's reputation as a short-story writer is secure. John Metcalf has accurately described *Flying a Red Kite* (1962), his first publication, as 'the first book of modern stories published in this country' (*Kicking* 149). But he will eventually be judged, I believe, by the quality of his ambitious novel series, *The New Age / Le nouveau siècle*, a twelve-volume, comprehensive, imaginative view of life in twentieth-century Canada. The central figure is the symbolically named Matthew Goderich, who is roughly the same age as Hood and shares many of his interests. Artistically, the most satisfying of the earlier volumes is *A New Athens*, perhaps the most profound study of eastern Canada in relation to its history, a book that convincingly evokes the 1950s and, with its protagonist's absorption in history, art, and archaeology, offers vivid examples of the way the present re-creates and reinterprets as well as replaces the past. Incidents are unified by image and emblem rather than by narrative succession, while the sequences involving the salvaging of the sunken ship of 1812 and May-Beth Codrington's inspired picture of the inhabitants of Stoverville (Hood's portrait of Brockville, Ontario) entering the New Jerusalem deftly set the novel against both time and eternity. The series as a whole aims to do the same for the century and for other parts of the country. It is an extraordinary undertaking, and, despite the difficulties involved in bringing the whole country within his scheme and imaginative range, *The New Age* as a whole will clearly provide impressive sequences in Hood's favoured vein that he calls 'documentary fantasy' (Struthers ed., 79; see also pp. 104–5 below).

Like so many contemporary writers, Hood blurred the distinctions between fiction and non-fiction. *The Swing in the Garden* reads like a personal memoir, and he can invest even statistical details with fascination. Although intrinsically Canadian, his world appears refreshingly different. Predominantly a novelist of urban life, whether he wrote about Toronto, Montréal, or the small towns of Ontario and Nova Scotia, he was unabashedly middle-class in his viewpoint, and his Catholicism (a more intellectual brand than Callaghan's) allowed him to view the life of the city with faith and hope. Above all, there is a healthy directness about Hood's prose that assiduously reflects his attitude to the world. He can offer precision of detail, delicacy of nuance, a smooth felicity of language, and warmly human compassion. Like Blaise and Metcalf (whose autobiographical re-creations are in many respects similar to his own), like Munro, whose psychological penetration he admired – and even, of course, like Davies – he had the capacity to irradiate and so exalt the commonplace.

Finally, Jack Hodgins has created his own inimitable world of wonder out of the unfamiliar area of northern Vancouver Island. Once he eventually burst into print, in just over five years between 1976 and 1981, with two novels and two short-story collections, he wrote himself into Canadian literature. Hodgins had found a way of combining the regional realistic with the magically fantastic; in his work the myth- and survival-ridden preoccupations of the Canadian literary consciousness have been transformed into something fresh and compelling, rich and strange. He has evolved a literary medium that can draw upon and successfully combine the magic realism associated with the Colombian novelist Gabriel García Márquez and the colloquial blarney of the traditional Irish storytellers. His narratives are hilarious, haunting, half comic, half disturbing, often touching, always technically assured.

Spit Delaney's Island (1976) contains a medley of stories unified by a common locale. The protagonists are all Vancouver Islanders, mostly from the logging and pulp-mill communities in the north; more to the point, the majority of them are vigorous, independent, irrepressible 'characters'. Spit himself appears in the first and last stories – 'bookends', Hodgins called them in an interview (Hancock 73) – and so provides a loose frame for the whole. But the stories are linked thematically as well. Images of breaking and separation recur throughout, topographically represented by the dividing line between sea and land but soon extended to embrace what separates human from animal, human from human – even, perhaps, what is and is not possible in fiction. *Spit Delaney's Island* is a magnificently vivid evocation of life in the country north of Nanaimo, but it transcends its regional origins to comment in its exuberant, unostentatious way on the general human condition.

The Invention of the World (1977) extended Hodgins's range remarkably. While the locale and the vigorous, fantastic, yet curiously convincing characters remain, Hodgins presents them with a new technical complexity. As the title suggests, it is a novel about invention – which includes deceit as well as creativity. And Hodgins's juxtaposition of myth and modern experience is also conspicuous. A key (though not central) character is Strabo Becker, who shares his first name with an ancient Greek historian, suggests Charon in his role of ferryman between mainland and island, attempts to record the local history of the region with his tape recorder, and, in the words of the opening section, 'wants to be God'. The story of Donal Keneally, the mythic villain figure, a false Messiah leading his deluded followers into a paradise-wilderness, is told in the style, and with all the miraculous accretions, of Irish epic. Yet the principal unifying figure is Maggie Kyle, endearing, promiscuous, resilient, life-affirming, whose cabin community on the site of Keneally's Revelations Colony of Truth is known as 'Kyle's Krazies' or 'The Revelations Colony of Kooks' ('Maggie' 1). Moreover, Hodgins's fantasy can blend with deeply moving pathos, as in the scene where, fulfilling his widow's request, Maggie returns Keneally's ashes to an ancient Irish hilltop; the subject of origins is explored at mythic, historical, and personal levels. We enjoy not only the characters and their bizarre adventures but the inventive gusto with which Hodgins tells his story.

With *The Resurrection of Joseph Bourne* (1979) and another collection of linked stories, *The Barclay Family Theatre* (1981), Hodgins consolidated his reputation. Both can be enjoyed at a simple level of zany make-believe, as one rip-roaring tall tale after another, and there is the same skillful and seemingly effortless mixture of comic and serious. But the novel is of special interest for its deliberate defiance of the doom-and-gloom school. Based on the conviction that there is 'lots of room for new ways of looking at things' (Part 1, Section 3), it undercuts the now conventional view of a meaningless world with disturbing intimations of mystery and purpose. Bourne himself even revives after apparently dying; miraculous and natural commingle. In 'More Than Conquerors', a dark story from *The Barclay Family Theatre,* however, an expected resurrection is revealed as a horrifying illusion. Indeed, this collection, which resembles *Spit Delaney's Island* in its loose formal and more rigorous thematic interrelations, impresses by the changes it rings on earlier Hodgins narratives. Mayor Wiens, an absurd figure in the previous novel, is presented in 'The Sumo Reversions' as a far more rounded character in a story which changes drastically from the farcical to the touchingly pathetic.

Hodgins has inevitably been classified as a magic realist, but the term is hardly an adequate pigeon-hole. His realism – and the books ultimately deserve that title – is neither 'magic' nor the official kind that reproduces the diurnal round, and certainly nothing like photographic realism. Instead he portrays, like Davies and Hood, that strange world of wonder, comedy, challenge, and terror which, whatever the literary systematizers may say, impinges upon us at all times and from all sides. Also, in the most profound sense, he is a regionalist, one who transforms his local backyard into an image of the whole creative universe. And he is a writer of relaxed 'postmodernist' novels that delight and move but never become self-indulgent or ponderously self-important. Hodgins's way is not, of course, everybody's way, but he is significant in demonstrating the seemingly endless possibilities for Canadian fiction.

Twenty Years After

In the twenty years or so since I wrote the previous chapters, there has been surprisingly little change in the careers and reputations of most of the more recent writers discussed. Some, of course, had already completed their work. Others continued writing, but consolidated what they had achieved without extending their range into new genres or new areas of experience. I shall make whatever minor adjustments to the record seem necessary in the following pages. What has changed, however, is our improved awareness of the character of the writings already produced. This has happened only occasionally as a result of recent literary-critical activity (I shall be offering comments on this topic in the concluding chapter). Most often it has occurred because illuminating literary biographies have appeared that reveal the shape of careers that had not been evident before, or, especially in the case of poets and short-story writers, because selected or collected editions have been published, thus facilitating a more confident overview. (These are recorded in the fully updated lists of 'Further Reading.') And sometimes, of course, the passage of time has made possible a more balanced assessment of a writer's *oeuvre.* I shall therefore proceed, as before, by genre, concentrating on writers who have added both quantitatively and qualitatively to their stature. In addition, I shall take note of what seem to me the more promising younger writers who had not yet achieved obvious distinction in the mid-1980s or, in some cases, had not even begun to publish. Needless to say, these judgments will be highly selective and tentative.

Of the poets discussed in Part Two who have continued to publish in the intervening years, P. K. Page has now won herself the unquestionably major status that she had not quite achieved earlier. *Hologram* (1994), which developed her love for poetic artifice to new heights, consists of fourteen *glosas,* poems elaborated out of four continuous lines selected from a previous poet. Page succeeds not merely in writing in the manner of the chosen poet but in remaining at the same time indisputably and splendidly herself. She responds exuberantly and memorably to the traditional challenge of the form, reminding us of the pleasure derived from recognition of verbal dexterity. In addition, her two-volume collected poems, *The Hidden Room* (1997), enables us to savour the full extent of her traditional poetic powers.

Some other seasoned poets, it has to be conceded, have been less successful. Although interest in Dorothy Livesay's work has continued, this has been for ideological (feminist) rather than for literary reasons, her later publications drawing attention more to her artistic weaknesses than to her strengths. Raymond Souster, though continuing to publish with enviable energy, has produced disappointingly slack volumes that have diluted his earlier reputation. And who would deny that Robert Kroetsch's later *Field Notes* fail to match the wit and originality of the earlier? On the other hand, several – notably George Johnston, Douglas Lochhead, Eli Mandel, John Newlove, and Anne Wilkinson – seem even more impressive now that substantial collected or selected volumes of their writings have appeared.

A few poets, moreover, have explored new pastures. Douglas LePan's *Weathering It* was offered as his complete poems in 1987, and though subsequent publications added nothing to his artistic reputation (and to some extent detracted from it), the 'Weathering It' sequence itself is a remarkable achievement that has not yet received the critical attention it deserves. A collection of fifty irregular and unrhymed sonnets, it is ostensibly autobiographical, proceeding from childhood memories in the remote past to his 'trying to be ready for death' in an anguished present (62). Yet it also constitutes a dour record of twentieth-century experience: the poet was born in 1914, and imagery of war dominates the sequence – even the opening sonnet is entitled 'Like a Battlefield'. Moreover, LePan here developed a style that, while retaining much of the formality and resonance of his earlier verse, has taken on an unexpected directness and flexibility. As a result, his whole contribution to Canadian poetry needs to be re-examined.

D. G. Jones (whose collected poems is in preparation) has moved in a comparable direction. In such volumes as *The Floating Garden* (1995) and *Grounding Sight* (1999), he appears to speak and write for himself, reproducing an important aspect of modern experience by showing how, in his apparently peaceful rural retreat, the violence of the contemporary world perpetually intrudes through radio, TV, books, conversation, and personal memories. Sometimes frustratingly allusive, these poems at their best offer a verbally fastidious, intellectually stimulating 'criticism of life'. George Bowering's career developed differently. In *Kerrisdale Elegies* (1984), he cleverly rewrites and transforms Rilke's *Duino Elegies* in terms of contemporary residential Vancouver, not only bestowing an important substantiality to his otherwise somewhat diffuse work but, by setting it firmly within a European as well as American context, paradoxically justifies his place within a recognizably Canadian tradition.

In addition, there are three poets who began publishing in the earlier period and who, I now realize, ought to have been included. While Charles Bruce's novel *The Channel Shore* was discussed, it is now clear that his poetry, especially *The Mulgrave Road* (1954), deserves similar recognition. His apparently straightforward yet highly sophisticated poetry about simple subjects is in fact an essential component of the Maritime poetic tradition remarkable for the flawless consonance between meaning and rhythm, every word – and the positioning of every word – carefully chosen to produce an appropriate cadence, a 'meshing of language and place', as Carmine Starnino notes (*Lover's* 145). Bruce himself insisted that, for him, poetry was 'the art of striking sparks from the common and usual' (*Mulgrave Road* [1985] 31). He wrote, as in his novel, about ordinary rural people gaining their livelihood from the land or the sea, and they are presented clearly, probingly, with a fine eye and ear for the detail that reveals character.

The late Richard Outram, a very different poet (Starnino calls him 'Canadian poetry's cleverest artificer' [115]), was similarly preoccupied with employing words and rhythms to their full effect. But his range is infinitely broader – though this has been, I suspect, an obstacle to proper recognition. An intensely religious poet, as his early title *Exsultate Jubilate* (1961) suggests, he could simultaneously be highly sensual; indeed, his God was made manifest through the whole creation in an almost Blake-like multiple vision. Though wholly serious as an artist, remarkably faithful to the discipline of his craft, his high spirits could lead to the creation of bizarre situations. Thus *Mogul Recollected* (1993) is a book-length poetic sequence commemorating the drowning of a circus elephant at sea. An unpromising subject, it might be thought, but Outram, while open to its grotesque aspects, invests it with deep pathos and even tragic significance. He is often difficult to interpret, and his allusions can become bafflingly obscure. As a result, he generally published his verse privately with his own Gauntlet Press, creating books and broadsheets of singular beauty, illustrated by Barbara Howard, his wife and a distinguished artist in her own right. But his second 'selected', *Dove Legend* (2001), will, one hopes, create wider interest in his work.

The writings of Gwendolyn MacEwen, initially recognized as relating to the so-called mythopoeic group of poets, were also marked by obscurity for various reasons: partly because her poems were often highly personal, partly because her generally arcane reference (Egyptology, alchemy, magic and the occult) rendered her work less easily accessible. She later admitted that her early verse was 'very enigmatic' even to herself (Pearce interview 69). It was not until publication of *The T. E. Lawrence Poems* (1982) that her writing fully matured. This poetic sequence presented an impressive portrait of Lawrence while at the same time revealing him as disturbingly representative of his age, in a manner curiously reminiscent of Atwood's *Journals of Susanna Moodie*. Since her early death, and the recent collection of her poetry in two volumes (co-edited by Atwood), it has been easier to appreciate the remarkable unity of her work, including her novels (*Julian the Magician* and especially *King of Egypt, King of Dreams*, the story of Akhenaton, the notorious monotheistic Pharaoh) and her short stories, particularly those devoted to Noman. Her imaginative presentation of male leaders, intellectually impressive yet vulnerably separated from the general attitudes of their time, provides her with a mirror image for her own situation as female poet. Her poetic language, like LePan's, combining the informal and the mysteriously resonant, reinforced her insistence that 'all of life is an act of magic' (*Noman's Land* 112).

At the end of chapter 6 I offered three hostages to poetic fortune: Stephen Scobie, Don Coles, and David Solway. Scobie has subsequently experimented with a variety of forms and styles, as his selected poems *The Spaces In Between* (2003) illustrates, but without in my opinion achieving a unified view – perhaps because, in 'postmodernist' fashion, he considers a unified view unattainable. He has, however, continued to produce interesting work, notably (though uncharacteristically) *Gospel* (1994), a poem sequence centred upon the life of Jesus, and has become a master of the seemingly casual but elegantly controlled poetic line.

Meanwhile, Coles and Solway have established themselves as the most talented poets of the past quarter of a century. Coles has evolved his own inimitable style that reproduces the hesitancies of everyday speech rhythms while at the same time catching the subtlest nuances of experience within a wry phrase. His range of subject is as wide as Scobie's – his most recent collection, *Kurgan* (2000), moves from a machine smoothing out ice at a local hockey rink to the excavation of an ancient grave in northern Russia – but is unified by a common intellectual curiosity expressed through distinctive diction and cadence. Perhaps his most original book, *Little Bird* (1991), is a dazzling display of tonal and syntactical pyrotechnics in a long poem-duel addressed to his dead father.

Solway, too, has distinguished himself through the discipline he brings to his poetry. He has spent a lifetime exploring the relation between his Canadian-Jewish upbringing and the isles of Greece in which he has spent so much of his time. More recently, he has even invented a hermit-like Greek poet, Andreas Karavis, whose poems, 'translated' by Solway, explore the modern world from one steeped by ancestry in the Greek past – an astonishing imaginative achievement carried off with a combination of playfulness and panache. In *Modern Marriage* (1987), he produced fifty technically regular sonnets recounting the crisis in a personal relationship with an amazing display of technical expertise. In *Franklin's Passage* (2003), exploiting almost all possible meanings of 'passage', Solway offers a multi-faceted focus on the third Franklin expedition in a style shifting cannily between the Victorian and the contemporary. His most recent book at the time of writing, *The Pallikari of Nesmine Rifat* (2005), continues his Karavis caper with poems supposedly written by Karavis's spurned lover. Solway appeals especially to poetic connoisseurs: his telling is all-important yet is always directed towards appropriate explications of his subject. He is especially important for his challenge to the technical slackness evident in so much free verse.

In an important article, 'Double Exile and Montreal English-Language Poetry', Solway notes that 'some of the best writing in English is [now] to be found in Montreal' (*Director's* 59). He argues that, because English-speaking writers are 'doubly cut off from an appreciative or at least available audience' by being a minority enclave in Québec and, so far as literature is concerned, in Canada (60), they have had to rely, healthily, on their own resources and so have established their own artistic freedoms.

Modestly, Solway does not list himself as a notable leader and practitioner within this group, but he draws our attention to an impressive collection of poets, including, among others, Michael Harris, Robyn Sarah, Eric Ormsby (recently relocated in England), and Carmine Starnino. Moreover, he insists that it is a group, not a school or a clique; they are 'individual poets ... free to choose their own sources, influences, usage, directions, and identities', building their home *'in the domain of language itself'* (60; Solway's emphasis).

That they are all distinctive as well as accomplished poets is true. At the same time, one can readily detect shared stylistic characteristics: sharp observation resulting in vivid presentations of detail, skillful combination of free verse with a deft employment of traditional verbal effects (especially assonance, along with internal and half rhymes), all of these serving a precision of statement that frequently (albeit unexpectedly) challenges modern minimalist tendencies with soaring flights of linguistic exuberance.

Michael Harris's subject matter ranges from 'Turning Out the Light', a harrowingly direct sequence about his brother's death from cancer to 'Death and Miss Emily', a detailed, poised, witty account of the last day in Emily Dickinson's life. His stylistic range is similarly broad. He can be elegantly balanced and restrained, as in this unusually distanced moment from 'Turning Out the Light' –

> Evenings we watch
> the darkness descend
> in its needle
>
> and the morphine
> rise in the drowse
> of his smile
>
> (*New and Selected Poems* 182)

– to the verbally and aurally inventive description of a 'bullfrog's *whump* which wells from the rotting / sump of the swamp' ('June'). Individual poems focus minutely on a specific, often natural object ('Barn Swallow', 'The Dolphin') and are often replete with startlingly original metaphor. He seldom employs regular metre, but his poems *look* regular by being divided into (unrhymed) couplets, triplets, quatrains, and sonnets that allow for flexibility within the illusion of a rigid structure.

Robyn Sarah began by training as a classical musician, and her early writing attracted the attention of the more discerning of her fellow poets by virtue of its fastidious search for the exact word within an appropriate rhythm. Her poems concentrate upon moments, insights, experiences that transcend the ordinariness of daily life. As she notes in 'The Face', 'a grace resides in mysteries like these'. 'Grace', indeed, is a recurrent and essential word in Sarah's writing; it is not accidental that a recent collection was entitled *A Day's Grace* (2003). Above all, she is adept at making 'much of something small' ('Bounty'), always eager to catch in verse what she calls 'the dance of things' ('Villanelle'). Her forms vary from free verse to sonnets and even sestinas. Her words seem simple, even commonplace – 'tinder words ... / the ones that / jump-start the heart', as she writes in 'Scratch' – but every vowel, every consonant fits into an elaborate pattern of sound. Her poems need to be read slowly, and preferably aloud; individual lines should be savoured, rolled around the tongue.

Eric Ormsby's earlier poems (in *Bavarian Shrine* and *Coastlines*) seem to originate in an almost Hopkinsian determination to achieve absolute precision, both scientifically accurate and poetically vibrant. They direct an eye-on-the-object gaze towards simple material objects ('Starfish', 'Foundry', 'Anhinga') in order to catch their essential qualities but also to establish their impact on the inquiring human mind. His stance may be detached, but his language is flamboyantly immediate. Solway has described it admirably as 'an eclectic fusion of precision and prodigality' (*Director's* 169). Believing that 'too much contemporary poetry in English [is] paltry and anorexic' (Bowling interview 201), he has developed his own verbal luxuriance that delights in a curious blend of exactitude and euphuism. (It is not accidental that he was responsible for the selection of poems in P. K. Page's *Planet Earth* [2002].) The smell of skunk cabbage, in the poem of that title, is 'smug and opulent', while in 'Grackle' the bird's 'acrid cackle' is 'a cacophony of slick and klaxon cries'. As Starnino remarks, 'Ormsby really loves words' (165).

Araby (2001), which draws upon his expertise as a professor of Islamic Studies, extends his range of subject matter while maintaining his verbal pyrotechnics. It consists of a series of interconnecting poems presenting the lives and attitudes of two Arabs, both auto mechanics (!), but one a poet, the other a religious fanatic. The traditional and the contemporary exist side by side; 'Scent of cardamom' (13) mingles with 'dense gasoline / ambrosial with oxygen' (31). Ormsby employs the whole range of traditional poetic style; as David O'Meara has observed, 'each poem is a plate heaped with alliteration, rhyme, sophisticated syntax, wild word-play and original dead-right metaphors' (28). Ormsby also insists on the pre-eminence of poetic form: 'Form isn't merely an ornament ... Form has to arise out of the necessity of the subject' (Bowling interview 201). But throughout his work, and nowhere more conspicuously than in the inventive and verbally luxuriant *Daybreak at the Straits* (2004), in which the poetic voices vary from the wife of Lazarus to a group of emperor penguins (!), his ultimate loyalty is to words: their engaging sound, flexible rhythms, exact meanings, their unpredictable oddity. Like Sarah, and more than most poets, he needs to be read aloud for his full quality to be recognized.

Carmine Starnino is the youngest of this group, and has clearly learned from them. His first book, *The New World* (1997), focuses on the traditional Italian family in which he grew up, and demonstrates an early mastery of poetic discipline surely deriving from Solway's example. Hence the control of rhythm within a verse line, the spare but apt use of adjectives, and a skillful orchestration of sound: 'This is my grandmother testing the hot iron with a spittled finger. / This is the hiss' (13). *Credo* (2000) displays an Ormsbyesque focus on a specific object ('Short Essay on a Tweed Cap') and a conspicuous interest in the range and variety of words, including even 'Words with a goat-stench to them' (43). All these features combine with an increased verbal luxuriance in *With English Subtitles* (2004), which is full of 'small / depth charges of phrasing' (25) and glories in 'a new word that shivers in the surprise / and risk of its arrival' (26). Here is a new and distinctive voice, one of the latest examples of the Canadian poetic tradition that he examines with critical verve and a healthy discrimination in his collection of essays, *A Lover's Quarrel*.

Montréal, of course, has no monopoly on contemporary Canadian verse, though there is little sign in other parts of the country of an equivalent group of poets, let alone a recognizable 'school'. An enormous amount of verse is being written – and published – but much of it seeks a perilous novelty more likely to result in eccentricity than distinctiveness. A number of poets, however, attempt to maintain the tradition of English by keeping open links with the earlier tradition, both Canadian and 'foreign', benefiting from techniques and craftsmanship derived from the past and helping to pass them on to the future. Though it is probably invidious to risk names in a situation where no clearly major figure is in evidence, a few representative talents are worth identifying. These include Richard Greene, drawing upon his Newfoundland heritage, John Reibetanz, Ricardo Sternberg, and the late Sheldon Zitner in Toronto, John Terpstra in Hamilton, Peter Stevens in Windsor, Christopher Wiseman in Calgary, and George Whipple in British Columbia. There are, however, three additional writers whose recent contributions deserve consideration in more detail, because each has an obvious and distinctive sense of purpose.

Like Dorothy Livesay and Miriam Waddington before her, the late Bronwen Wallace was social worker (ultimately, in a home for battered women) as well as poet, and the tension between the communal and the solitary is never far from the surface of her work. Because she wrote invariably about women and their responses to the challenge of everyday life, she is understandably placed within the feminist camp, but she was a feminist with a difference: in her best work human realities always take precedence over political precept. Indeed, a remarkably high percentage of her poems is domestic in reference; her subjects are presented preparing meals in the kitchen, working in their gardens, keeping an eye on the children outside, gossiping over the back fence. 'Ordinary' and 'common' are recurrent words: 'Ordinary Moving', 'Common Magic', 'the awkward tangle of an ordinary growing up' ('Red Light, Green Light'). As a consequence, her quietly conversational poems avoid the conspicuous artifice of rhyme and regular metre; they are unusual in being almost totally devoid of metaphor, and when similes are used they are seldom original but derived instead from popular speech. They employ plural pronouns ('we', 'you') as often as the personal 'I', but those addressed are sometimes 'we women writers' (as in the central 'A Simple Poem for Virginia Woolf'), sometimes the neighbours (as in the equally central 'All That Uneasy Spring'). Wallace's poems vividly evoke the atmosphere of small communities, whether rural or suburban, and (especially in the later poems) the sense of frustration and limited horizons that can accompany them. Such emphasis can sometimes become oppressive, yet, because she made no grand or over-generalized statements, she could successfully communicate the feelings, insights, and yearnings of her generation.

Jeffery Donaldson's distinctiveness could not be more different. The Yeatsian title of his first volume, *Once Out of Nature* (1991), indicates that he is concerned, in a corresponding phrase from 'Sailing to Byzantium', with 'Monuments of unageing intellect'. His most characteristic poems present artists and thinkers at significant moments in their careers that provide notable revelations about their work: Monet (on the occasion of his funeral), Vitruvius (after his retirement speech), Heidegger (a wickedly contrived situation that challenges his philosophy), a superb sequence of poems offering a commentary on Mahler's life and attitudes. This Nature/Art dichotomy is further explored in *Waterglass* (1999), where the moving water is an emblem for the ever-changing world of nature, and the inert glass represents the created human product that preserves it within the artifice of eternity. Here the chosen subjects include Bonnard's paintings of his wife, the Vienna Secessionist exhibition of 1902, a painting by Caspar David Friedrich, and an incident from Freud's last days in London. Donaldson presents these moments in a deliberately impersonal, unemotional style that focuses on the essentials and wittily revives dead metaphors. Peter Sanger (147) has rightly praised his 'precise mixing of predictability and unpredictability in rhyme and pace', while Cynthia Messenger (112) remarks that there is 'simply no ego at the heart of his poems' and that he 'defers almost always to other voices', voices which belong as often as not to acute observers of the subjects concerned. To be sure, Donaldson's speakers are all characterized by the same combination of precision and restraint, but this serves to suggest how the creative mind tends to work – inquisitive, vigilant, sensitive to the ambiguities of words and their effects. His poems, it should be stressed, do not yield their secrets easily, but they invite intrigued and intellectually curious readers to return to them again and again.

Finally, notice should be taken of the inimitable, gossipy poetry of Mary Dalton because it too places a welcome emphasis on the power and expressiveness of language, especially the Newfoundland dialect. Here (a rarity in the twenty-first century), we experience the sense of a vivacious community expressed within its own unique speech. In her earlier books, *The Time of Icicles* and *Allowing the Light*, she confines herself for the most part to standard English, often gaining effects through the juxtaposition of language levels, as in 'Rosicrucian software' ('Buttercup Poem'), though we occasionally notice dialect phrases like 'on mauzy days' ('Your Absence Palpable'). But in *Merrybegot* (2003) the local vocabulary comes into its own. These are short poems (none extends over a single page, and they average less than twelve lines apiece). They consist of brief samples of oral speech, laced with proverbial phrases and salty dialogue refreshing to hear in the generally homogenized present. Unexpectedly, Dalton, though referring readers to the *Dictionary of Newfoundland English,* does not offer a glossary, yet this hardly matters. One can appreciate a phrase like 'Conceited as a punt's piggin' ('Devil's Fashion') or 'That rawny ghost of a gommil' ('The Tangler') without inquiring into subtle niceties of meaning. And many of her best effects depend not on obscure dialect but on feisty rural speech: 'He'd the face of a robber's horse' ('Elt'), 'They'd dazzle a blind horse with blinkers on' ('Rosella and Bride'). Dalton forces us to acknowledge and revel in the all-essential variety and quality of words.

Many established writers of fiction, like their counterparts in poetry, added to their list of publications without notably altering the overall pattern of their work. Yet some developments occurred. Morley Callaghan broke new ground with *A Time for Judas,* set in Palestine in the first century AD and offering a reinterpretation of the motives and actions of Judas Iscariot, though it threw light on Callaghan's liberal Catholicism rather than indicating any change in his art or style. W. O. Mitchell published much in the last decade of his life, but only to demonstrate a further sad descent from the standard of *Who Has Seen the Wind.* Brian Moore used Canada as the setting for two experiments, a historical documentary of the 1970 Montréal kidnappings, *The Revolution Script* (1972), and the historical novel *Black Robe* (1985) deriving from *The Jesuit Relations,* but the rest of his later work revealed him as, at heart, an Irish novelist. Sheila Watson unexpectedly published *Deep Hollow Creek,* a conventional novel written in the 1930s using material later transformed in *The Double Hook* but important only for the way it highlights the quality of her classic work. Alistair MacLeod reinforced the promise of *The Lost Salt Gift of Blood* with another short-story collection, *As Birds Bring Forth the Sun* (1986) but his full-length *No Great Mischief* (1999), though highly impressive in its individual parts, betrays formal weaknesses when presented as a novel.

Robertson Davies, of course, added substantially to his already extensive body of work by completing his Cornish trilogy. The central volume, *What's Bred in the Bone* (1985), is now regarded as one of his most satisfying books. His final trilogy was left incomplete at his death, but the second novel, *The Cunning Man* (1994), displays a strength and vitality remarkable for a writer in his eighties. Interestingly, in his later fiction he abandoned the first-person narrative of the Deptford trilogy, returning to the omniscient narration of the Salterton books, devising all sorts of bizarre (and, to his admirers, delightful) preternatural machinery that enabled him to view the human comedy *sub specie aeternitatis.*

Mordecai Richler published two widely acclaimed novels towards the end of his career: *Solomon Gursky Was Here* (1989) and *Barney's Version* (1997). Personally, I consider that the former, like *St. Urbain's Horseman,* suffers because its satirical subjects – materialistic greed, sexual indulgence, etc. – are so clearly relished for most of the book that their exposure is difficult to take seriously. The novel is also too close-packed (readers are recommended to use a later edition furnished with a genealogical table). *Barney's Version,* on the other hand, is a triumph, clearly qualifying, with *The Apprenticeship of Duddy Kravitz,* as Richler at his best. One quickly realizes that nothing is sacred and that the book is less a narrative than an anthology of the absurdities of the contemporary age. Richler's only foray into first-person narrative, it succeeds because it avoids any pretence to a dubious moralism. The title is crucial. This is Barney Panofsky's version of his life experience. Richler has created a character who can share the full resources of his own stylistic dexterity. As a result, no modern folly, Canadian or otherwise, escapes unmentioned or unscathed.

Like Richler's, Rudy Wiebe's most recent novels reveal an evolving shape to his work as a whole. *A Discovery of Strangers* (1994) is another novel about white/Indian relations, this time going back to the first Franklin expedition, but *Sweeter Than All the World* (2001) brings his career full circle. It is an epic- or saga-like novel about the history of the Mennonites from seventeenth-century Europe to contemporary North America. Perhaps significantly, the main character is now a secularized Mennonite. Though its craggy prose style and constant shifts of time and place make it a challenge to the reader, this novel's visionary scope sets it alongside *The Blue Mountains of China* as a major fictional statement.

In 1984, just after the first edition of this book went to press, Timothy Findley published *Not Wanted on the Voyage*, his brilliantly imaginative moral fable about the biblical Noah and the abuse of human power over the animal kingdom. At once a thought-provoking allegorical fantasy and a creative *jeu d'esprit* (including fairies, unicorns, and talking opossums), it was unfortunately the last of Findley's major works. Henceforward, his dependence on melodrama and his conspiracy-theory attitude to the world took centre stage. His books were compulsively readable, and many of the situations (like the reincarnation of Conrad's Kurtz in *Headhunter*) are wonderfully bold in conception, but towards the end his work became damagingly predictable. Stephen Henighan has noticed an 'adjustment of Findley's reputation that has begun in recent years' (44), and I suspect that his later work will not sustain the praise heaped on it at the time of publication.

Jack Hodgins has published new novels regularly, his work always energetic, humorous, though with serious and even threatening undertones, and he continually experiments with bizarre effects containing aspects of magic realism and 'postmodern' metafictional parody. *The Honorary Patron* considers Vancouver from the viewpoint of a returning B.C.-born art critic, while *Innocent Cities* explores the multiple meanings of 'Victoria' by way of the British queen who gave her name to an age, a Canadian city, and an Australian state. His most recent novels form a loose trilogy united by the irrepressible Macken family that has appeared in his work from *Spit Delaney's Island* onwards. The most successful of these is *Broken Ground* which, while filled with Hodginsian exuberance, sounds darker and deeper notes with its emphasis on the protagonist's experience in the First World War, a sequence recounted with deeply moving immediacy. Although the last, *Distance*, seemed ill-focused and lumbering, *Damage Done by the Storm* (2004), his third volume of short stories (including a Macken novella), displays all the invention and vitality of his early work, and may well cause readers to wonder whether he is not at his best in the shorter form.

Margaret Atwood has clearly succeeded in becoming, at least for the moment, the most widely known Canadian writer of her generation, but the probing originality and richness of Canadian texture of her early work have been depleted in the process. She has experimented with a dystopia (*The Handmaid's Tale*), and forms of thriller (*The Blind Assassin*) and science fiction (*Oryx and Crake*), though she prefers to call the last 'speculative fiction' (*Moving Targets* 330), but thinness and repetition – sometimes, as in *The Robber Bride*, amounting to self-parody – are becoming evident. Perhaps significantly, *Cat's Eye*, which draws creatively upon autobiographical elements in her childhood, and *Alias Grace*, set in the place and time of Susanna Moodie, have been her most appealing recent efforts. Atwood may have paid a heavy price for world-wide recognition. As early as 1984, in a predominantly positive essay, B. W. Powe observed: 'It is amazing to watch how time and again Atwood will go for the flip remark, the tight-lipped murmured suggestion, the parody that passes for satire, the political sentimental "yes", the lyrical phrase that opts for polish and gloss' (152). Since that time, alas, these tendencies have proliferated.

Other writers, already established, developed their talents conspicuously, and one of these was John Metcalf, who completed the forging of a new style to fit his new circumstances. *General Ludd* had dramatized an outsider's almost apoplectic response to the vulgarity and blatancy of North America while at the same time recognizing and acknowledging its pulsing energy. In his subsequent short fiction gathered (and sometimes recycled) in *Adult Entertainment, Shooting the Stars, Forde Abroad* and *Standing Stones,* he has disciplined his reaction by creating the precise cadences, appropriate pacing, and subtle control implicit in such seemingly small technical details as punctuation and italics, to provide a virtually definitive critique of contemporary experience. Perhaps ironically, this has been attained by harnessing the finest virtues of modern *English* prose – the prose of Evelyn Waugh, Anthony Powell, and P. G. Wodehouse. To borrow from one of M. G. Vassanji's titles, the 'In-Between World' of the Canadian present has helped to make this achievement possible.

One of the most prolific, and certainly the most ambitious fiction-writer of the period was Hugh Hood. He not only continued to publish collections of short stories, but also completed his twelve-volume roman fleuve, *The New Age / Le nouveau siècle*, just before his death in 2000. *The New Age* (despite the full title, all the novels are in English) follows the fortunes of an intellectually curious art historian, half English-, half French-Canadian, who lives through the main political, social, and artistic events in Canada (including Québec) from the 1930s to modern times. The series has not yet received the detailed attention it deserves because it presents readers with an unusual literary challenge: the 'plot' continues from book to book, yet each volume belongs to a different fictional subgenre. There are specimens of fictional memoir, situational comedy, *Künstlerroman,* science fiction, even spiritual allegory. Readers need to be dedicated, intellectually flexible, and sensitive to literary nuance. It is a highly original work strong enough to dictate the unique way in which it must be read. When more literary critics come to recognize its artistic satisfactions, and its profundities, *The New Age* will come into its own.

I made only passing reference to Leon Rooke's writings in Chapter 11 because, as Keith Garebian wrote later, 'Rooke was too strange, too idiosyncratic a virtuoso for many Canadian critics' (CWTW Fiction 8, 1989, 133). That situation has now changed, partly because his prolific output has forced itself on our attention, but also because 'postmodernist' attitudes have now provided a more responsive context for his work. Yet Rooke is no ordinary postmodernist – or, rather, his postmodernism partakes of creative paradox rather than reductive parody. He offers a clue to his independent position when he remarks in an interview (itself an opportunity for paradox) that he holds 'the old-fashioned notion that one of the writer's jobs is to project a multitude of voices, of identities, and not simply to write of the self' (Hancock 165).

It is impossible to offer any satisfactory generalization about Rooke's art, because every story is different and so needs to be read and appreciated in a different way. Moreover, each story presents a separate and unique world, complete with its appropriate style and sometimes even its own language. Some (like the quirky but ambitious *Shakespeare's Dog*) are characterized by an original perspective, others (like 'Mama Tuddi Done Over' in *Death Suite* [1981]) by an unforgettably distinctive idiolect or personal speech. Yet although Rooke is often experimental, he is rarely guilty of innovation for innovation's sake. He is most remarkable, perhaps, for his energy and the amazing fertility of his imagination. There is enough invention in each short story to fill the average full-length novel. The impish quality so characteristic of his writing is sufficiently indicated by the title 'The Birth-Control King of the Upper Volta';

even his apparently flippant stories often conceal a serious purpose. Significantly, few of his admirers can agree on what they consider his best stories. Furthermore, Rooke is a superb reader – or, rather, performer – of his own work, and many readers have testified that they recognized his artistic quality only after having heard him in person.

A prominent feature of recent Canadian literary history has been the emergence of a heartening number of gifted writers whose ancestral origins are non-European. Coming to terms with their work is, however, difficult because literary criticism has not yet developed an adequate way to discuss it. Many of these writers naturally favour different emphases and follow different literary conventions, and these must be understood, accepted, and absorbed. On the other hand, such writers have to learn to adapt their own traditions to the possibilities, challenges, and exigencies of the English language. So far, unfortunately, commentary has been obsessed with questions of race, and has fallen back on oversimplified ideological judgments that lead to serious misreadings. The following discussions attempt to place these new writings within the Canadian literary context of which they now form a part.

Joy Kogawa's *Obasan* has attracted considerable attention since it first appeared in 1981. A searing account of the experience of the Japanese Canadians dispossessed and uprooted immediately after the attack on Pearl Harbor in 1941, it is a supremely effective and deeply moving human document. That said, however, we may still question whether the book fully succeeds as fiction. It involves an uneasy combination of three genres: autobiographical memoir (the story of Naomi, the narrator), documentary history (the political crusade of Aunt Emily), and contrived fiction (the fate of Naomi's mother in Nagasaki). Yet the title refers to another aunt, "Ayako, my Obasan" (ch.4), an essentially passive presence, enduring rather than acting, who supposedly offers a unifying centre, a still point in a tragically turning world.

There is a superb subject here that could well form the basis for a great novel. Kogawa, previously known as a writer of delicate imagistic verse, writes sensitively, effectively, even poetically, yet, as her decidedly less impressive later fiction indicates, she lacks the skills of a major novelist. She provides the necessary dignity required by the subject, yet the process of memory and recollection remains at odds with the justifiable anger of protest. Above all, one can legitimately ask whether fiction is an appropriate medium for the topic, and doubt the extent to which it adds to the revelation of tragic historical events. Ultimately, the poignant subject is inevitably more compelling than the art that presents it; the fictional interest is always in danger of obscuring the shocking actuality of the events recorded.

Of all these writers, Michael Ondaatje has, at least temporarily, achieved the greatest literary recognition, though for reasons that are not immediately obvious. The success of the film version of *The English Patient* (along with accompanying media 'hype') is clearly one factor. Others doubtless include the current openness to Gothic-style melodrama (cf. Findley and the later Atwood), a taste for exotic settings (Egypt here, and the Sri Lanka of *Anil's Ghost*), and the trendy liking for a combination of sex and violence seemingly endemic to modern popular culture. On the other hand, he has been faulted by Philip Marchand for 'inflated sentiment' and 'grotesquely inapt metaphor' (28), while Henighan goes so far as to claim that he 'has little grasp of the novel as a literary form' and cannot present 'interaction between people' (140). Henighan, as a novelist himself, could be vulnerable to the charge of professional jealousy, but he is only one of many to suspect 'that most people who start reading [*The English Patient*] do not finish it' (138). Moreover, I have heard Ondaatje's prose described as so beautiful as to be unreadable.

Ondaatje is, however, nothing if not 'postmodernist' with his fragmented action, borrowings from popular arts (notably B movies), and politically correct attitudes to war and racial issues (though Kip's response to the bombing of Hiroshima at the close of *The English Patient* seems embarrassingly flimsy and factitious after a reading of *Obasan*). A rather cosy aura of cynical pessimism and the romance of rebellion – both dear to armchair intellectuals – pervades his work. None the less, he is an accomplished writer, and *Anil's Ghost* is effective in evoking a strong sense of what was traditionally known as 'local colour'. His Sri Lankan scenes and people are presented with a vivid immediacy very different from the artful and artificial glamour of *The English Patient,* and with less emphasis on surrealist fantasy than their equivalents in *In the Skin of a Lion.* But the taste for Gothic effects has risen and fallen several times in the history of the novel, and it remains to be seen whether Ondaatje's work will date quickly or whether it will be found to possess lasting interest.

Three immigrant fiction-writers from non-European origins who have attained distinction in recent years are Rohinton Mistry, M. G. Vassanji, and Neil Bissoondath. It can hardly be coincidental that all three have personal histories involving complex interracial relations which make any straightforward colonial/imperial assumptions hopelessly simplistic. As a Parsi, Mistry writes from the perspective of a people who long ago fled religious persecution in Iran, and have more recently suffered political intolerance in post-Independence India. Vassanji lived as an Indian in both Kenya and Tanzania, and so is in a position to provide unique insights into African/British relations. Bissoondath has a comparable history as an Indian born in Trinidad.

Moreover, despite coming to prominence within a supposedly 'postmodernist' age, all fit comfortably within the supposedly old-fashioned realist tradition of fiction. This should come as a surprise only to those who are slaves to the vagaries of literary fashion. Just as an earlier generation of Canadian writers, finding a wealth of story that had not been exploited in literature, wrote readily and effectively in modes that appeared exhausted elsewhere, so Mistry, Vassanji, and Bissoondath have stories to tell which are excitingly unfamiliar to non-Indian Canadian readers. In addition, their work can also appeal to those who share their origins but are fearful of losing their cultural heritage in a new land. Such material has no need for postmodern tricks and trends; the few exceptions, notably the metafictional last story in Mistry's *Tales from Firozsha Baag*, merely serve to confirm the general rule. There is therefore no excuse for any condescending attitude towards the traditional strengths of these probing and original fictions.

Of the three, Mistry, although he has so far written exclusively of Bombay (Mumbai) life, is closest in form to the traditional English novel; whatever Asian influences he may reflect, we clearly recognize a kinship with Charles Dickens. There is the same capacity to create an absorbing, intricate, and well-rounded narrative. He can manipulate a large cast of characters, all readily differentiated, and, in particular, is able to convey a convincing sense of crowdedness. The short stories in *Tales from Firozsha Baag*, all set in the same apartment block, are interlinked not merely for the sake of artistic effect (though the technique *is* effective), but to take full advantage, for novelistic purposes, of the hard fact of people forced to live close together and interrelate, easily or uncomfortably, with each other. Above all, Mistry's work is Dickensian in its tonal variety, in the skilled juxtaposition of the farcical and the poignant, the tragic and the resilient. His prose, while clear and adequate for his purpose, rarely draws attention to itself like Ondaatje's; Mistry is more remarkable for his structure and control than for style or euphony.

All these, alas, are qualities that are too often ignored by 'postcolonial' commentators. As for politics, his books are all set in post-Independence India, where ideological oppression comes from within – the 1971 war with Pakistan in *Such a Long Journey,* and Indira Gandhi's 1975 'Emergency' in *A Fine Balance.* Mistry's emphasis, even in scenes of political crisis, is on the human, a characteristic he shares with Vassanji. For all their sense of political tensions, his books focus on such topics as the clash between the generations (especially between the values of the old and the new India) or the difficulties involved in tending the aged (as in the significantly titled *Family Matters*). Concentration on these topics, without in any way detracting from the specificity of the instances, performs the additional function of demonstrating to non-Indian readers that the major human problems, whatever 'postmodernist' theory asserts, are universal in relevance.

M. G. Vassanji is preoccupied with movements of history and the ways in which these impinge upon individual lives. His novels might better be described as sagas or family chronicles. His protagonists are usually Indians in Tanzania or Kenya, under British and/or African rule, with complex and uneasy relations to the other races. When Independence comes to Africa, they find themselves caught in an 'In-Between World' as victims of racial suspicion that they not uncommonly practise themselves, a 'visible minority' whether in Africa or in the New World. 'Why do you call me "Indian"? I too am an African' (*Gunny Sack* 211) is a crucial remark that sets up resonant echoes for immigrants to contemporary Canada.

The gunny sack that provides the title for his first novel contains objects that spark bittersweet memories from the past history of Tanzania and the lives and sufferings of its peoples. The novel itself, impressive yet confusing to non-Indian readers because of the numerous characters with puzzling names connected by bewildering family ties, acts as a repository for themes and situations that recur continually in his later work. Thus Salim encounters bitter atavistic opposition when he wishes to marry an African, and Deepa faces a similar crisis in *The In-Between World of Vikram Lall.* A recurring pattern involves youthful dreams of freedom and unbounded possibility doomed to frustration by prejudice and corruption in both governmental circles and private families.

For Western readers, Vassanji's most satisfying novels are likely to be *The Book of Secrets* (1994) and *The In-Between World of Vikram Lall* (2003). The title of the former refers initially to a diary kept by a British administrator, and the attempts of an Indian to interpret what it says and what it does not say. As a result, it refers ultimately to the novel we are reading. *The Book of Secrets* is a deftly structured novel set for the most part in Dar es Salaam, which is presented as a bustling hive of activity comparable to Mistry's Bombay. *The In-Between World* takes us on an extended journey through time from the horror of the Mau Mau killings in Kenya in the 1950s to the 'Years of Betrayal' (Part 3) in the now independent country as well as in personal lives, both Asian and African. *No New Land* and *Amriika,* less original in form, nevertheless treat Afro-Asian experience in suburban Toronto and the United States respectively. All Vassanji's books present their protagonists (strong or weak, Indian or African or white) with credibility, understanding, and compassion.

'Writers have one function, and that is to tell a good story.' In itself, Neil Bissoondath's comment in an interview (Allen and Carr 90) is a non-controversial statement that most serious writers, including Mistry and Vassanji, would surely accept. It is certainly the conviction upon which the present book is based. What makes the remark supremely significant here is that a writer of Bissoondath's background should make it. At one stroke he shatters and transcends the whole 'postcolonial' debate. By refusing to 'play ethnic' (Allen and Carr 86), he points the way to a new – yet, ironically, age-old – literary dispensation.

Mistry and Vassanji write out of their own experience about the people and situations that they know best, as writers (from Jane Austen to Alice Munro, from Henry James to Robertson Davies) have always written. But Bissoondath is confident enough, and courageous enough, to venture further. He has broken down theoretical barriers by writing novels and short stories about people of all backgrounds, colours, and creeds, and has done so with convincingness and stylistic ease. Some of his best short stories, like the interlinked 'Insecurity' (*Digging Up the Mountains*) and 'Security' (*On the Eve of Uncertain Tomorrows*), show an Indian-Caribbean having to choose between danger and violence in his native place or safety and boredom in Canada. But he can also portray a Viennese Jewish caretaker ('Goodnight, Mr. Slade') and in 'The Cage' writes across the divide of gender as well as nation and race by presenting a narrator who is not only female but Japanese.

His novels display a similar variety and independence. His first, *A Casual Brutality* (1988), confines itself to his own people and place, but *The Innocence of Age* (1992), set in a Toronto of shabby restaurants and cut-throat materialist competition, while containing scenes of racial conflict (significantly balanced so far as aggressors and victims are concerned), concentrates on white Canadians and is more interested in the hostility arising between generations than provoked by skin colour. *The Worlds Within Her* (1998) returns to Indian/Caribbean material but focuses on the heroine's mixed marriage with a white Canadian. The central figure in *Doing the Heart Good* (2002), where all the characters are white, is a sympathetic but crusty seventy-five-year-old widower with a number of English-Canadian prejudices and obsessions that are presented clearly but without fuss or conspicuous comment. All Bissoondath's novels are strongly plotted and well-crafted, and draw upon the sanctioned qualities of traditional fiction. This may make him appear old-fashioned in the trendy 'postmodernist' present, but, if one takes a larger view, he is clearly a precursor of a healthier literary world where writers are cherished for their artistry rather than for their origins or ideology.

If we look for the more satisfying examples of the postmodernist mode as expressed in fiction, we shall find it most readily in playful and exuberant comedy. One engaging example is Leon Rooke's novel *The Fall of Gravity* (2001), in which a father and daughter leave the security of their gated apartment residence to travel the length and breadth of the United States in search of the absconding mother. Conspicuously defiant of 'the realistic mode nearly everyone prefers' (ch.2), it is ironically traditional in offering an updated version of eighteenth-century picaresque. It becomes a fictive roller-coaster through an absurd America, a veritable anthology of satirical 'takes' on American images, clichés, myths, and sacred cows.

Yet its success depends not so much on its zany inventiveness as on Rooke's capacity to make his lightly etched characters both convincing and appealing, as well as on the zippy wit and precision of his prose by which, as Keath Fraser has noted, his 'common language' is made 'uncommon' (Gorjup ed. 290).

But perhaps the most absorbing of these texts is Thomas King's *Green Grass, Running Water* (1993). King is half Cherokee, half Greek, but he offers here a firm yet good-natured spoof on western literature and attitudes from the native 'Indian' viewpoint. The book revels in cartoon-like parody, with little regard for either realism or credibility. Coyote, the trickster-god, is prominent, and is accompanied by a chorus of white/native stereotypes: out of *Robinson Crusoe,* Fenimore Cooper's Leatherstocking novels, *Moby-Dick,* and the Lone Ranger movies. As allusive as any high-modernist text, the nothing-is-sacred (yet, paradoxically, all-is-sacred) approach to human lives and human myths is as exhilarating as it is amusing. The book is packed with literary and historical references ranging from Genesis to contemporary political allusions, both American and Canadian, together with outrageous and witty puns (Nasty Bumppo, 'Hosanna da our home on Natives' land' [Ch. 11]). The intellectual element is both intense and sophisticated, though few readers can be relied upon to recognize all the allusions. *Green Grass, Running Water* is a dazzlingly original work, unrepeatable. King's other fiction pales beside it, but he has stated, sadly but doubtless wisely, that he is unlikely to write anything similar.

The postmodernist mode, it seems, though suitable for satire and comedy, is ill-equipped for tragic insights or the presentation of deep emotions. However, the younger writers with roots in other cultures have already demonstrated that construction is ultimately more important than deconstruction, that traditionally sanctioned modes of writing still have much to offer. The twenty-first century will doubtless bring new developments. It has already, indeed, produced one writer of remarkable literary promise. I refer to Mary Swan, author of a novella, *The Deep* (2000), and a collection of short stories, *Emma's Hands* (2003). *The Deep* recounts the experience of two young women, identical twins, who leave Canada in 1918 to tend the wounded in the trenches. It is remarkable for highlighting an aspect of (and viewpoint on) the First World War that has been generally ignored. The stories in *Emma's Hands* focus mainly on women looking back over their lives with special reference to their own loves and, in particular, the deaths of their loved ones. Swan has a comparatively limited palette – one is reminded of Jane Austen's four-inch-wide piece of ivory – but is remarkable for a delicate, beautifully cadenced prose, much less mannered and self-conscious than Ondaatje's, that conveys nuances of unparalleled subtlety. Swan's style is inseparable from her content. She is a strong, independent writer who recognizes the importance and relevance of the past, and knows that adherence to (con)temporary preferences is no substitute for quality of writing.

My original chapter on Drama was brief, and this update will follow suit. It is true that certain aspects of Canadian drama have developed over the past twenty years: playwrights have gained more practical theatrical experience, and more Canadian actors, directors, and dramatists have been produced. Yet the main obstacles to an indigenous drama are still present: the seductions of didacticism and the sensational; the splintering of dramatic emphases (women's drama, socially committed drama, homosexual drama); too many playwrights and directors with specific political agendas. To make the point baldly, if one applies the same standards to drama that have been applied in this book to other genres, the pickings are modest. Canadian drama has enjoyed a few international successes, but little enduring recognition. When a New York critic describes Sharon Pollock as 'a prize-winning playwright in her native Canada' but then adds, 'a fact that may say more about the Canadian theatre than the quality of her work' (qtd in Conolly 265), one wants to protest and deny. Unfortunately, I find it difficult to do so.

The premature deaths of George Ryga and Michael Cook were also serious setbacks. Of the established dramatists discussed in Chapter 7, only David French has produced a significant number of new plays. The most successful have been the three additional 'Mercer family' plays: *Saltwater Moon, 1949,* and *Soldier's Heart.* French has always managed to find a suitable language for the family members, and been able to present creative challenges to his actors. Both *Saltwater Moon* and *Soldier's Heart* are fairly static plays with small casts (two and three characters respectively). The latter, which focuses on memories of the First World War trenches, demands especially experienced actors, but French provides them with excellent opportunities for changes of pace and tone as jokes intermingle with the horror. But his non-Mercer plays have been disappointing. *That Summer* lapses into the tear-jerkingly sentimental, while *Silver Dagger*, a thriller in which individual fortunes shift so rapidly that the last act of Shakespeare's *Cymbeline* seems relaxed by comparison, though highly theatrical, remains no more than a thriller.

The recent playwrights who have quantitatively built up a large body of work are Sharon Pollock and George F. Walker, both of whom began writing in the early 1970s. Perhaps Pollock's most successful plays, both historical, are *Walsh,* which presents the betrayal of Sitting Bull after Custer's defeat in 1876, and *Blood Relations,* which explores the notorious Lizzie Borden murder trial of 1892. She shows considerable dramatic invention in both plays, but little striking dialogue, and her liking for melodrama and the didactic tends to dominate her work. Too often one gets the impression that a play is written primarily to make a social or political point.

Unlike many contemporary dramatists, Walker has evolved a dramatic speech which suits his own work, whether the jungle-colonial setting of *Beyond Mozambique,* the Italianate European world of *Zastrozzi,* or the Nova Scotia of *The Art of War.* Dialogue is clipped, pared down to the minimum, firmly adapted for stage delivery. Walker is blessed, moreover, with an apparently innate sense of the theatrical. Yet his concentration, to quote Chris Johnson, upon 'electronic media, pop culture, street slang' (56), as well as his obsession with the conventions of B movies, ultimately proves limiting. For all its surface brilliance, his work seems curiously empty. This is a drama of intellectual caricature, with clichés exaggerated to the point of grotesquerie. As a result it tends to produce no more than monuments of its own extravagance. His audiences are encouraged not so much to think or judge as to congratulate themselves on their supposed sophistication. His populist reaction against 'taste' and 'high art' is likely to irritate traditionally educated playgoers, and it is hardly surprising that his plays appear incongruous within the context of this book. The tradition of drama in English, we might say, is not a club of which Walker would want to become a member.

Of all the literary genres, drama, with its special techniques and effects (not to mention the number of skilled participants needed in bringing a play to dramatic life), may well present the greatest challenge to writers attempting to express themselves in a new language and a radically different culture. Some years ago Tomson Highway provoked considerable interest and attention with *The Rez Sisters* and *Dry Lips Oughta Move to Kapuskasing*. These plays had the attraction of novelty, though one would have thought that a Cree playwright might find a more pressing subject than, for instance, an epic journey of seven women to 'The Biggest Bingo in the World'. Satire? Perhaps. Profundity and insight? No. But Highway has made a valid point about the situation in which he found himself: 'The difficulty Native writers encounter as writers ... is that we must use English if our voice is to be heard by a large enough audience ... we are working in a language that we must reshape to our particular purpose' (qtd. in Conolly 370). Precisely. It is a task that many creative people will have to undertake in the so-called 'postcolonial' age. Such mastery will, one hopes, eventually come. There are already pioneers embarking on the first stage of the crusade. But, in drama, the goal has not yet been reached.

The writing of non-fiction has been unusually active in the past twenty-five years, and only time can tell which of the numerous publications will achieve more than passing interest. Of the established writers, Northrop Frye and George Grant have both been honoured since their deaths with handsome collected editions (still in progress), so it is becoming possible to obtain a far more rounded sense of their achievements. Scholars have also published generous collections of literary letters, especially those of Malcolm Lowry and Robertson Davies, both of whom distinguished themselves in a form of expression for which Canadians are not generally known. Writers in other genres have also produced stimulating works of non-fiction that illuminate their own writing as well as being of interest in their own right. These include Clark Blaise's *I Had a Father*, subtitled 'A Post-Modern Autobiography', which returns once again to the theme of his relation with his father, which has been the focus for so much of his fiction. Blaise has always exploited a tricky borderland between fiction and non-fiction, but in this book the emphasis tilts more clearly in the direction of verifiable experience. Similarly, David Solway's *The Anatomy of Arcadia* is partly a travel book and partly a provocative meditation on the distinction between travellers and tourists. In addition, it provides an essential context for the poet's fascinating inquiry into Greek life and landscape within his poetry.

Among new writers of non-fiction, Sharon Butala is unquestionably the most original. The pattern of her life is itself instructive. Born in a rural area of central Saskatchewan, she moved to the city, became urbanized, worked as a psychologist, and produced a number of competent but relatively undistinguished novels that earnestly explore women's issues (unplanned pregnancies, abortions, etc.). But a time came when she urgently felt that she 'needed to re-create [her]self' (*Wild Stone Heart* 29), and so made a new life on the open prairie. Her non-fiction writings, beginning with *The Perfection of the Morning*, take the first tentative steps in a process described in the subtitle as 'An Apprenticeship in Nature'. In *Wild Stone Heart*, for instance, she attempts to learn about a single field by the simple method of continually walking over it and meditating until it revealed its secrets. Ultimately, she came to understand 'the profound meaning of land' (88).

As a result of this experience, her viewpoint is decidedly unsettling. 'I had so much to learn before I could call this place home', she writes, yet she also had much to unlearn, commenting bitterly: 'I had been trained to understand human nature from Freud and pop psychology' (*Perfection* 57, 88). Once a fairly conventional feminist, she came to advocate a 'natural' feminism, because Nature's rhythm 'is the rhythm of the feminine' (182). Her new, non-conforming attitude insists, controversially, that a (rural) woman's true place is in the home. Her remarks on native peoples are similarly independent. Addressing the agronomic rape of the land, she notes forcefully that the 'postcolonial' concern for aboriginals rarely includes listening to their advice about the way we live on the earth, and remarks: 'This land makes [i.e., should make] Crees of us all' (*Perfection* 100). Our customary assumptions are continually being questioned.

But Butala is of special interest because her work recalls so many earlier Canadian writers who have found a place in this book. Her life in central Saskatchewan in the 1940s, though possessing a few modern conveniences, was not all that far removed from the pioneering world of Traill and Moodie a century earlier. Her description of a journey across windswept plains accompanying cattle to the winter feeding grounds, albeit in a truck, recalls Grove's rides 'over prairie trails'. Her spiritual insights – what she calls 'a *frisson* of the numinous' (*Coyote* 97) – bear a fascinating resemblance (though she may not have been aware of it) to those in Emily Carr's journals. All in all, like Patrick Lane in his impressive memoir *There Is a Season* (2004), she represents a healthy retort to Frye's urban insistence on terror as a characteristic Canadian response to Nature.

The main socio-political concerns of recent decades have given rise to two of the finest specimens of argumentative prose written in Canada. The first is Mordecai Richler's *Oh Canada! Oh Quebec! Requiem for a Divided Nation,* published in 1992 at the height of the separatist controversy. As a Québec-born, English-speaking Jew, Richler had the advantage of a unique perspective. He makes his political position abundantly clear: 'If I thought that Francophone Quebeckers were oppressed in Canada, I would be out there in the streets demonstrating with them' (239). But as a member of a race that recognizes oppression when it sees it, he knows better. He can penetrate the specious rhetoric of both sides of the debate, whether 'conservative' or 'progressive', English-born or Québécois. His journalistic reporting (representing journalism at its best) can be interpreted as either hilarious or frightening as he zeroes in on one political *gaucherie* after another. One soon becomes convinced that his sometimes cheeky, sometimes bitterly satirical style is the only viable way to describe the absurdities of the quarrel. An informatively anecdotal book, open to ironies and inconsistencies yet aware of its own complexity, it can be enjoyed for its style as much as for the cogency of its arguments. Somewhat surprisingly, for all its depressing revelations, it turns into a celebration of 'this cockeyed country I grew up in and still call home' (108).

Equally effective, and for comparable reasons, on the even more contentious issue of race is Neil Bissoondath's *Selling Illusions* (1994, rev. 2002), an intellectually powerful challenge to official governmental advocacy of 'multiculturalism'. He argues that the Canadian Multiculturalism Act is based upon 'several unexamined assumptions: that people, coming from elsewhere, wish to remain what they have been; that personalities and ways of doing things, ways of looking at the world, can be frozen in time; that Canadian cultural influences pale before the exoticism of the foreign' (39 [2002 ed. qtd. throughout]). While this legislation was probably well-intentioned, Bissoondath points out that it had the (possibly convenient) effect of keeping immigrants from other cultures separate. Ironically, such a policy can lead unwittingly to the creation of cultural ghettoes. He refuses to mince matters: 'The psychology and politics of multiculturalism has ... given legitimacy here to what was once deplored in racially segregated South Africa' (176).

These arguments, radical in the best sense of the word, are assembled coolly and convincingly. If one should not suffer discrimination because of (say) skin colour, he insists, one should not benefit from it either. Oddly, quotas once imposed to restrict entrance to institutions are now invoked, in the name of 'affirmative action', to facilitate entrance – also for racist reasons, the insidious implication being that the people involved would not succeed in open competition. Bissoondath himself naturally wants to be judged as a writer, recognized for his literary ability, not coddled and protected as (vile phrase) 'a writer of colour'. Moreover, by insisting that 'to define yourself' – rather than to be defined – by your colour 'is to be a racist' (163), he suggests that those who campaign most vigorously for 'minorities' carry the seed of racism within themselves. Such arguments are anathema in some quarters, but they are difficult to subvert.

Compared with Richler, Bissoondath appeals more to reason and logic and less to humour and exaggeration, but he has a gift for witty illustration, as when he declines to be relegated to 'Caribbean North' (24), or refers to the 'best example of cultural appropriation ever seen: the Jamaican bobsled team' (169). His courage to speak out, and to speak out so persuasively, is exemplary: his own achievements justify his arguments that no immigrant either deserves or needs any condescending special treatment. *Selling Illusions* should be compulsory reading for all Canadian politicians.

Finally mention should be made of a series of literary-critical books that have begun to appear recently and offer a healthy challenge to current approaches to Canadian literature. These are for the most part writers' books about writing. The first was the vigorously titled *Kicking Against the Pricks* (1982), the precursor of several similar compilations by John Metcalf. This was closely followed in 1984 by Paul Stuewe's *Clearing the Ground,* a much-needed attack on thematically centred criticism, and B. W. Powe's *A Climate Charged,* an eloquent plea for more rigorous scrutinies of major writers. Then, after a decade of absorption, there has been a flurry of similar books, all fostered by Metcalf and the Porcupine's Quill: first, with a primary though not exclusive emphasis on fiction, Philip Marchand's *Ripostes* (1998), then T. F. Rigelhof's *This Is Our Writing* (2000), and Stephen Henighan's *When Words Deny the World* (2002), closely followed by their companions focusing on poetry, David Solway's *Director's Cut* (2003) and Carmine Starnino's *A Lover's Quarrel* (2004).

I have quoted several of these writers earlier in the chapter, and I shall be quoting others in the chapter to follow. Suffice it here to state that these critics are concerned, first and foremost, with good writing; they have no patience with criticism that is content to be 'a book of patterns' (Atwood, *Survival* 11) or with slavish academic loyalty to an imposed theory. You will not find them prattling about signifiers or becoming obsessed with marginality; moreover, if they discuss racism or 'appropriation of voice', they do so to expose their baleful presence in such institutions as the Writers' Union of Canada (see p. 130). The sole axe they have to grind is the need to nurture excellence. They may be opinionated, but they have independent minds and high, though not rigid standards (see the conflicting evaluations of Robertson Davies, negative in Rigelhof 45, positive in Powe 155). Above all, they demonstrate unquestionably that there is something wrong with current attitudes to Canadian literature on the part of academics, publishers, journalists, and (if such an entity still exists) the educated reading public. But these are issues to be explored in the concluding chapter.

Polemical Conclusion

The dream of tory origins
Is full of lies and blanks,
Though what remains when it is gone,
To prove that we're not Yanks?

*Dennis Lee's deeply serious quip in 'When I Went Up to Rosedale' demonstrates both his debt to and independence of the thought of George Grant (and so provides an excellent instance of the continuity of Canadian literary tradition). It offers evidence of a Canadian myth (the country, we may now feel, is no longer without a mythology), yet, in typically Canadian fashion, it raises the question of the variety of meanings that the word 'myth' can encompass (from a story of origins to a pack of lies). But, more insistently, Lee's quatrain also draws attention to the problems inherent in a tradition that is essentially negative. If it is fair to define a Canadian as one who has rejected the American Revolution and its implications, then – at least from a North American perspective – Canadians have no alternative but to insist upon what they are not rather than what they are. Moreover, Lee reminds us of the resemblances that, for reasons of geography and the politics of close contact, inevitably exist between the Canadian and American peoples. As the British impress upon Canadian life gradually fades – and this is as much the result of change in the ethnic mix over many decades of immigration as of the waning of political influence – the problem increases. We come to realize that assimilation or annexation (a political solution regularly raised and rejected from the earliest period of Canadian history down to recent times) is not just a matter of treaties and governmental agreements. Psychologically, we are indisputably a North American people; at the same time, we are anxious to distinguish ourselves from those whom the rest of the world recognizes as *the* American people.

A healthy and vigorous Canadian literature is therefore of immense

---

* The first section of this chapter reproduces my 1985 'Conclusion'.

importance because it helps to clarify and so to maintain the distinction. If literature holds a mirror up to our Canadian nature, it plays a significant role in proving 'that we're not Yanks'. It can only do so, however, if it exists as a living part of the nation's culture – not a mere museum of words from the past but a genuine reflection of the country's attitudes, hopes, and aspirations. And here a serious weakness in the current Canadian literary situation becomes painfully evident.

To put the matter bluntly, the impressive literary activity that has given us so many talented poets, novelists, and other writers since the late 1950s has been artificially induced by massive subsidies from the Canada Council. The standard pattern is easily constructed. A Canadian writer, well known or not so well known, is awarded a generous grant to write a particular book; when it is finished, a publisher is provided with a subvention to assist with the costs of printing and distribution – and as often as not the writer in question is then awarded an additional grant for a cross-country tour to help publicize it. And we may add to all this the patent fact that a significant percentage of the eventual readers will be part of the university community, itself largely government-supported. I would not, of course, wish to be interpreted as criticizing this support. Artists have always needed patrons, and governments that take over the functions of regal court and hereditary aristocracy must also take over the cultural sponsorship that they once provided. But if the whole expensive process does not create a body of educated and discriminating readers prepared to support its native literature in a more direct and unforced way, then these efforts will have been made in vain.

Canada is not, of course, alone in being a country where the standard of literacy is officially high, but in which the quantity and quality of reading are depressingly low. And the prospects are not all gloomy. Although the best-known Canadian writers within the country as a whole are those who have become media personalities (Atwood, Cohen, Layton), there is at least a growing awareness that a native literature exists and that this is something to be proud of. That is an important first stage. Again, increasing emphasis is being laid on Canadian studies in schools and universities, though the extent to which this is offset by neglect of the masterpieces of world literature and the current materialist emphasis on the natural and social sciences at the expense of humanistic studies has yet to be seen. The difficulty, as always, is to create an appropriate balance: those who know only their Canadian literature know little of that, but those who neglect it are stifling an important part of their heritage.

It would be unwise, then, to end this book on a note of conspicuous optimism, let alone euphoria, though excessive caution is also an old-fashioned Canadian trait and similarly needs to be resisted. Two contemporary Canadian writers have recently painted a gloomy scenario for the immediate prospects of the nation's literature. John Metcalf has analyzed what (in 1982) he called 'the last twelve years of Canada's literary renaissance, growth, decline, and fall' (*Kicking* 131), while Matt Cohen wrote an article originally published in *Saturday Night* (May 1979) that was entitled 'The Rise and Fall of Serious CanLit'. The language seems melodramatic or (to say the least) premature. A body of impressive literature has been written and will continue to give pleasure and provide intellectual and emotional sustenance even if its quality and quantity are not equalled in the coming years. But it is important for the cultural health of the nation that the recent momentum be maintained, and it is important (indeed, essential) for Canadian writers themselves that a firm nucleus of a reliable and informed Canadian critical readership come into being. Given the experience of the fairly recent past, the prospects for the future are not unpromising, but they are by no means clear either. This being so, it seems appropriate that I should end by repeating a remark that A. J. M. Smith, at a time when Canadian literature was still in its infancy, employed when introducing his *Book of Canadian Poetry* (1943): 'In a sense this book is an act of faith.'

Such a conclusion was justifiable in 1985 but is no longer appropriate. Now, twenty years later, the balance between confidence and concern, between faith and a nagging fear, is decidedly more difficult to maintain. As the preceding (added) chapter indicated, senior Canadian writers have in the interim reinforced their achievements while a number of gifted young authors have appeared on the scene. So far, so good. At the same time, certain developments within Canada – and, indeed, within the western world as a whole – leave no room for complacency and raise serious anxieties about the future.

I quoted Metcalf's *Kicking Against the Pricks* in my original 'Conclusion', and I shall be drawing upon the book more than once in the pages to follow because it anticipated so accurately many of the main problems that confront us today. Most prominent among his concerns was the virtual absence of what I there called 'a body of educated and discriminating readers prepared to support its national literature'. In Metcalf's words: 'What concerns me as a writer – and I emphasize that – *as a writer* – is what happens to the gifted and literate minority' (*Kicking* 57). A pessimistic, melodramatic, but not altogether inaccurate answer to Metcalf's query is that, to the extent that it ever existed, it has collapsed. In short, we are facing a real threat to cultural continuity. The reasons for this collapse are intricate, and involve trends in modern history extending back over several centuries. Even a brief discussion of them will lead into areas apparently far removed from the Canadian literary tradition. These include the domination of science in the contemporary world, drastic changes in the size, character, and emphases of our universities, the equivocal influence of governments, and the actions of academics. I am now embarking on a dark and for the most part depressing journey, but it needs to be made if we are to understand the dilemma in which we find ourselves.

Wolfe's defeat of Montcalm in 1759 may be said to mark the beginning of modern Canada. Historically, this means that the country as we now know it started to emerge when literature in English was already well established and when science was well on the way towards intellectual ascendancy. The development of Canadian literature over the last two and a half centuries has therefore occurred at a time when humanistic attitudes and assumptions were noticeably on the defensive. We can now see that a major shift in values was taking place. The poet, claimed Dr Johnson, does not number the streaks of the tulip, yet science, by its very nature, focuses primarily on what is measurable, and trusts only what can be proven. But how does one measure the impact of a great novel or prove the effectiveness of a major poem? Moreover, sciences progress while the arts do not, as the respective histories of drama and science since the flowering of ancient Greek civilization in the sixth century BC make abundantly clear. Set against the current achievements in science, those of the arts can seem modest and even peripheral. Above all, the sciences have evolved for their own purposes a series of standard procedures known collectively as the scientific *method,* while the arts and humanities are better approached, more flexibly, in terms of *discipline,* of mastering more than one way in which an art form can be examined and appreciated. In many respects, the fact that scientific method has imposed itself upon other areas of human experience, for which it was not designed and to which it is not perfectly suited, explains many of the tensions that now exist between what in the 1950s C. P. Snow christened 'the two cultures'.

It is only a slight exaggeration to claim that universities in the past focused on the attaining of wisdom while their modern equivalents concentrate on the acquisition of knowledge and practical skills. This change, of course, occurred in direct response to the rise of science and the scientific habit of mind. Subsequently, when administrative convenience led to standardization of university procedures, scientific models, needless to say, were adopted. Among these was the installation of Research (capital R) as a main scholarly activity that soon became as important as (if not more important than) the traditional teaching function. In other words, 'scholarship', which could seek out facts and produce genuine and permanent contributions to knowledge, was judged to be more substantial than 'criticism', which disseminated merely subjective opinions and unprovable impressions. This development, as we shall see, had a profound and drastic effect upon the operation of arts disciplines in general and, for our present purposes, the cause of Canadian literature in particular.

The previous two paragraphs, though presenting an all-too-brief and oversimplified account of a complex situation, outline the essentials necessary for an understanding of what has happened in the last forty years or so, and what has led to the current crisis. This is no time to mince words. Scholarly detachment and propriety may be admirable in certain circumstances, but, no longer recognizing the need to spare the blushes of my profession, I now feel the need to speak out. There are many interrelating factors that have contributed to the seriousness of the situation. In addition to governmental priorities and the decisions of university administrators, these include the increasingly influential 'media', as well as general and often disturbing tendencies within the age. But a major part of the responsibility must be laid at the doors of educators, scholars, teachers, and literary critics. It is no exaggeration to claim that we have witnessed a massive contemporary *trahison des clercs*.

Here is the story as I see it.

The most significant social and educational development of the 1960s may well have been the dramatic increase in universities and in the percentage of the population that attended them, an increase that has continued to the present day. Governments, both federal and provincial, recognizing voter approval, supported the process; unfortunately, however, by showing more concern for the mere numbers of students and less for their qualifications, they failed to anticipate long-term consequences. These consequences, negligible in the sciences and in subjects like engineering in which instruction virtually begins at university level, placed a particular strain on departments in the arts and the humanities. Many new students came from backgrounds in which traditional cultural activities (not to mention proficiency in the language) had not been a natural component of their way of life from childhood. As a result, literary and intellectual awareness that was once taken for granted could no longer be assumed. A general dilution of expectation occurred, and, not surprisingly, this was followed by a perceptible drop in academic standards. Metcalf was, I am convinced, accurate when he insisted: 'The quality of education has declined everywhere in the last 50 years as the number to be educated has risen' (*Kicking* 2). Moreover, the situation has now worsened. Needless to say, government statistics about the increased number of degrees granted by Canadian universities (many of them artificially upgraded from polytechnical institutions in, frankly, a 'book-cooking' operation) avoid any admission that their criteria for counting have changed and that academic requirements have been quietly readjusted. In short, to quote Metcalf yet again, 'the degrees [the universities] confer have become debased coinage' (*Kicking* 60).

Related difficulties arose from 'politically correct' initiatives relating to multiculturalism and an increasingly secular stamp impressed upon public education. These policies are understandable in context, but long-term results have not been happy. The multicultural concern to protect the heritage of immigrants (see pp. 117–18) has all too often discouraged 'new Canadians' from entering the cultural mainstream. In addition, the possible effect upon historical continuity and the maintenance of the *Canadian* heritage passed unnoted. For many students nowadays, the history of Canada (including its literary history), though referring to their country, is not *their* history; 'tradition' in such circumstances becomes meaningless. Similarly, the secularization issue concealed potential dangers. Fear of unwelcome religious indoctrination has led to difficulties when non-western students find themselves unfamiliar with the religious tradition upon which understanding of so much literature in English – including, of course, Canadian literature – depends. Ironically, it is now considered improper for western readers to fail to appreciate the Hindu and Buddhist references in T. S. Eliot's *The Waste Land* but permissible for Asian students to be ignorant of Christian concepts underlying his *Four Quartets.* Or, if a Canadian example is preferred, contemporary attention to Sheila Watson's *The Double Hook* tends to emphasize the 'Coyote' background at the expense of the far more frequent biblical echoes and allusions. Margaret Avison recently drew timely attention to the anomaly by which students are often taught Greek and primitive but not Christian myths in school. (Double standards can raise their heads in unexpected places.)

Spurred on by financial inducements, universities responded to all these challenges by abandoning their position as centres of excellence and independent inquiry to become employment-oriented training institutions emphasizing marketable skills. The once-traditional centrality of the arts disciplines shifted dramatically towards more practical subjects: science, engineering, social studies, business administration. After all, an array of completed arts courses, however impressive in theory, did not guarantee success in job interviews. As a result, a disturbingly high percentage of university students, though well-trained in computer technology and scientific procedures, may now be considered culturally deprived.

From these ranks, however, the reading public of the future, so essential to the survival of a living literature, has traditionally been drawn. What now?

The impact of all these shifts and developments upon the arts, and especially on literary studies in English, has been cataclysmic. Although a modest number of well-qualified, talented, and dedicated students is still encountered, the general standard of English proficiency declined drastically as technical abilities took precedence in schools over reading and writing skills and the nurturing of the human imagination. (David Solway's impassioned and embittered books on education are relevant here.) Curiously, the precision expected in scientific procedure is not considered essential in the use of English. Writing 'labs' (the very word is imported from the sciences) are now routinely provided by universities for students who, after twelve years of secondary-school education, are grossly deficient in the language of basic information and instruction. It is impossible to imagine aspiring science students believing that they could gain university entrance without having mastered basic skills in mathematics. The attitudes of education authorities to the relative importance of scientific and literary skills are here illustrated all too clearly.

Worse follows, so far as the prospects for a literate reading public are concerned. Because the various faculties within universities compete with each other for their share of students and accompanying financial support, English departments are now forced by circumstances to accept into literary courses students who display little or no aptitude for the subject and even lack the habit of regular and unforced reading. Such students are obviously ill-equipped to respond to literature containing complex allusions or employing subtle artistic effects. No wonder that the standard of modern writing (sadly reflected, it might be added, in contemporary journalism) is dominated by what Solway, in a wonderfully apt and evocative phrase, calls 'backwards-baseball-cap language' (*Director's* 152). In consequence, to talk to most students about style, Metcalf has observed, 'is to incur the deepest suspicion and hostility' (*Kicking* 129).

At this point, we must necessarily engage with the actions and reactions of university teaching personnel. In the mid-1960s the cause of Canadian literature, scandalously neglected in traditional curricula, had been attracting public discussion, and new courses devoted to the subject were hastily introduced. Inevitably, the emphasis fell on 'Canadianness', a feature that was considered by many to take precedence over literary quality. So began the exaggerated emphasis on thematic criticism in 'CanLit' (as it came to be called), and this was stimulated by the publication in 1972 of *Survival* by Margaret Atwood, then a fast-rising star in the national artistic firmament. For all its inadequacies and inaccuracies, *Survival* constituted a ready-to-hand guide for modelling courses and assigning set texts. Despite occasional protests from the independent-minded, mainly from the more thoughtful practising writers who insisted that literary excellence could not be confined by political boundaries and that a writer's overriding responsibility was, simply, to write well, this approach flourished virtually unchallenged for over a decade.

Yet Paul Stuewe has argued – justifiably, in my view – that 'most of what passes for "thematic criticism" was simply a mask for superficial thinking and analysis' (22). Certainly it was far less demanding – on teachers as well as students – than the delicate, controversial, and (perhaps most significant in an age dominated by science) non-measurable process of literary evaluation. Evaluative criticism has, indeed, always been suspect in Canada, initially because of a fear that the national achievement, if examined rigorously, might prove slight, more recently as a result of the pervasive influence of Northrop Frye, whose disapproval of comparative value judgments was notorious. In pragmatic terms, the emphasis on nationalistic and thematic issues, focusing on content rather than treatment, fitted all too conveniently into the new pedagogic situation.

The following interpretation of the sequence of events may seem excessively cynical, but it conforms accurately enough, I fear, to the hard facts of the case. First, Canadian literature was taught within a social and political but not a historical context because students displayed no knowledge of or interest in history. This was the *now* generation; everything had to be 'relevant'. Second, faced with students inexperienced in the reading of literature, poorly equipped to appreciate the structure of an elaborate novel or the manipulation of rhythm and cadence within an accomplished poem, many instructors – there were, of course, honourable exceptions – abandoned literary considerations, content to allow them to ferret out uniquely Canadian references – or later, when ideological approaches came into vogue, to praise politically correct attitudes and condemn unsanctioned views. For similar reasons, less demanding texts were often chosen for study. If the fiction of (say) Mavis Gallant or Rudy Wiebe seemed too complex for students inexperienced in what Metcalf calls 'literature performing at high voltage' (*Freedom* 219), work by (say) W. P. Kinsella or Lucy Maud Montgomery could be substituted. Inevitably, these were soon treated as if they were writings of comparable literary importance. An emphasis on language and style, how words are employed – the qualities that have always distinguished major creative work – was strategically avoided. And, in the process, Canadian literature, along with its potential reading public, was sold short.

Scholarly (as distinct from pedagogic) activity in the discipline took a very different turn. Canadian literary criticism had hitherto been preoccupied with what used to be known as 'missionary work', aimed at the creation and fostering of a readership aware of the scope and history of the nation's achieved body of writing. Perhaps disillusioned by the lack of interest and even comprehension on the part of their students, many publishing scholars tended to move at that time into either the ivory tower of abstruse aesthetics or (more recently) the dubious arena of political ideology. In so doing, they have abandoned Metcalf's 'gifted and literate minority' and left the continuity of the Canadian tradition in jeopardy. The result of both endeavours has been the publication of numerous books directed exclusively towards narrow fellow-specialists and couched in a jargon inaccessible to the general reader. All this in the interests of (and justified by) the new buzz-word: 'Postmodernism'. This is a controversial topic, but one which, important as it undoubtedly is, can easily distract us from our primary concerns here, the prospects of Canadian literature in the future and the fortunes of the Canadian reading public. I have therefore placed further discussion of it in the Appendix that immediately follows this chapter.

It must be admitted, however, that academics are not alone in deserving censure. I noted earlier that a number of writers protested against the attempt by excessively nationalistic critics to confine literature within artificial political boundaries, and one would like to think that the artistic community consistently defended its rights and freedoms against academic or bureaucratic narrowness. Unfortunately, this is not the case. Perhaps the most bizarre literary controversies of our time have been those involving 'appropriation of voice' and the classification (and consequent separation) of writers according to race. 'Appropriation of voice', the idea that writers of one race should not draw upon the cultural traditions of another, or even portray characters of a different race from their own, is obviously absurd in practice since, if pressed to its logical conclusion, it would prevent the presentation of *any* interchange between races and so create a strict literary *apartheid*. Yet a resolution to this effect was passed by no less a body than the Writers' Union of Canada (see Henighan 59–69), and the same organization made itself doubly ridiculous by approving a non-whites-only conference organized to protest racial discrimination (see Marchand 158–62)!

Such attitudes could have potentially horrendous consequences, and have already had deleterious effects. Henighan recounts a personal instance. One of his own novel manuscripts was rejected by a timid (I am tempted to say craven) publisher, despite a reader's positive recommendation in terms of literary quality, because its protagonist was 'Ecuadorian, dark-skinned and female' while Henighan himself is 'Canadian, white-skinned and male'. He quotes a senior editor as saying: 'I would rather publish an *inferior* novel by a real Ecuadorian woman than this novel' (59, my italics). In other words, in this brave new politically correct Canada, literary evaluation takes second place to the dictates of racist and sexist ideology.

While I firmly believe that too many academic scholars and critics (as well as the more ideologically obsessed writers) have betrayed their trust by abandoning their hallowed roles as guardians of cultural continuity, it must be admitted that contemporary social and political tendencies have conspired against the preservation of traditional values.* Philip Marchand is probably correct in claiming that we live 'in a period unfavourable to the production of great literature' (12). At the same time, when Henighan complains that the new literary generation 'writes with a faulty knowledge of what has gone before' (163), it is not illegitimate to blame the academics for allowing the historical break to occur without vigorous protest. No literature, however, can ignore or escape the dominant characteristics of the age in which it is produced; it is now time to explore what Dudek called the 'total confusion between popular culture and what was once called art' (*In Defence* 37).

A yawning gap between the world of 'best-sellers' and that of 'minority culture' has been an accepted fact of literary life for generations. None the less, interconnections occur regularly, and it is generally agreed that the traditions of 'high art' were profoundly influenced by aspects of 'popular culture' during the last century, and that this trend has continued, even accelerated, in our own time. Moreover, it has been one of the

* Even official governmental recognition of the arts can degenerate into a bureaucratic smokescreen obscuring practical neglect – hence the absurdity of the recent inauguration of the Laureateship at a time when poetry, in Carmine Starnino's words, not only 'does not enjoy wide circulation' but is 'an utterly unwanted article of trade' (*Lover's* 34).

professed aims of the 'postmodernist' critical movement to break down the barriers that were seen to exist between the two extremes. The Canadian literary tradition needs, therefore, to be considered alongside the main cultural trends within the contemporary world.

Interconnections between 'high art' and 'popular culture' have, of course, been characteristic of all the arts throughout the western world. Examples include the impact of jazz on classical music (Ravel, Shostakovich), the points of intersection between grand opera and Broadway musical (Gershwin's *Porgy and Bess,* Bernstein's *West Side Story*), the employment of distinguished composers to write music for film scores (Korngold, Walton), the 'crossover' phenomenon in contemporary recording practice, the influence of cartoons and comic strips on modern painters (Warhol, Lichtenstein), etc., etc. In Canadian literature, one thinks of the impact of film techniques on novelists as diverse as Lowry and Ondaatje, Hollywood as the subject of fiction in Hood's *The Camera Always Lies* and Findley's *The Butterfly Plague,* Atwood's treatment of the modern Gothic-romance tradition in *Lady Oracle,* Livesay's *Poems for People,* Acorn's *More Poems for People* – and, of course, Leonard Cohen in his twin roles as poet and pop singer.

Cohen's work as a whole is in fact central to any serious discussion of this topic. When commenting on *Beautiful Losers,* Linda Hutcheon properly notes that pop culture is there 'set in opposition to the official culture of the eternal and the serious', but continues: 'Charles Axis (Charles Atlas), Plastic Man, Blue Bottle, "Smash! Wham! Pow!" – these are all presented (albeit with irony) as intertextual references of comparable weight to those from the Bible or Nietzsche' (*Canadian Postmodern,* 1988, 33). True enough, yet this neutral listing sidesteps the crucial matter of evaluation: in what way are the two 'of comparable weight'?

In popular culture, as much as in any other form of creative endeavour, discriminations need to be made. It is the infiltration of *tasteless* popular culture into serious literature that is so destructive of authentic standards (see Dudek's interview in Hildebrand 109). The phrase 'popular culture' combines an astonishing variety of activities ranging from detective fiction, *Anne of Green Gables,* and the art of Walt Disney, through TV evangelists, hockey games, and bingo halls, to the visual and audio 'entertainment' provided on intercontinental flights, the magazines available at convenience stores, and hard porn. Any art form dealing with contemporary life will need to consider that same life's varied manifestations, but it will judge them, at least implicitly, at the same time. Notable examples include the hilarious bar-mitzvah film-sequence in Richler's *The Apprenticeship of Duddy Kravitz* (Pt. 2, Ch. 6), Metcalf's presentation of the aging-father-and-hippie-son confrontation in *Polly Ongle,* and, more positively, the delicate and profound treatment of jazz and early radio in the growth of a talented musician in Hood's *Be Sure to Close Your Eyes.* Whether 'Smash! Wham! Pow!' can be satisfactorily transformed into high art is, however, arguable.

Juxtaposition of the high and the low, the dignified and the disreputable, the exalted and the vulgar, has characterized literature from time immemorial (consider the role of the satyr play in ancient Greek dramatic festivals or the comic moments that punctuate, and enhance, Shakespearean tragedy). Canadian literature is no exception, and contemporary writing exploits its potentialities to the full. When Ondaatje refers to both King Kong and Wallace Stevens (see Vol. 1, p. 161), the cultural range, though surprising and somewhat disturbing, is impressive, and the same is true, as Hutcheon has reminded us, of Cohen's *Beautiful Losers,* whatever reservations we may have about its ultimate quality. Increasingly, however, the main allusions and references in modern writing are *confined* to the popular – and ephemeral – forms. Troubling questions arise. Is such writing itself doomed to be equally impermanent and disposable? What happens when the popular culture represented by TV and rented DVDs itself *becomes* the literary tradition? Can Canadian literature flourish – or even survive – under such circumstances?

At this point, it may be useful to consider the case of an aspiring contemporary young writer who does not come from a bookish environment. Where does he or she turn for literary experience or for stylistic models? First, most probably, to newspapers. But the last half-century has seen a noticeable decline in journalistic style and in the discussion of books of high quality. Even in the supposedly better newspapers, writing has become more demotic, with an increased use of slang, recalling Solway's 'backwards-baseball-cap language' once again – to such an extent that the serious discussion of serious topics, requiring precision of speech and subtle distinctions of meaning, becomes almost impossible.

Besides, as Dudek lamented years ago, there has been an increasing tendency for book-review pages to shrink in size and, worse, to be banished to a relatively inconspicuous part of the 'Entertainment' section. A decline in the *choice* of books accepted for review has also occurred, serious and thought-provoking publications all too often giving place to the brash and the trendy. When 'literary' material is included, the work of a select group of favoured authors (but favoured by whom?) is given fulsome attention, while the less fashionable are routinely ignored. I use the word 'favoured' advisedly; Henighan (45–9) records being dropped from a newspaper's reviewing roster for several years because he presumed to criticize a disappointing novel by Timothy Findley. Similarly, Starnino makes reference to 'an all-star team of Canadian poets whose work one may *not* find objectionable' (*Lover's* 14). In addition, reviewers, I suspect, tend now to be less qualified – though this may in part be blamed on the academies. Reviewing is rarely recognized as an important public service by university administrators – it isn't regarded as commensurate with 'Research' – so many professors are loath to devote much time to it. (In any case, such critics are less adept in accommodating their style and attitudes to the needs of interested but non-specialist readers.)

Another factor of contemporary critical journalism is the increased emphasis placed on best-seller lists and literary awards as a basis for attention and approval. Both must be regarded as insidious. Best-seller lists in particular involve a vicious circle. Publishers flourish on them for obvious reasons, so their appearance is accompanied by a battery of media 'hype', including prominent advertising and highly exaggerated press releases. Newspapers vigorously support the process (after all, advertising revenue is essential to their survival) by devoting reviewing-space to books that are claimed to be making – or about to make – news, and carefully selected reviewers will be expected to reflect the general enthusiasm. Naturally, booksellers (especially the larger chain stores) then get into the act. Unfortunately, as Henighan has documented (51–7), the best-seller lists, supposedly based on bookshop sales, may not be statistically pure. He discovered that lists sometimes appeared even before copies of the books in question had arrived in stores, thus giving the lie to the whole enterprise. One bookseller summed up the situation with devastating directness: 'A best-seller … is a book that is meant to be a best-seller' (52).

Comparable objections need to be made concerning literary prizes. These have escalated in recent years, and the more financially valuable are now accompanied by all the publicity hoopla (and much of the vulgarity) associated with the Academy Awards. And they are equally unreliable. Awards, after all, depend upon juries, which are at best fallible and at worst decidedly suspect (see Marchand 65–6, Henighan 84, and especially Solway, who cites an instance when a 'well-known and influential Canadian poet handpicked a provincial writers' guild jury and then – received the award', *Director's* 147). Moreover, the track record of even the more reputable awards is notoriously unimpressive. An extensive reading list might, for example, readily be compiled of Canadian novels of unquestioned quality that did *not* win the Governor General's Award for Fiction. These would include *The Apprenticeship of Duddy Kravitz, The Stone Angel,* and *Fifth Business.* The fact that neither Ethel Wilson nor Hugh Hood ever won a single Governor General's Award speaks volumes about the reliability not only of the awards themselves but of the commentators who take them seriously. It is frankly amazing how those who are reluctant to make value judgments themselves are nevertheless prepared to take over the evaluations of others. The acknowledgment of prizes is now proclaimed prominently not only in advertising material but in academic listings (especially on blurbs and contributors' pages) and encyclopedia entries. No wonder Henighan complains that criticism 'has become simply one wing of the publicity machine' (164).

So far as entertainment is concerned, our potential writer will hardly escape a perpetual bombardment of film, TV, and computer technology, and these are likely to exert a powerful (and almost certainly disastrous) influence on any creative effort. Those who have served on university committees responsible for assigning student literary awards will have recognized the 'cultural malnutrition' (Davies, *A Mixture of Frailties,* Pt. 2, Ch. 8) that such a diet produces. It manifests itself in a slick but superficial style, cliché situations (the discovery of sex in high school is an especially tired – and tiresome – subject), a chronic lack of deep feeling, a tin (or at least untrained) ear for the rhythms of both prose and verse, and, where fiction or drama is involved, inarticulate dialogue and characters with severely limited intellectual and imaginative horizons. 'Good poetry,' Eric Ormsby has observed, 'cannot flourish where bad standards prevail' (Bowling interview 209), and the remark can be extended to cover most literary creation. Add to all this the impact, dictated by 'peer pressure', of such anti-literary distractions as video games, partying, discothèques, surfing the Internet, and the cult of sports, and one realizes the overwhelming odds against such experience resulting in any creative work of originality or even interest.

Pessimists can hardly be blamed for considering the prospect bleak.

And yet . . .

When Sam Solecki, in the title of his study of Al Purdy, called him 'the last Canadian poet', he did not mean that the writing of poetry in this country would subsequently come to a complete halt. Rather, he was suggesting that Purdy might well be the last poet to produce a body of work that could reasonably be described as speaking from a generally accepted national perspective. Any common denominator linking the array of younger writers discussed in the previous chapter is likely to reflect global rather than nationalist features.

This statement does not, however, imply that I look with either horrified distaste or complacent satisfaction at the currently fashionable prospect of 'globalization'; I prefer Starnino's attitude towards what he calls 'the exciting chemistry between local legacies and cosmopolitan perspectives' (*Lover's* 35). After all, there is abundant evidence to indicate that the high-quality international fiction of the twentieth century – from Joyce's *Ulysses* to García Márquez's *One Hundred Years of Solitude,* and even, albeit at a fantasy remove, Tolkien's *Lord of the Rings* – paid intense allegiance to a local habitation and a name. Moreover, works that challenge the concept of a narrowly geographical Canadianness – such as Mistry's *A Fine Balance* and Clarke's *The Polished Hoe* – are notable for a highly specific and meticulously realized sense of a place elsewhere. (The same argument applies to poetry; consider Solway's Karavis poems set in Greece, or Ormsby's *Araby.*) There is therefore no reason why Canadian writing, whatever the setting, should not become the subject of international attention and approval. Gallant's and Munro's contributions to the *New Yorker* (the former mainly set in Europe, the latter in Canada) and Atwood's recent popularity have already lighted the way. Indeed, an ironic paradox seems to operate here. Literature written deliberately for the international market, and therefore dedicated to 'rootless cosmopolitanism', may well achieve short-term success; in the long run, however, writings of imaginative and stylistic quality characterized by local but not limited settings are likely to prove more enduring.

Finally, literary-critical (as well as academic) fashions rarely last long, and there are already signs that the current emphasis on the dourly 'theoretic' and 'problematic' is encountering increased resistance. Those of us who remember the battle against the entrenched thematists of a generation ago can reasonably anticipate a revolt in the not-too-distant future against the current equivalent pedantries. In particular, the seemingly abandoned notion among academics that literature is intended primarily for pleasure is surely ripe for revival. There is nothing trivial or low-pitched about such a hope. I would be the last to advocate literature as a mere pastime, on the level served by run-of-the-mill detective fiction or those tiresomely flippant works widely advertised as 'humorous'. I am referring instead to the experience of exalted tragedy or subtle comedy that fully involves both the emotions and the intellect, and especially to works that give pleasure by employing language vividly, precisely, and inventively – that 'pleasure-in-words' which, to quote Starnino yet again, is 'a *sine qua non* but more often *sine* in contemporary Canadian poetry' (*Lover's* 127). The realm of literature needs to be won back from the sociological, the ideological, and the politically approved, and restored to the human spirit of delight, originality, imagination, and, above all, the love of what can be achieved through verbal sensitivity and dexterity. There is no inherent reason why Canadian writing, prose or verse, should not take a major part in this endeavour.

Appendix (2006):

A Note on 'Postmodernism', Jargon, etc.

A prominent feature of the last few decades of literary commentary in the Western world has been a preoccupation with the phenomenon known as 'postmodernism', and an increasing emphasis on 'literary theory' as an intellectual and scholarly advance over the supposedly old-fashioned and discredited 'practical' and (in North America) 'new' criticisms. In addition, alongside these developments came the stylistic shift towards heavy terminology generally known (though not, of course, by its practitioners) as jargon. I wish to explain here why both the approach and its accompanying vocabulary have been generally avoided in the revised edition of this book as well as in the original text.

By 'jargon' I am not referring simply to specialist terminology, which is at least sometimes unavoidable, but to the mind-deadening assemblage of clotted abstractions. Nowadays virtually any scholarly book or learned journal will yield examples. To cite an almost random instance, a writer's work is described in *The Cambridge Companion to Canadian Literature* (2004) as representing 'the totalizing formalist containment of disciplinary difference within an overriding master vision rather than any more open or inter-discursive hybridity' (118). I do not understand what this means, and am not, frankly, eager to find out. I sympathize with John Metcalf, who recommends a drastic personal response to this sort of thing: 'I see no reason to pay attention to those who analyse, criticize and explicate, if they themselves seem incapable of journeyman English' (*Kicking* 182). This is a sentiment, I might add, that has influenced the choice of recommended readings that follows this appendix (hence the absence of the volume just quoted).

What is particularly disturbing about so much contemporary scholarly writing is that it is not merely obscure and unattractive but vague and ambiguous. Take, for instance, the now ubiquitous 'postmodernism' itself. To add 'post-' to a word literally meaning 'current' or 'up-to-date' is bound to cause confusion with the passing of time; when shall we enter post-postmodernism – or have we done so already – and what will come after that? Moreover, 'postmodernism' is commonly used, to quote the relevant entry from the *Encyclopedia of Literature in Canada,* to indicate 'either a radical break from or a continuation of modernism', a confusing practice which hardly encourages clarity or precision. Even Linda Hutcheon, author of *The Canadian Postmodern* (1988), grants that the definition of the word 'remains decidedly vague' (1), and admits 'the ironies and contradictions [*sic*] of postmodernism' (4). Occasionally, as in the entry for Thomas King in the just-cited *Encyclopedia,* we are informed in a discussion of 'postcolonialism' that 'post-' is sometimes considered to mean 'against' rather than 'after'; but this usage only compounds ambiguity, and in any case is not supported by the standard dictionaries. As for 'postcolonialism' itself, one wonders how anybody who has read today's newspaper can believe that we are now living in a postcolonial age. (Those prone to conspiracy theories could be forgiven for suspecting that the term was coined by the CIA or FBI.)

Other fashionable words should be treated with caution and even suspicion. Thus 'canon' is frequently used to suggest a body of officially sanctioned literature on the model of the Christian or Jewish scriptures, as if 'classic' literature had been eternally fixed at a moment in time by an authoritative (= authoritarian) assembly. This is, of course, inaccurate, and displays an ignorance of the process of literary history. Indeed, if one talks of the 'Western canon' in terms implying either favouritism or limitation, one is interpreting an image with an insensitive literalness in much the same way as strict fundamentalists read the Bible. Furthermore, to claim, as some theorists have done, that the canon has been destroyed is obviously false. As Sam Solecki has written: 'It still exists, and most of the figures in it are self-evident, but postmodernist critics ... are simply pretending that it isn't there' (*The Last Canadian Poet: An Essay on Al Purdy* x).

Similarly, 'Eurocentric' is all too often employed as a term of abuse by writers who conveniently forget that they are making their protests in a 'Eurocentric' (and often appropriated) language. The British influence on Canadian literature, however diminished politically, is still strong because of the qualities represented by and inherent in the language. Moreover, while English remains the predominant language (and the same is true, of course, of French in Québec), the influence will continue to operate. In the same way 'marginalization' has recently become popular as a blanket charge directed at anyone who prefers some authors to others; this is illogical since a centre cannot possibly contain everyone, and critically irresponsible since it fails to acknowledge that certain writers deserve to be marginalized. 'Elite' has also come to be interpreted as a 'bad' word indicative of unearned privilege. Ironically, many of those who use the term so glibly constitute a powerful and even oppressive élite themselves, while virtually all of them are connected with universities, which are by definition élite institutions. More insidiously, contemporary usage makes no distinction between groups who have gained their influence through demonstrated excellence (compare the 'clerisy' celebrated in Robertson Davies's *A Voice from the Attic,* Part 1) and those who govern through raw political power.

Modern critical writing, it will be noticed, generally downgrades the meanings and dignity of the words it both emphasizes and over-uses. One exception, not perhaps *up*graded but clearly welcomed as an excuse for theoretical elaboration, is 'problematic', extended to make a new verb: problematize. Once an aspect of a work of art has been 'problematized' all details concentrating on language and style can be abandoned in favour of socio-political commentary. The word seems infectious; it has spread alarmingly, like a disease, through recent criticism. What troubles here is not so much the word itself as the fact that a problem, once noticed, is pounced upon with unbecoming eagerness in the manner of a dog worrying a bone. Just about anything can be turned into a problem if one is sufficiently ingenious, and the word thereby loses any usefulness it may once have possessed. Its meaning and its tone are not only unfortunate but vague, or rather ... well ... how else can one describe it? ... problematic.

'Postmodernism' was creeping into the language while the first version of this book was being written. I use it sparingly and neutrally, for the most part in warning quotation-marks, to imply contemporaneity. The other terms are either shunned or used in contexts where the meaning is direct and unambiguous. As for jargon, I fervently hope that I have avoided it totally.

Further Reading

The following list is intended to guide interested readers in the direction of reliable critical commentary and specific information about the publications of individual authors. It is, naturally, highly selective, making no claims to be either comprehensive or 'objective'. Since readers who consult it have presumably found the preceding text helpful, I concentrate for the most part on critical books and articles that I have myself found useful and stimulating, and omitted those that seem outdated, uninspired, or even wrong-headed and perverse. Wherever possible I have avoided highly theoretical discussions, most thematic and conspicuously ideological studies, as well as writings that employ complicated and obscure jargon, though encyclopedias and collections of essays inevitably include items of varying quality.

Reference Books (and Multi-Volume Series)

Annotated Bibliography of Canada's Major Authors [ABCMA] (ed. Robert Lecker and Jack David, 8 vols. Downsview, ON [later, Toronto]: ECW, 1979–94). Bibliographies of major writers also listing selected reviews and critical articles about them, averaging 5 authors per volume.

Canadian Books in Print. Published annually by UTP.

The Canadian Encyclopedia (3 vols. Edmonton: Hurtig, 1985; revised and updated in 4 vols., 1988; further updated in 1 vol., M&S, 1999).

Canadian Writers and Their Works [CWTW] (ed. Robert Lecker, Jack David, and Ellen Quigley. 24 vols., 12 covering fiction, 12 poetry. Downsview, ON [later, Toronto]: ECW, 1983–95). Individual literary-critical studies, averaging 5 authors per volume. Contain brief biographies and bibliographical check-lists for each writer.

Dictionary of Canadian Biography (UTP 1966–). Continuing project modelled on the British *Dictionary of National Biography.* 15 vols. to date. Complete up to the end of the nineteenth century, now proceeding into the early decades of the twentieth.

NB: In full entries, unless indicated, place of publication (or co-publication) is Toronto.

Dictionary of Literary Biography [DLB] (Detroit: Gale Research, 1978–). Multi-volume series on writers in English. Volumes devoted to Canadian writers (all ed. W. H. New) are: Vol. 53, *Canadian Writers Since 1960,* first series (1986); Vol. 60, *Canadian Writers Since 1960,* second series (1987); Vol. 68, *Canadian Writers, 1920–1959,* first series (1988); Vol. 88, *Canadian Writers, 1920–1959,* second series (1989); Vol. 92, *Canadian Writers, 1890–1920* (1990); Vol. 99, *Canadian Writers Before 1890* (1990). Generally concise surveys, biographical and critical, usually illustrated, with bibliographical check-lists.

Encyclopedia of Literature in Canada (ed. W. H. New, UTP, 2002). Emphasizes political and sociological issues; somewhat spotty on literary matters.

Literary History of Canada: Canadian Literature in English (gen. ed. Carl F. Klinck, UTP, 1965). Second ed., 3 vols., 1976 (revised throughout, the third vol. new). A fourth additional vol. (ed. W. H. New) appeared in 1990.

The Oxford Companion to Canadian History (ed. Gerald Hallowell, OUP, 2004).

The Oxford Companion to Canadian Literature (ed. William Toye, OUP, 1983); revised (eds. Eugene Benson and Toye), 1997. *The Concise Oxford Companion to Canadian Literature* (ed. Toye), abridged but updated, appeared in 2001.

Profiles in Canadian Literature [PCL] (ed. Jeffrey M. Heath, 8 vols. Dundurn, 1980–91). Basic introductory guides to individual authors, illustrated, with bibliographical check-lists, averaging 14 authors per volume.

General Literary and Cultural Studies

Although this bibliography has been completely revised and reconstructed since the first edition, it will be noted that a number of the studies recommended in this and subsequent sections are by no means recent. But the most up-to-date is not necessarily the best, and the earlier titles that have been retained, though looked down upon as old-fashioned in some quarters, are, I believe, more valuable and reliable than many more recent studies.

In the present section I have included a considerable number of non- and even anti-academic studies that challenge the current status quo because I consider that these provocative challenges to contemporary orthodoxy have more to say about the essentially literary character of their subjects.

Daymond, Douglas M. and Leslie G. Monkman, eds. *Towards a Canadian Literature: Essays, Editorials and Manifestos* (2 vols. Ottawa: Tecumseh, 1984, 1985). Extremely useful gathering of significant documents.

Frye, Northrop. *The Bush Garden: Essays on the Canadian Imagination* (Anansi, 1971). Influential collection of writings on Canadian literature.

——. *Divisions on a Ground* (Anansi, 1982). Essays on Canadian culture.

——. *Northrop Frye on Canada* (ed. Jean O'Grady and David Staines. Vol. 12 of *Collected Works of Northrop Frye*. UTP, 2003). Collection of virtually all Frye's writings on Canada, including the whole of *The Bush Garden* and most essays from *Divisions on a Ground.*

Henighan, Stephen. *When Words Deny the World: The Reshaping of Canadian Writing* (Erin, ON: Porcupine's Quill, 2002). Incisive essays on contemporary literature and literary politics in Canada.

Keith, W. J. *An Independent Stance: Essays on English-Canadian Criticism and Fiction* (Erin, ON: Porcupine's Quill, 1991).

Lee, Dennis. *Body Music* (Anansi, 1998). Thoughtful essays, mainly though not exclusively on poetry, by a thoughtful poet.

Mandel, Eli, ed. *Contexts of Canadian Criticism* (Chicago: University of Chicago Press, 1971). Thoughtful, wide-ranging essays on Canadian history and culture.

Marchand, Philip. *Ripostes: Reflections on Canadian Literature* (Erin, ON: Porcupine's Quill, 1998). No-nonsense, independent essays by a literate literary journalist.

Metcalf, John. *Kicking Against the Pricks* (Downsview, ON: ECW, 1982; revised ed., Guelph: Red Kite, 1986). Independent, thought-provoking essays on Canadian writing.

——. *What Is a Canadian Literature?* (Guelph, ON: Red Kite, 1988). Challenging long essay on the concept of 'Canadian Literature'.

——. *Freedom from Culture: Selected Essays 1982–92* (ECW, 1994). Provocative essays on Canadian literature and culture.

New, W. H. *A History of Canadian Literature* (Macmillan, 1989; second ed., updated, MQUP, 2003). Too sociological and ideological, but covers Native and Québécois writing.

Powe, B. W. *A Climate Charged: Essays on Canadian Writing* (Oakville, ON: Mosaic, 1984). One of the earlier independent scrutinies of the Canadian literary status quo.

Rigelhof, T. F. *This Is Our Writing* (Erin, ON: Porcupine's Quill, 2000). Personal, independent-minded essays on Canadian writing.

Solecki, Sam, John Metcalf, and W. J. Keith. *Volleys* (Erin, ON: Porcupine's Quill, 1990). Significant literary-critical exchange on the perennial question of substance versus style in Canadian literature.

Staines, David, ed. *The Canadian Imagination: Dimensions of a Literary Culture* (Cambridge, MA: Harvard University Press, 1977).

Stuewe, Paul. *Clearing the Ground: English-Canadian Literature after 'Survival'* (Proper Tales, 1984). Healthy, early challenge to the thematic emphasis on Canadian criticism.

Warkentin, Germaine, ed. *Canadian Exploration Literature: An Anthology* (OUP, 1993). A gathering of writing not easily accessible, accompanied by informative commentary.

Woodcock, George. *Odysseus Ever Returning: Essays on Canadian Writers and Writing* (M&S, 1970). Wide-ranging critical essays.

——. *The World of Canadian Writing: Critiques & Recollections* (Vancouver: Douglas & McIntyre, 1980). More wide-ranging critical essays.

——. *A Northern Spring: The Flowering of Canadian Literature* (Vancouver: Douglas & McIntyre, 1987). Essays on fiction and poetry.

Interviews

Canadian authors must be among the most frequently interviewed writers on earth, and I have therefore listed the main interviews that have been collected in book form. Others, of course, are scattered in literary journals. Personally, I find interviews highly revealing (though not always positively); they should, like all literary criticism, be themselves read critically.

Allen, R. E. M. and Angela Carr, eds. *The Matrix Interviews* (Montréal: DC Books, 2001).

Bowling, Tim, ed. *Where the Words Come From: Canadian Poets in Conversation* (Roberts Creek, BC: Nightwood, 2002).

Cameron, Donald, ed. *Conversations with Canadian Novelists* (Macmillan, 1973 [cloth edition in 1 vol., paperback in 2, but with separate pagination in both]).

Daurio, Beverley, ed. *The Power to Bend Spoons: Interviews with Canadian Novelists* (Mercury, 1998).

Garrod, Andrew, ed. *Speaking for Myself: Interviews with Contemporary Canadian Writers* (St. John's, NL: Breakwater, 1986).

Gibson, Graeme, ed. *Eleven Canadian Novelists* (Anansi, 1973).

Hancock, Geoff., ed. *Canadian Writers at Work* (OUP, 1987).

Kruk, Laurie, ed. *The Voice Is the Story: Conversations with Canadian Writers of Short Fiction* (Oakville, ON: Mosaic, 2003).

Meyer, Bruce, and Brian O'Riordan, eds. *In Their Words: Interviews with Fourteen Canadian Writers* (Anansi, 1984).

——. *Lives & Works: Interviews* (Windsor, ON: Black Moss, 1992.

O'Brien, Peter, ed. *So to Speak: Interviews with Canadian Writers* (Montréal: Véhicule, 1987).

Pearce, Jon, ed. *Twelve Voices: Interviews with Canadian Poets* (Ottawa: Borealis, 1980).

Twigg, Alan, ed. *Strong Voices: Conversations with 50 Canadian Authors* (Madeira Park, BC: Harbour Publishing, 1988). Enlarged version of *For Openers* (1981).

Wallace, Robert, and Cynthia Zimmerman, eds. *The Work: Conversations with English-Canadian Playwrights* (Coach House, 1982).

Poetry

Bentley, D. M. R. *The Confederation Group of Canadian Poets*, 1880–1897 (UTP, 2004). Authoritative study of the first Canadian literary movement.

Brown, E. K. *On Canadian Poetry*. 1943, rev. 1944 (Ottawa: Tecumseh, 1973). Historically important early study.

Davey, Frank, ed. *Tish No. 1–19* (Vancouver: Talonbooks, 1975). Reprinting of the initial issues of the Vancouver poetry magazine.

Dudek, Louis. *Selected Essays and Criticism* (Ottawa: Tecumseh, 1978). Important collection, mainly on poetry, by a distinguished poet and thinker.

Dudek, Louis, and Michael Gnarowski, eds. *The Making of Modern Poetry in Canada* (Ryerson: 1967). Essential articles on modern Canadian poetry in English.

Smith, A. J. M. *Towards a View of Canadian Letters: Selected Critical Essays 1928–1971* (Vancouver: University of British Columbia Press, 1973). Important series of essays by a distinguished poet and influential anthologist.

——. *On Poetry and Poets* (M&S, 1977).

——. ed. *Masks of Poetry* (M&S, 1962).

Solway, David. *Director's Cut* (Erin, ON: Porcupine's Quill, 2003). A contemporary poet's polemical essays on recent Canadian poetry.

Starnino, Carmine. *A Lover's Quarrel* (Erin, ON: Porcupine's Quill, 2004). Challenging essays by a young poet-critic.

Sutherland, John. *Essays, Controversies and Poems* (ed. Miriam Waddington, M&S, 1972). Stimulating critiques of Canadian poetry in the 1940s and 1950s.

Trehearne, Brian. *Aestheticism and the Canadian Modernists: Aspects of a Poetic Influence* (MQUP, 1989). Admirable study of the main Canadian poets of the 1920s and 1930s.

——. *The Montreal Forties: Modernist Poetry in Transition* (UTP, 1999). Equally admirable study of the main poets of the 1940s.

Fiction

Daymond, Douglas, and Leslie Monkman, eds. *Canadian Novelists and the Novel* (Ottawa: Borealis, 1981). Useful anthology of Canadian novelists writing about fiction.

Dooley, D. J. *Moral Vision and the Canadian Novel* (Clarke Irwin, 1979). Study of individual works in relation to traditional moral thought.

Harrison, Dick. *Unnamed Country: The Struggle for a Canadian Prairie Fiction* (Edmonton: University of Alberta Press, 1977).

Keith, W. J. *A Sense of Style: Studies in the Art of Fiction in English-Speaking Canada* (ECW, 1989).

Steele, Charles, ed. *Taking Stock: The Calgary Conference on the Canadian Novel* (Downsview: ON: ECW, 1982). Papers from a controversial but stimulating conference.

Woodcock, George, ed. *The Canadian Novel in the Twentieth Century* (M&S, 1975).

Drama

Anthony, Geraldine. *Stage Voices: Twelve Canadian Playwrights Talk about Their Lives and Work* (Doubleday, 1978).

Benson, Eugene, ed. *The Oxford Companion to Canadian Theatre* (OUP, 1989).

Benson, Eugene, and L. W. Conolly. *English-Canadian Theatre* (OUP, 1987). A useful, concise survey.

Conolly, L. W., ed. *Canadian Drama and the Critics* (Vancouver: Talonbooks, 1995). Reviews, articles, and often authorial commentary on individual plays.

Davies, Robertson. *The Well-Tempered Critic: One Man's View of Theatre and Letters in Canada* (ed. Judith Skelton Grant, M&S, 1981).

New, W. H., ed. *Dramatists in Canada* (Vancouver: University of British Columbia Press, 1972). Critical essays, mainly from *Canadian Literature*.

Plant, Richard, ed. *The Penguin Book of Modern Canadian Drama* (Penguin, 1984). Useful introductory anthology.

Rubin, Don, ed. *Canadian Theatrical History: Selected Readings* (Copp Clark, 1996).

Rubin, Don, and Alison Cranmer-Byng, eds., *Canada's Playwrights: A Biographical Guide* (Canadian Theatre Review Publications, 1980).

Wagner, Anton, ed., *The Brock Bibliography of Published Canadian Plays in English, 1766–1978* (Playwrights Press, 1980). Useful checklist, with plot summaries.

Individual Authors

I confine myself in these entries to the more significant works. Where possible, in genres other than the novel, I recommend an accessible and useful 'collected' or 'selected' volume. For further literary discussion, I list, wherever available, a good biography, a straightforward and (preferably) *introductory* critical discussion, and (for those who want it) a place to turn for more detailed bibliographical information.

Acorn, Milton (1923–86)

Dig Up My Heart: Selected Poems 1952–83 (M&S, 1983) is a good introduction to his work. Subsequent publications include *Captain Neal MacDougal & the Naked Goddess* (1982), *Whiskey Jack* (1986), and *The Uncollected Acorn: Poems 1950–1986* (ed. James Deahl, 1987).

Interview: Meyer and O'Riordan 1984 (125–33).

Jewinski, Ed. 'Milton Acorn'. CWTW Poetry 7 (1990), 21–74.

Lemm, Richard. *Milton Acorn in Love and Anger* (Ottawa: Carleton University Press, 1999). Excellent biography.

Atwood, Margaret (1939–)

Poetry: *Selected Poems 1966–1984* (OUP, 1990) contains *The Journals of Susanna Moodie* complete (though unillustrated and without the prose afterword), and selections from her other volumes of verse. *Morning in the Burned House: New Poems* appeared in 1995.

Fiction: *The Edible Woman* (1969), *Surfacing* (1972), *Lady Oracle* (1976), *Dancing Girls* (short stories, 1977), *Life Before Man* (1978), *Bodily Harm* (1981), *Bluebeard's Egg* (short stories, 1983), *The Handmaid's Tale* (1985), *Cat's Eye* (1988), *Wilderness Tips* (short stories, 1991), *The Robber Bride* (1993), *Alias Grace* (1996), *The Blind Assassin* (2000), *Oryx and Crake* (2003), *Moral Disorder* (short stories, 2006). *The Penelopiad* (2005) is a flippant, feminist retelling of Homer's *Odyssey*.

Selected Criticism: *Survival: A Thematic Guide to Canadian Literature* (1972). Highly influential study, now considered by many to have done more harm than good. *Second Words: Selected Critical Prose* (1983), *Moving Targets: Writing with Intent, 1982–2004* (2004). In the U.S., *Writing with Intent: Essays, Reviews, Personal Prose: 1983–2005* (2005) contains a different selection of items from *Moving Targets*; in England, *Curious Pursuits: Occasional Writing 1970–2005* (2005) selects from all three.

Interviews: Bowling (213–24), Daurio (20–24), Gibson (5–31), Hancock (256–87), Meyer and O'Riordan 1992 (1–8), O'Brien (175–93) Twigg (6–11). See also *Margaret Atwood: Conversations* (ed. Earl G. Ingersoll, Firefly, 1990).

Cooke, Nathalie. *Margaret Atwood: A Biography* (ECW, 1998).

Davidson, Arnold E. and C. N., eds. *The Art of Margaret Atwood: Essays in Criticism* (Anansi, 1981). See especially Sandra Djwa on poetry, Robert Lecker on fiction, George Woodcock on criticism.

Horne, Alan J. 'Margaret Atwood' (Prose). ABCMA 1 (1979), 13–46; 'Margaret Atwood' (Poetry). ABCMA 2 (1980), 13–53.

Keith, W. J. 'Atwood as (Infuriating) Critic.' *An Independent Stance* (Erin, ON: Porcupine's Quill, 54–61.

McCombs, Judith, ed. *Critical Essays on Margaret Atwood* (Boston: Hall, 1982). Includes a selection of reviews.

Stein, Karen F. *Margaret Atwood Revisited* (Boston: Twayne, 1999). Wide-ranging overview.

Avison, Margaret (1918–)

The first volume of *Always Now: The Collected Poems* (Erin, ON: Porcupine's Quill, 2003–2005) reprints *Winter Sun* (1960) and *The Dumbfounding* (1966), uncollected poems and translations, the second *Sunblue* (1978) and *No Name* (1989), the third *Not Yet But Still* (1997), *Concrete and Wild Carrot* (2002), and new poems.

See also *A Kind of Perseverance: The Pascal Lectures on Christianity and the University* (1994).

Interviews: Bowling (159–73), Meyer and O'Riordan 1992 (9–15).

Kent, David, ed. *'Lighting Up the Terrain': The Poetry of Margaret Avison* (ECW, 1987).

Mansbridge, Francis. 'Margaret Avison'. ABCMA 6 (1985), 13–66.

Belaney, Archie. See 'Grey Owl'.

Birney, Earle (1904–95)

The Collected Poems (2 vols., M&S, 1975) reprints selections of his earlier poetry.

For later poetry, see *Fall by Fury* (M&S, 1978) and *Last Makings* (M&S, 1991).

Fiction: *Turvey: A Military Picaresque* (1949; rev. [unexpurgated] ed., 1976) and *Down the Long Table* (1955).

See also *Spreading Time* (memoir, 1980).

Cameron Elspeth. *Earle Birney: A Life* (Viking, 1994).

Nesbitt Bruce, ed. *Earle Birney* (McGraw-Hill Ryerson, 1974).

Noel-Bentley, Peter. 'Earle Birney'. ABCMA 4 (1983), 13–128.

Bissoondath, Neil (1955–)

Digging Up the Mountains (short stories, 1985), *A Casual Brutality* (1988), *On the Eve of Uncertain Tomorrows* (short stories, 1990), *The Innocence of Age* (1992), *The Worlds Within Her* (1998), *Doing the Heart Good* (2002), *The Unyielding Clamour of the Night* (2005).

Selling Illusions: The Cult of Multiculturalism in Canada appeared in 1994 (expanded 2002).

Interviews: Allen and Carr (85–94), Garrod (35–55), Meyer and O'Riordan 1992 (16–25).

Blaise, Clark (1940–)

Novels: *Lunar Attractions* (1979), *Lusts* (1983), *If I Were Me* (1997).

Short Stories: *A North American Education* (1973), *Tribal Justice* (1974), *Resident Alien* (1986), and *Man and His World* (1992). Now republished in rearranged form as *The Selected Stories* (Erin, ON: Porcupine's Quill); *Southern Stories* appeared in 2000, *Pittsburgh Stories* in 2001, *Montreal Stories* in 2003, *World Body* in 2006. Previously uncollected stories are also included.

See also *I Had a Father: A Post-Modern Autobiography* (1993), *Days and Nights in Calcutta* (travel narrative, 1977, with his wife Bharati Mukherjee), and 'Clark Blaise, 1940– ', *Contemporary Authors Autobiography Series 31* (Detroit, Gale Research, 1986), 15–30.

Interview: Hancock (146–63).

Cameron, Barry. 'Clarke Blaise'. CWTW Fiction 7 (1985), 21–89.

Canadian Notes & Queries 67 (2005). Special Blaise issue.

Lecker, Robert. *An Other I: The Fiction of Clark Blaise* (ECW, 1988).

Bodsworth, Fred (1918–)

Last of the Curlews (1955), *The Strange One* (1959), *The Atonement of Ashley Morden* (1964), *The Sparrow's Fall* (1967).

Keith, W. J. 'Fred Bodsworth'. DLB 68 (1986), 22–26.

Bowering, George (1935–)

George Bowering Selected: Poems 1961–92 (M&S, 1993) offers representative selections from numerous earlier volumes. Subsequent books include *His Life: A Poem* (2000), etc.

Fiction: *A Short Sad Book* (1977), *Burning Water* (1986), *Caprice* (1987), etc.

Critical writing includes *A Way with Words* (on Canadian poetry, 1982), *The Mask in Place* (on North American fiction, 1982), *Craft Slices* (1985) and *Imaginary Hand* (1988), both on North American literature.

Interviews: Cameron (II 3–16), Twigg (31–4).

Harris, John. 'George Bowering'. CWTW Poetry 8 (1992), 113–85.

Miki, Roy. *A Record of Writing: An Annotated and Illustrated Bibliography of George Bowering* (Vancouver: Talonbooks, 1989). Also contains much information on Bowering's literary biography.

Brewster, Elizabeth (1922–)

Selected Poems 1944–1977 and *1977–85* (2 vols. Ottawa: Oberon 1985) reprint selections from her earlier work. More recent volumes include *Entertaining Angels* (1988), *Spring Again* (1990), *Wheel of Change* (1993), *Footnote to the Book of Job* (1995), *Garden of Sculpture* (1998), *Burning Bush* (2000), *Jacob's Dream* (2002). Oberon Press published the first two volumes of *Collected Poems* (up to 1977) in 2003.

Has also published novels, short stories, and two autobiographical miscellanies, *Invention of Truth* (1991) and *Away from Home* (1995). See also 'Elizabeth Brewster, 1922– ', *Contemporary Authors Autobiography Series 15* (Detroit: Gale Research, 1992), 149–63.

Interviews: Garrod (57–77), Pearce (7–23).

Cogswell, Fred. 'Elizabeth Brewster'. DLB 60 (1987), 20–23.

Brooke, Frances (1723–89)

The History of Emily Montague (1769; ed. Mary Jane Edwards, CEECT, 1985) is her only novel that concerns Canada. *The Excursion* (1777; ed. Paula R. Backscheider and Hope D. Cotton, Lexington, KY: University Press of Kentucky, 1997) is also accessible.

McMullen, Lorraine. *An Odd Attempt in a Woman: The Literary Life of Frances Brooke* (Vancouver: University of British Columbia Press, 1983).

——. 'Frances Brooke'. CWTW Fiction 1 (1983), 25–60.

Bruce, Charles (1906–71)

Poetry: *The Mulgrave Road* (ed. Andy Wainwright and Lesley Choice, Porters Lake, NS: Potterfield, 1985) reprints poems from *Wild Apples* (1927), *Tomorrow's Tide* (1932), *Grey Ship Moving* (1945), *The Flowing Summer* (1947), and *The Mulgrave Road* (1951).

Fiction: *The Channel Shore* (novel, 1954), *The Township of Time* (linked short stories, 1959).

Starnino, Carmine. 'The Farmer-Fisher Bard: A Look at Charles Bruce'. *A Lover's Quarrel* (Erin, ON: Porcupine's Quill, 2004), 137–46.

Wainwright, Andrew. *World Enough and Time: Charles Bruce, a Literary Biography* (Halifax, NS: Formac, 1988). Detailed if somewhat rambling biography.

Buckler, Ernest (1908–84)

Novels: *The Mountain and the Valley* (1952) and *The Cruelest Month* (1963).

Short stories: *Thanks for Listening* (ed. Martha Dvorak, Waterloo, ON: Wilfrid Laurier University Press, 2004) reprints stories originally published in *The Rebellion of Young David and Other Stories* (ed. Robert D. Chalmers, 1975), sometimes in improved versions, and includes previously unpublished material.

See also *Ox Bells and Fireflies* (memoir, 1968).

Interview: Cameron (I 3–12).

Bissell, Claude. *Ernest Buckler Remembered* (UTP, 1989).

Cook, Gregory M., ed. *Ernest Buckler* (McGraw-Hill Ryerson, 1972).

Orange, John. 'Ernest Buckler'. ABCMA 3 (1981), 13–56.

——. 'Ernest Buckler'. CWTW Fiction 5 (1990), 23–75.

Butala, Sharon (1940–)

The Perfection of the Morning (1994), *Coyote's Morning Cry* (1995), *Wild Stone Heart* (2000), *Old Man on his Bed* (2002), *Lilac Moon: Dreaming of the Real West* (2005).

Has also published novels and short stories.

Butler, William Francis (1838–1910)

The Great Lone Land (1872), *The Wild North Land* (1873).

See also *An Autobiography* (1911).

Ryan, Martin. *William Francis Butler: A Life, 1838–1910* (Dublin: Lilliput, 2003).

Callaghan, Morley (1903–90)

Novels: *Strange Fugitive* (1928), *It's Never Over* (1930), *A Broken Journey* (1932), *Such Is My Beloved* (1934), *They Shall Inherit the Earth* (1935), *More Joy in Heaven* (1937), *The Loved and the Lost* (1951), *The Many Colored Coat* (1960), *A Passion in Rome* (1961), *A Fine and Private Place* (1975), *Close to the Sun Again* (1977), *The Enchanted Pimp* (1978, rev. as *Our Lady of the Snows* 1990), *A Time for Judas* (1983), *A Wild Old Man on the Road* (novella, 1988).

Short stories: *The Complete Stories* (4 vols., ed. Barry Callaghan, Exile, 2003).

See also *That Summer in Paris* (memoir, 1963).

Interview: Cameron (II 17–33).

Boire, Gary. 'Morley Callaghan'. CWTW 5 (1990), 79–145.

——. *Morley Callaghan: Literary Anarchist* (ECW, 1994). Succinct biography.

Kendle, Judith. 'Morley Callaghan'. ABCMA 5 (1984), 13–177.

Carman, Bliss (1861–1929)

His numerous volumes of poems include *Low Tide on Grand Pré* (1893), *Behind the Arras* (1895), *Songs from Vagabondia* (with Richard Hovey, 1895), *Sappho: One Hundred Lyrics* (1904), *Pipes of Pan* (1906), *Bliss Carman's Poems* (1931).

See also *The Letters of Bliss Carman* (ed. H. P. Gundy, 1982).

Lynch, Gerald, ed. *Bliss Carman: A Reappraisal* (Ottawa: University of Ottawa Press, 1990). Uneven collection, but contains John R. Sorfleet's 'A Primary and Secondary Bibliography of Bliss Carman's Work' (193–204).

Stephens, Donald. 'Bliss Carman'. DLB 92 (1990), 38–44.

Carr, Emily (1871–1945)

The Emily Carr Omnibus (Vancouver: Douglas & McIntyre, 1993, rpt. as *The Complete Writings of Emily Carr,* 1997) reprints all her published writing, but should be read alongside *Opposite Contraries: The Unknown Journals of Emily Carr and Other Writings* (ed. Susan Crean, 2003), which prints unexpurgated passages from previously published writings as well as selected letters.

Blanchard, Paula. *The Life of Emily Carr* (Vancouver: Douglas & McIntyre, 1987).

Shadbolt, Doris. *Emily Carr* (Vancouver: Douglas & McIntyre, 1990). On Carr's painting.

Child, Philip (1898–1978)

Novels: *The Village of Souls* (1933), *God's Sparrows* (1937), *Day of Wrath* (1948), *Mr. Ames against Time* (1949).

Poetry: *The Victorian House* (1951), *The Wood of the Nightingale* (1965).

Duffy, Dennis. 'Memory Pain: The Haunted World of Philip Child's Fiction.' *Canadian Literature* 84 (Spring 1980), 41–56.

Clarke, Austin (1934–)

The Austin Clarke Reader (Exile 1996) contains short stories, newspaper columns contributed to the *Nation* (Barbados), and selected prose, including the complete *Public Enemies.*

Selected Novels: *The Meeting Point* (1967), *Storm of Fortune* (1973), *The Bigger Light* (1975), *Proud Empires* (1986), *The Origin of Waves* (1997), *The Question* (1999), *The Polished Hoe* (2002).

Choosing His Coffin: The Best Stories of Austin Clarke (Thomas Allen, 2002) is a convenient recent collection of short stories.

See also *Growing Up Stupid Under the Union Jack* (autobiography, 1980), *Public Enemies* (on racial issues, 1992), and 'Austin Clarke, 1934– ', *Contemporary Authors Autobiography Series 16* (Detroit: Gale Research, 1992), 71–88.

Interview: Gibson (37–54).

Algoo-Baksh, Stella. *Austin C. Clarke* (ECW, 1994). Concise biography.

Brown, Lloyd W. *El Dorado and Paradise: Canada and the Caribbean in Austin Clarke's Fiction* (London, ON: University of Western Ontario, 1989). Important for political, social, and psychological background.

Sanders, Leslie. 'Austin Clarke'. PCL 4 (1982), 93–100. Early but excellent introduction.

Cogswell, Fred (1917–2004)

A Long Apprenticeship: The Collected Poems (Fredericton, NB: Fiddlehead, 1980) reprints poetry from early volumes. Numerous subsequent volumes (Ottawa: Borealis Press) include *As I See It* (1994) and *The Trouble with Light* (1995). His translations include *The Poetry of Modern Quebec* (1976) and *The Complete Poems of Emile Nelligan* (1983).

'Fred Cogswell: Poet, Translator, Publisher, Friend of Poets'. Special issue of *Ellipse* (68, Autumn 2002). Articles, interview, tributes, poems.

Cohen, Leonard (1934–)

The most accessible edition of his verse is *Stranger Music: Selected Poems and Songs* (M&S, 1993). *Book of Longing* appeared in 2006.

Novels: *The Favourite Game* (1963), *Beautiful Losers* (1966).

Interviews: Meyer and O'Riordan 1984 (27–42), Twigg (41–7).

Gnarowski, Michael, ed. *Leonard Cohen: The Artist and the Critics* (McGraw-Hill Ryerson, 1976).

Nadel, Ira Bruce. *Various Positions: A Life of Leonard Cohen* (Random House, 1996).

Scobie, Stephen. *Leonard Cohen* (Vancouver: Douglas & McIntyre, 1978).

Coles, Don (1928–)

How We All Swiftly: The First Six Books (Montréal: Véhicule, 2005) reprints the best of Coles's earlier verse from *Sometimes All Over* (1975), *Anniversaries* (1979), *The Prinzhorn Collection* (1982), *Landslides: Collected Poems 1975–85* (1986), *K. in Love* (1987), and *Little Bird* (1991). His later work consists of *Forests of the Medieval World* (1993) and *Kurgan* (2000).

Novel: *Doctor Bloom's Story* (2004).

Interview: Bowling (87–102).

'Don Coles at 75, *Arc* at 25'. Special issue of *Arc* (50, Summer 2003).

Keith, W. J. Introduction to *How We All Swiftly*, a revised version of 'A Preference for the Classical: Notes on the Art of Don Coles'. *Canadian Poetry* 48 (Spring/Summer 2001), 13–37.

Connor, Ralph (Gordon, Rev. Charles William, 1860–1937)

Published numerous novels, including *Black Rock* (1898), *The Sky Pilot* (1899), *The Man from Glengarry* (1899), also a collection of short stories, *Glengarry Schooldays* (1902) and an autobiography, *Postscript to Adventure* (1938).

Lennox, John. 'Charles W. Gordon ["Ralph Connor"]'. CWTW Fiction 3 (1988), 103–59.

Wilson, Keith. *Charles William Gordon* (Winnipeg: Peguis, 1981).

Cook, Michael (1933–94)

Colour the Flesh the Colour of Dust (1972), *Jacob's Wake* (1975), *Tiln and Other Plays* (*Tiln; Quiller; Therese's Creed*, 1976), *Three Plays* (*On the Rim of the Curve; The Head, Guts and Soundbone Dance; Therese's Creed*, 1977), *The Gayden Chronicles* (1979), *The Fisherman's Revenge* (1984).

Interview: Wallace and Zimmerman (157–71).

Johnson, Chris. 'Michael Cook'. DLB 53 (1986), 147–52.

Wallace, Robert. 'Michael Cook'. PCL 4 (1982), 109–116.

Coulter, John (1888–1980)

Riel (1962, rev. 1975 [performed 1950]), *The Trial of Louis Riel* (1968), *The Crime of Louis Riel* (1976 [performed 1966]).

See also *In My Days: Memoirs* (1980).

Anthony, Geraldine. *John Coulter* (Boston: Twayne, 1976).

Crawford, Isabella Valancy (1850–87)

Old Spookses' Pass, Malcolm's Katie, and Other Poems (1884), *The Collected Poems of Isabella Valancy Crawford* (ed. J. W. Garvin, Briggs, 1905), *Hugh and Ion* (ed. Glenn Clever, Ottawa: Borealis, 1977), *Malcolm's Katie* (ed. D. M. R. Bentley, CPP, 1987).

Burns, Robert Alan. 'Isabella Valancy Crawford'. CWTW Poetry 1 (1988), 21–71.

Galvin, Elizabeth. *Isabella Valancy Crawford: We Hardly Knew Her* (Natural History / National Heritage, 1994). Brief biography, with selection of poems.

Suo, Lynne. 'Isabella Valancy Crawford: An Annotated Bibliography'. *ECW* 11 (Summer 1978), 289–314.

Dalton, Mary (1950–)

The Time of Icicles (1989), *Allowing the Light* (1993), *Merrybegot* (2003).

Nickel, Barbara. 'There's a Carnival for You: Interview with Mary Dalton'. *Books in Canada* 31.4 (June/July 2002), 27–9.

Davies, Robertson (1913–95)

Fiction: *Tempest-Tost* (1951), *Leaven of Malice* (1954), *A Mixture of Frailties* (1958), *Fifth Business* (1970), *The Manticore* (1972), *World of Wonders* (1975), *The Rebel Angels* (1981), *What's Bred in the Bone* (1985), *The Lyre of Orpheus* (1988), *Murther and Walking Spirits* (1991), *The Cunning Man* (1994).

Drama: *Eros at Breakfast and Other Plays* (1949, also containing 'The Voice of the People', 'Hope Deferred', 'At the Gates of the Righteous', and 'Overlaid', all one-act), *A Jig for the Gypsy* (1949), *At My Heart's Core* [1950] *& Overlaid* [1948] (1966), *Four Favourite Plays* (1968, also containing 'At the Gates of the Righteous', 'The Voice of the People', and *Fortune My Foe* [1949]), *Hunting Stuart and Other Plays* (1972, also containing *King Phoenix* and *General Confession*), *Question Time* (1975).

Prose: *A Voice from the Attic* (1960), *Stephen Leacock* (1970), *One Half of Robertson Davies* (1977), *The Enthusiasms of Robertson Davies* (ed. Judith Skelton Grant, 1979), *The Well-Tempered Critic: One Man's View of Theatre and Letters in Canada* (ed. Grant, 1981), *The Papers of Samuel Marchbanks* (1985, comprising *The Diary of Samuel Marchbanks*, 1947, *The Table Talk of Samuel Marchbanks*, 1949, and *Marchbanks' Almanack*, 1967), *The Merry Heart: Selections 1980–1995* (1996), *Happy Alchemy: Writings on the Theatre and Other Lively Arts* (ed. Jennifer Surridge and Brenda Davies, 1997), *For Your Eye Alone: Letters 1976–1995* (ed. Grant, 1999), *Discoveries: Early Letters 1938–1975* (ed. Grant, 2002).

Interviews: Cameron (I 30–48), Twigg (54–60). See also *Conversations with Robertson Davies* (ed. J. Madison Davis, Jackson, MS: University of Mississippi Press, 1989).

Grant, Judith Skelton. *Robertson Davies: Man of Myth* (Viking, 1994). Magisterial biography.

La Bossière, Camille, and Linda M. Morra, eds., *Robertson Davies: A Mingling of Contraries* (Ottawa: University of Ottawa Press, 2001). Solid collection of critical essays.

Little, Dave. *Catching the Wind in a Net: The Religious Vision of Robertson Davies* (ECW, 1996).

Ryrie, John (with Judith Skelton Grant). 'Robertson Davies'. ABCMA 3 (1981), 57–279.

Stone-Blackburn, Susan. *Robertson Davies, Playwright: A Search for the Self on the Canadian Stage* (Vancouver: University of British Columbia Press, 1985).

de la Roche, Mazo (1879–1961)

Her fourth novel, *Jalna* (1927), became the first of a sixteen-novel cycle that ended with *Morning at Jalna* (1960). Also wrote plays and an autobiography, *Ringing the Changes* (1957). A collection of short stories, *Selected Stories* (ed. Douglas Daymond), appeared in 1979.

Bratton, Daniel L. *Thirty-Two Short Views of Mazo de la Roche* (ECW, 1996). The most recent and most balanced biography.

De Mille, James (1833–80)

A Strange Manuscript Found in a Copper Cylinder (1880; ed. Malcolm Parks, CEECT, 1986) and a poem, *Behind the Veil* (ed. Archibald MacMechan, 1893), are his only works that remain at all well known.

Monk, Patricia. *The Gilded Beaver: An Introduction to the Life and Work of James De Mille* (ECW, 1991). Also contains detailed bibliographical check-list.

Denison, Merrill (1893–1975)

The Unheroic North (M&S, 1923) collects his early plays ('Brothers in Arms', 'From Their Own Place', 'The Weather Breeder', and *Marsh Hay*). Later, he turned his attention to radio drama.

MacDonald, Dick. *Mugwump Canadian: The Merrill Denison Story* (Montréal: Content, 1973).

Tait, Michael S. 'Merrill Denison'. PLC 3 (1982), 65–72.

Donaldson, Jeffery (1960–)

Once Out of Nature (1991), *Waterglass* (1999).

Messenger, Cynthia. '"Confluence and Separation": The Poetry of Jeffery Donaldson.' ECW 48 (Winter 1992–3), 111–115.

Sanger, Peter. '"Allowance for all": On Jeffery Donaldson's *Once Out of Nature*.' *Antigonish Review* 95 (Autumn 1993), 145–51.

Dudek, Louis (1918–2001)

Collected Poetry (Montréal: Delta Canada, 1981) contains an adequate selection of his early poetry, including selections from *Europe* (1956; rpt. in full, Erin, ON: Porcupine's Quill, 1991), *En México* (1958), *Atlantis* (1967), and an incomplete version of *Continuation 1*. For his later poetry, the best source is *The Poetry of Louis Dudek: Definitive Edition* (Ottawa: Golden Dog, 1998), though this is, despite its title, a 'selected poems'. *Continuation I* appeared in 1981, *Continuation II* in 1990. Parts of 'Continuation III' are contained in *The Caged Tiger* (1997) and *The Surface of Time* (2000).

His critical writings include *Selected Essays and Criticism* (1978) and *In Defence of Art* (1988). See also Frank Davey and bp Nichol, eds., 'Louis Dudek: Texts

& Essays', a special issue of *Open Letter,* Fourth Series 8–9 (Spring & Summer 1981). See also 'Louis Dudek, 1918– ', *Contemporary Authors Autobiography Series 14* (Detroit: Gale Research, 1991), 121–42.

Hildebrand, George, ed. *Louis Dudek: Essays on His Works* (Guernica, 2001). Includes interview.

Starnino, Carmine. 'Didactic Simplicities'. *A Lover's Quarrel* (Erin ON: Porcupine's Quill, 2004), 191–96.

Stromberg, Susan. *Louis Dudek: A Biographical Introduction to His Poetry* (Ottawa: Golden Dog, 1983).

Duncan, Sara Jeannette (Mrs. Everard Cotes, 1861–1922)

An American Girl in London (1891), *Those Delightful Americans* (1902), *The Pool in the Desert* (short stories, 1903), *The Imperialist* (1904; ed. Thomas E. Tausky, 1996), *Cousin Cinderella: A Canadian Girl in London* (1908), etc.

See also *Selected Journalism* (ed. Tausky, Ottawa: Tecumseh, 1978).

Fowler, Marian. *Redney: A Life of Sara Jeannette Duncan* (Anansi, 1983).

Tausky, Thomas E. *Sara Jeannette Duncan: Novelist of Empire* (Port Credit, ON: Meany, 1980).

——. 'Sara Jeannette Duncan'. CWTW Fiction 3 (1988), 23–100.

Dunlop, William 'Tiger' (1792–1848)

Statistical Sketches of Upper Canada (1832) and *Recollections of the American War, 1812–14* (1905, serialized 1847), both rpt. in *Tiger Dunlop's Upper Canada* (M&S, 1967).

Draper, Gary. 'William "Tiger" Dunlop'. PCL 3 (1980), 17–24. Useful introduction.

Graham, W. S. *The Tiger of Canada West* (Clarke Irwin, 1962). Biography.

Klinck, Carl F., ed. *William 'Tiger' Dunlop: Blackwoodian Backwoodsman.* (Ryerson, 1958). Essays by and about Dunlop.

Findley, Timothy (1930–2002)

Novels: *The Last of the Crazy People* (1967), *The Butterfly Plague* (1969), *The Wars* (1977), *Famous Last Words* (1981), *Not Wanted on the Voyage* (1984), *The Telling of Lies* (1986), *Headhunter* (1993), *The Piano Man's Daughter* (1995), *You Went Away* (novella, 1996), *Pilgrim* (1999), *Spadework* (2001).

Short stories: *Dinner Along the Amazon* (1984), *Stones* (1988), *Dust to Dust* (1997).

See also *Inside Memory: Pages from a Writer's Notebook* (1990), and *From Stone Orchard: A Collection of Memories* (1998), both autobiographical, and *Journeyman: Travels of a Writer* (2003), containing Findley's discussions of his own work.

Plays: *Can You See Me Yet?* (1977), *The Stillborn Lover* (1993), *The Trials of Ezra Pound* (1994), *Elizabeth Rex* (2000).

Interviews: Cameron (I 49–63), Daurio (59–68), Gibson (119–49), Kruk (77–99), Meyer and O'Riordan 1984 (45–54), Twigg (83–9).

Hulcoop, John F. 'Timothy Findley'. DLB 53 (1986), 181–91.

Roberts, Carol, and Lynne Macdonald. *Timothy Findley: An Annotated Bibliography* (ECW, 1990).

Roberts, Carol. *Timothy Findley: Stories from a Life* (ECW, 1994). Concise biography.

French, David (1939–)

The five 'Mercer' plays consist of *Leaving Home* (1972), *Of the Fields, Lately* (1975), *Saltwater Moon* (1985), *1949* (1989), and *Soldier's Heart* (2002). Other plays include *One Crack Out* (1976; rev. ed. 2003), *Jitters* (1980), *Silver Dagger* (1993), *That Summer* (2000), and *The Riddle of the World* (2003). His translation of Chekhov's *The Seagull* appeared in 1977 (rpt. 1993).

Interview: Wallace and Zimmerman (305–16).

Johnson, Chris. 'David French'. DLB 53 (1986), 191–94.

Zimmerman, Cynthia. 'David French'. PCL 4 (1982), 117–23.

Frye, Northrop (1912–91)

Collected Works of Northrop Frye (gen. ed. Alvin A. Lee, UTP, 1991–) has so far published 21 volumes, including letters, articles, notebooks, and Canadian and biblical writings. His numerous books on literary theory and criticism include *Fearful Symmetry* (on Blake, 1947; *Collected Works 14*), *Anatomy of Criticism* (1957), *The Bush Garden* (on Canadian literature, 1971; fuller text in *Collected Works 12*), *The Great Code* (on the Bible, 1982; *Collected Works 19*), *Divisions on a Ground* (on Canadian culture, 1982; mainly rpt. in *Collected Works 12*), *Words with Power* (on the Bible, 1990), and (with Jay Macpherson) *Biblical and Classical Myths: The Mythological Framework of Western Culture* (2004; Frye's contribution also available in *Collected Works 13*).

Adamson, Joseph. *Northrop Frye: A Visionary Life* (ECW, 1993). Concise biography.

Cayley, David, ed. *Northrop Frye in Conversation* (Anansi, 1992).

Denham, Robert D. *Northrop Frye: An Annotated Bibliography of Primary and Secondary Sources* (UTP, 1987).

Gallant, Mavis (1922–)

The Selected Stories (M&S, 1996) provides an excellent introduction to her short stories, but three later stories are contained in *Montreal Stories* (M&S, 2004).

She also wrote two novels, *Green Water, Green Sky* (1959) and *A Fairly Good Time* (1970),

See also *What Is to Be Done?* (play, 1984) and *Paris Notebooks* (non-fiction, 1986).

Interviews: Hancock (79–126), O'Brien (251–82), Twigg (102–7).

Grant, Judith Skelton. 'Mavis Gallant'. CWTW Fiction 8 (1989), 23–80.

Grant, Judith Skelton, and Douglas Malcolm. 'Mavis Gallant'. ABCMA 5 (1984), 179–230.

Keefer, Janice Kulyk. *Reading Mavis Gallant* (OUP, 1989).

Garner, Hugh (1913–79)

Garner's work is best sampled in *The Hugh Garner Omnibus* (McGraw-Hill Ryerson, 1978), which reprints his short stories, *Cabbagetown* in full, and selected journalism.

Selected novels: *Storm Below* (1949), *Cabbagetown* (1950; complete text 1968), *The Silence on the Shore* (1962).

See also *One Damn Thing After Another* (autobiography, 1973).

Stuewe, Paul. *The Storms Below: The Turbulent Life and Times of Hugh Garner* (James Lorimer, 1988).

——. 'Hugh Garner'. CWTW Fiction 6 (1985), 81–127.

Glassco, John (1909–81)

Selected Poems with Three Notes on the Poetic Process (ed. Michael Gnarowski, Ottawa: Golden Dog, 1970) offers a good selection of his verse. Best known for *Memoirs of Montparnasse* (fictional memoir, 1970; ed. Gnarowski, OUP, 1995). His translations include *The Complete Poems of Hector Saint-Denys Garneau* (1962) and *The Poetry of French Canada in English* (1970). He also published works of pornography.

Canadian Poetry 13 (Fall/Winter 1983). Special Glassco memorial issue.

Kokotailo, Philip. *John Glassco's Richer World: 'Memoirs of Montparnasse'* (ECW, 1988).

Sutherland, Fraser. *John Glassco: An Essay and a Bibliography* (ECW, 1984).

Goldsmith, Oliver (1794–1861)

The Rising Village (1825; ed. Gerald Lynch, CPP, 1989), *Autobiography* (ed. W. E. Myatt, 1943).

Bentley, D. M. R. 'Oliver Goldsmith and *The Rising Village*'. *Studies in Canadian Literature* 15.1 (1990), 21–61.

Keith, W. J. '*The Rising Village* Again'. *Canadian Poetry* 3 (Fall/Winter 1978), 1–13.

Gordon, Rev. Charles William (See Connor, Ralph)

Grant, George Monro (1835–1902)

Ocean to Ocean: Sandford Fleming's Expedition through Canada in 1872 (1873).

Jackel, David. '*Ocean to Ocean*: G. M. Grant's "round unvarnish'd tale"'. *Canadian Literature 81* (Summer 1979), 7–23.

Jackel, Susan. 'George Monro Grant'. DLB 99 (1990), 131–33.

Grant, George Parkin (1918–88)

The George Grant Reader (ed. William Christian and Sheila Grant, UTP, 1998) provides an excellent introduction to his work. *Collected Works of George Grant* (UTP, 2000–) has currently published 3 vols.: vol. 1 (ed. Arthur Davis and Peter Emberly) includes early writings, 1933–50, vol. 2 (ed. Davis) prints articles, etc., 1951–9, including *Philosophy in the Mass Age*, vol. 3 (ed. Davis and Henry Roper) writings 1960–69, including *Lament for a Nation.*

Philosophy in the Mass Age (1959), *Lament for a Nation* (1965), *Technology and Empire* (1969), *Time as History* (1971), *English-Speaking Justice* (1978). *Selected Letters* (ed. William Christian) appeared in 1996.

Cayley, David, ed. *George Grant in Conversation* (Anansi, 1995).

Christian, William. *George Grant: A Biography* (UTP, 1993).

Schmidt, Larry, ed. *George Grant in Process: Essays and Conversations* (Anansi, 1978).

'Grey Owl' (Archie Belaney, 1888–1938)

The Men of the Last Frontier (1931), *Pilgrims of the Wild* (1935), *The Adventures of Sajo and Her Beaver People* (1935), *Tales of an Empty Cabin* (1936).

Dickson, Lovat. *Wilderness Man* (Macmillan, 1973).

Smith, Donald B. *From the Land of the Shadows: The Making of Grey Owl* (Saskatoon: Western Producer, 1990).

Grove, Frederick Philip (1879–1948)

Settlers of the Marsh (1925), *A Search for America* (1927), *Our Daily Bread* (1928), *The Yoke of Life* (1930), *Fruits of the Earth* (1933), *Two Generations* (1939), *The Master of the Mill* (1944).

Other writings include *Over Prairie Trails* (non-fiction, 1922), *In Search of Myself* (fictional autobiography, 1946), *Consider Her Ways* (satirical fantasy, 1947), *Tales from the Margin* (ed. Desmond Pacey, short stories, 1971), and *The Letters of Frederick Philip Grove* (ed. Pacey, 1976). The two novels Grove published in Germany under his original name, Felix Paul Greve, have been translated: *Fanny Essler* (2 vols., 1984) and *Mauermeister Ihles Haus* (as *The Master Mason's House*, 1976).

Hjartarson, Paul, ed. *A Stranger to My Time: Essays by and about Frederick Philip Grove* (Edmonton: NeWest Press), 1986.

Keith, W. J. 'Frederick Philip Grove'. CWTW Fiction 4 (1991), 21–70.

Martens, Klaus. *F. P. Grove in Europe and Canada: Translated Lives* (Edmonton: University of Alberta Press, 2001).

Gustafson, Ralph (1909–95)

The Collected Poems (3 vols. Victoria: Sono Nis, 1987, 1994) is now the standard edition of his verse. *Visions Fugitive* (1996) appeared posthumously, as did *Selected Poems* (Montréal: Véhicule, 2001), chosen by himself.

McCarthy, Dermot. *The Poetics of Place: The Poetry of Ralph Gustafson* (MQUP, 1991). Exhaustive academic study.

——. 'Ralph Gustafson'. CWTW Poetry 6 (1989), 85–170.

Gutteridge, Don (1937–)

Dreams and Visions: The Land consists of *Riel* (1968), *Coppermine* (1973), *Borderlands* (1975), and *Tecumseh* (1976). *Time Is a Metaphor*, a later series of both prose and verse volumes, is made up of *Bus Ride* (1974), *A True History of Lambton County* (1977), *All in Good Time* (1980), *St. Vitus Dance* (1987), *Shaman's Ground* (1988), and *How the World Began* (1991). *The Exiled Heart: Selected Narratives 1968–1992* (1993) reprints the *Dreams and Visions* tetralogy and other works. *Something More Miraculous* (2004) contains recent poems.

Garebian, Keith. 'Don Gutteridge's Mythic Tetralogy'. *Canadian Literature 87* (Winter, 1980), 25–41.

Haig-Brown, Roderick (1908–76)

Haig-Brown's prime interests are reflected in three posthumous anthologies (all M&S): *Woods and River Tales* (1980), *The Master and His Fish* (1981), and *Writings and Reflections* (1982). His main works are *Pool and Rapid* (1932), *The Western Angler* (1939), *Return to the River* (1941), *A River Never Sleeps* (1946), *Measure of the Year* (1950), *Fisherman's Spring* (1951), *Fisherman's Winter* (1954), *Fisherman's Summer* (1959), *Fisherman's Fall* (1964).

Cave, Robert Bruce. *Roderick Haig-Brown: A Descriptive Bibliography* (Curtis Heights, CA: privately published, 2000).

Haig-Brown, Valerie. *Deep Currents: Roderick and Ann Haig-Brown* (Victoria, BC: Orca, 1997). Intimate biography by their daughter.

Robertson, Anthony. *Above Tide: Reflections on Roderick Haig-Brown* (Madeira Park, BC: Harbour Publishing, 1984).

Haliburton, Thomas Chandler (1796–1865)

The Clockmaker (1st series 1836, 2nd series 1838, 3rd series 1840; ed. George L. Parker, CEECT, 1995), *The Attaché; or, Sam Slick in England* (1st series 1843, 2nd series 1844), *The Old Judge* (1849).

See also *The Letters of Thomas Chandler Haliburton* (ed. Richard A. Davies, 1988).

Davies, Richard A. *Inventing Sam Slick: A Biography of Thomas Chandler Haliburton* (UTP, 2005).

——, ed. *On Thomas Chandler Haliburton: Selected Criticism* (Ottawa: Borealis, 1979).

McMullin, Stanley E. 'Thomas Chandler Haliburton'. CWTW Fiction 2 (1989), 27–76).

Harris, Michael (1944–)

New and Selected Poems (Montréal: Véhicule/Signet, 1992) includes well-chosen selections from his main earlier volumes, *Grace* (1977) and *In Transit* (1985).

Has also published *Veiled Countries/Lives*, translations from Marie-Claire Blais (1984).

Interview: Allen and Carr, 31–36.

Harrison, Charles Yale (1898–1956)

Relevant here for *Generals Die in Bed* (1930).

Besner, Neil. 'Charles Yale Harrison'. DLB 68 (1988), 164–65.

Hearne, Samuel (1745–92)

A Journey from Prince of Wales's Fort to Hudson's Bay in the Northern Ocean (1795).

Hamilton, Mary E. 'Samuel Hearne'. PCL 3 (1982), 9–16.

McGoogan, Ken. *Ancient Mariner: The Amazing Adventures of Samuel Hearne, The Sailor Who Walked to the Arctic Ocean* (Harper*Flamingo*, 2003). Semi-fictionalized but well-researched biography.

Nuffield, Edward W. *Samuel Hearne: Journey to the Coppermine River, 1769–1772* (Vancouver: Haro Books, 2000).

Heavysege, Charles (1816–76)

Heavysege's work is best sampled in *Saul and Selected Poems* (ed. Sandra Djwa, UTP, 1976).

Woodcock, George. 'Charles Heavysege'. CWTW Poetry 1 (1988), 75–116.

Henry, Alexander (1739–1824)

Travels and Adventures in Canada and the Indian Territories between the Years 1760 and 1776 (1809).

Besner, Neil. 'Alexander Henry'. DLB 99 (1990), 161–63.

Hiebert, Paul (1892–1987)

Best known for *Sarah Binks* (1947). Other books include *Willows Revisited* (1967) and *For the Birds* (1980).

MacKendrick, Louis K. 'Paul Hiebert'. DLB 68 (1988), 180–84.

Hodgins, Jack (1938–)

Short stories: *Spit Delaney's Island* (1976), *The Barclay Family Theatre* (1981), *Damage Done by the Storm* (2004).

Novels: *The Invention of the World* (1977), *The Resurrection of Joseph Bourne* (1979), *The Honorary Patron* (1987), *Innocent Cities* (1990), *The Macken Charm* (1995), *Broken Ground* (1998), *Distance* (2003).

Interviews: Hancock (51–78), Kruk (126–58), O'Brien (195–228), Twigg (124–29).

Jeffrey, David. 'Jack Hodgins'. CWTW 10 (1989), 187–239.

Struthers, J. R. (Tim), ed. *On Coasts of Eternity: Jack Hodgins' Fictional Universe* (Lantzville, BC: Oolichan, 1996). Includes critical essays, four interviews, and a bibliographical check-list.

Hood, Hugh (1928–2000)

Short stories (best sampled in *Light Shining Out of Darkness and Other Stories*, M&S, 2001): *Flying a Red Kite* (1962; *Collected Short Stories I*, 1987), *Around the Mountain: Scenes from Montreal Life* (1967; *Collected Short Stories IV*, 1994), *The Fruit Man, the Meat Man & the Manager* (1971), *Dark Glasses* (1976), *None Genuine Without This Signature* (1980), *August Nights* (1985), *A Short Walk in the Rain* (*Collected Short Stories II*, 1989), *The Isolation Booth* (*Collected Short Stories III*, 1991), *You'll Catch Your Death* (1992), *After All!* (*Collected Short Stories V*, 2003).

Novels: *White Figure, White Ground* (1964), *The Camera Always Lies* (1967), *A Game of Touch* (1970), *You Cant Get There from Here* (1972), *The New Age/Le nouveau siècle*: 12 novels, comprising *The Swing in the Garden* (1975), *A New Athens* (1977), *Reservoir Ravine* (1979), *Black and White Keys* (1982), *The Scenic Art* (1984), *The Motor Boys in Ottawa* (1986), *Tony's Book* (1988), *Property and Value* (1990), *Be Sure to Close Your Eyes* (1993), *Dead Men's Watches* (1995), *Great Realizations* (1997), *Near Water* (2000). Also, *Five New Facts about Giorgione* (novella, 1987).

Essays: *The Governor's Bridge Is Closed* (1973), *Unsupported Assertions* (1991). See also 'Hugh Hood, 1928– ', *Contemporary Authors Autobiography Series 17* (Detroit: Gale Research, 1993), 75–94.

Keith, W. J. *Canadian Odyssey: A Reading of Hugh Hood's 'The New Age/Le nouveau siècle'* (MQUP, 2002).

Struthers, J. R. (Tim), ed. 'Hugh Hood's Work in Progress'. Special issue of ECW, 13–14 (Spring–Summer 1978–79). Rpt. as *Before the Flood* (ECW, 1979). Contains an important and extensive interview.

——. 'Hugh Hood'. ABCMA 5 (1984), 231–353.

Howe, Joseph (1804–73)

Speeches and Public Letters (1858), *Poems and Essays* (1874), *Acadia* (1833–4; ed. M. G. Parks, CPP, 1989), *Western and Eastern Rambles: Travel Sketches in Nova Scotia* (serialized 1828–31; ed. Parks, 1973).

Beck, J. Murray. *Joseph Howe* (2 vols. MQUP, 1982, 1983). Full biography.

Vincent, Thomas B. 'Joseph Howe'. DLB 99 (1990), 167–70.

Innis, Harold (1894–1952)

The Fur Trade in Canada (1930), *The Cod Fisheries* (1940), *Empire and Communication* (1951), *The Bias of Communication* (1956), *Changing Concepts of Time* (1952), *Staples, Markets and Cultural Change: Selected Essays* (ed. Daniel Drache, 1995).

Creighton, Donald. *Harold Innis: Portrait of a Scholar* (UTP, 1957).

Watson, Alexander John. *Marginal Man: The Dark Vision of Harold Innis* (UTP, 2005). Detailed biography.

Jameson, Anna (1794–1860)

Winter Studies and Summer Rambles in Upper Canada (3 vols., 1838).

Thomas, Clara. *Love and Work Enough: The Life of Anna Jameson* (UTP, 1967).

Johnston, George (1913–2004)

Endeared by Dark: Collected Poems (Erin, ON: Porcupine's Quill, 1990) reprints his earlier verse. *What Is to Come: Selected and New Poems* followed in 1996.

Also translated Norse sagas and other works of Scandinavian literature.

Cameron, M. I., et al., eds. *The Old Enchanter: A Portrait of George Johnston* (Manitock, ON: Penumbra, 1999).

Keith, W. J. 'The Later Poetry of George Johnston'. *Canadian Poetry 31* (Fall/Winter 1992), 8–27. Rpt. in *Canadian Notes & Queries 64* (2003), 10–18.

Malahat Review 78 (March 1987). Special Johnston issue.

Sarah, Robyn. 'In Star-Warm Dusk: The Poems of George Johnston'. *Canadian Notes & Queries 69* (Spring/Summer 2006), 32–43. Useful introduction.

Jones, D. G. (Douglas Gordon, 1929–)

Frost on the Sun (1957), *The Sun Is Axeman* (1961), *Phrases from Orpheus* (1967), *Under the Thunder the Flowers Light Up the Earth* (1977), *A Throw of Particles: New and Selected Poetry* (1983), *Balthazar and Other Poems* (1988), *The Floating Garden* (1995), *Wild Asterisks in Cloud* (1997), *Grounding Sight* (1999). A *Collected Poems* is forthcoming (Montréal: Véhicule).

His thematic study of Canadian literature, *Butterfly on Rock*, appeared in 1970.

Interviews: Allen and Carr (37–47), Meyer and O'Riordan 1992 (37–44).

Bowering, George, 'Coming Home to the World: The Poetry of D. G. Jones'.

A Way with Words (Ottawa: Oberon, 1982), 60–87.

Steele, Charles R. 'D. G. Jones'. DLB 53 (1986), 232–37.

Kane, Paul (1810–71)

Wanderings of an Artist among the Indians of North America (1859).

Harper, J. Russell. *Paul Kane's Frontier* (Austin: University of Texas Press, 1971). Biographical as well as artistic.

King, Thomas (1943–)

Medicine River (1990), *One Good Story, That One* (short stories) and *Green Grass, Running Water* (both 1993), *Truth and Bright Water* (1999), *A Short History of Indians in Canada* (short stories, 2005).

Interview: Daurio (90–97).

See also *The Truth About Stories: A Native Narrative* (2003). A rather quirky series of lectures about storytelling.

Canadian Literature 161–62 (Summer/Autumn 1999). Important for 'Peter Gzowski Interviews Thomas King on *Green Grass, Running Water*' and Jane Fleck's invaluable 'Reading Notes for Thomas King's *Green Grass, Running Water*'.

Kirby, William (1817–1906)

The U. E.: A Tale of Upper Canada (verse, 1859), *The Golden Dog (Le Chien d'or)* (fiction, 1877).

Northey, Margot. 'William Kirby'. CWTW Fiction 2 (1989), 79–104.

Pierce, Lorne. *William Kirby: Portrait of a Tory Loyalist* (Macmillan, 1929).

Klein, A. M. (Abraham Moses, 1909–72)

The Collected Works of A. M. Klein (UTP) includes *Complete Poems* (2 vols., 1990), excellently edited and annotated by Zailig Pollock. Other volumes in the edition are *Beyond Sambation: Selected Essays and Editorials, 1928–1953* (ed. M. W. Steinberg and Usher Caplan, 1982), *The Short Stories of A. M. Klein* (ed. Steinberg, 1983), *Literary Essays and Reviews* (ed. Usher and Steinberg, 1987), *The Second Scroll* (ed. Elizabeth Popham and Pollock, 2000).

Caplan, Usher. *Like One Who Dreamed: A Portrait of A. M. Klein* (McGraw-Hill Ryerson, 1982).

Marshall, Tom, ed. *A. M. Klein* (Ryerson, 1970).

Pollock, Zailig. *A. M. Klein: An Annotated Bibliography* (ECW, 1993).

——. *A. M. Klein: The Story of a Poet* (UTP, 1994).

Starnino, Carmine. 'The Colours of Abe's Fancy'. *A Lover's Quarrel* (Erin, ON: Porcupine's Quill, 2004), 197–215.

Knister, Raymond (1899–1932)

After Exile: A Raymond Knister Poetry Reader (Exile, 2003) is a useful recent selection. See also *Collected Poems* (ed. Dorothy Livesay, 1949), *White Narcissus* (novel, 1929), *My Star Predominant* (novel, 1934), *Selected Stories* (ed. Michael Gnarowski, 1972), *Raymond Knister: Stories and Essays* (ed. David Arnason, *Journal of Canadian Fiction* special issue 1972); *The First Day of Spring: Stories and Other Prose* (ed. Peter Stevens, 1975), *Windfalls for Cider* (poems, ed. Joy Kuropatwa, 1983).

Burke, Anne. 'Raymond Knister'. ABCMA 3 (1981), 281–322.

Thompson, Lee Briscoe. 'Raymond Knister'. DLB 68 (1988), 206–10.

Kogawa, Joy (1935–)

Obasan (1981), *Itsuka* (1992, rev. 1993), *The Rain Ascends* (1995, rev. 2003).

For her poetry, see *A Garden of Anchors: Selected Poems* (Oakville, ON: Mosaic, 2003). Her long poem *A Song of Lilith* appeared in 2000.

Interviews: Daurio (98–104), Meyer and O'Riordan 1992 (45–52).

Davidson, Arnold. *Writing Against the Silence: Joy Kogawa's 'Obasan'* (ECW, 1993). Emphasizes politics more than artistry, but useful for background and bibliography.

Kreisel, Henry (1922–91)

The Rich Man (1948), *The Betrayal* (1964), *The Almost Meeting and Other Stories* (short stories, 1981).

Another Country: Writings by and about Henry Kreisel (ed. Shirley Neuman, Edmonton: NeWest, 1985) contains Kreisel's internment diary as well as essays, short stories, letters, and two interviews.

Hlus, Carolyn. 'Henry Kreisel'. PCL 5 (1986), 113–20.

Kroetsch, Robert (1927–)

Kroetsch's poetry is now gathered in *Completed Field Notes* (M&S, 1989), but see *Stone Hammer Poems* (1975) for 'F. P. Grove: A Finding' and 'Old Man Stories'. Subsequent volumes are *The Hornbooks of Rita K.* (2001) and *The Snowbird Poems* (2004).

Novels: *But We Are Exiles* (1965), *The Words of My Roaring* (1966), *The Studhorse Man* (1969), *Gone Indian* (1973), *Badlands* (1975), *What the Crow Said* (1978), *Alibi* (1983), *The Puppeteer* (1992), *The Man from the Creeks* (1998).

See also *A Likely Story: The Writing Life* (1995). Idiosyncratic personal essays about writing.

Interviews: Cameron (I 81–95), Hancock (127–45), Twigg (149–54). See also *Labyrinths of Voice: Conversations with Robert Kroetsch* (ed. Shirley Neuman and Robert Wilson, Edmonton: NeWest, 1982).

Lecker, Robert. 'Robert Kroetsch'. ABCMA 7 (1987), 271–401.

Thomas, Peter. *Robert Kroetsch and His Works* (ECW, 1988).

Lampman, Archibald (1861–99)

Selected Poetry of Archibald Lampman (ed. Michael Gnarowski, Ottawa: Tecumseh, 1990) provides a good introduction. *The Poems of Archibald Lampman* (ed. Duncan Campbell Scott, 1900) collects the contents of *Among the Millet* (1888), *Lyrics of Earth* (1895), and prints uncollected poems. Reprinted (UTP, 1974) along with *At the Long Sault* (ed. Scott and E. K. Brown, 1943), this is still the most complete edition of Lampman's poetry, though supplemented by *Lampman's Kate: Late Love Poems, 1887–1897* (ed. Margaret Coulby Whitridge, 1975) and *Lampman's Sonnets, 1884–1899* (ed. Whitridge, 1976).

See also *Essays and Reviews of Archibald Lampman* (ed. D. M. R. Bentley, CPP, 1996).

Early, L. R. 'Archibald Lampman'. CWTW Poetry 2 (1983), 135–85.

Wicken, George. 'Archibald Lampman'. ABCMA 2 (1980), 97–146.

Lane, Patrick (1939–)

Poems New & Selected (OUP, 1978) reprints from his earlier volumes, *Selected Poems 1978–1997* (Madeira Park, BC: Harbour Publishing, 1997) from his later. Subsequent volumes: *The Bare Plum of Winter Rain* (2000) and *Go Leaving Strange* (2004).

See also *There Is a Season: A Memoir in a Garden* (2004; published in U.S. as *What the Stones Remember: A Life Rediscovered*).

Interviews: Bowling (62–74), Meyer and O'Riordan 1992 (53–64), Twigg (155–60).

Woodcock, George. 'Patrick Lane'. CWTW Poetry 9 (1985), 133–85.

Laurence, Margaret (1926–87)

This Side Jordan (1960), *The Tomorrow-Tamer* (short stories, 1963), *The Stone Angel* (1964), *A Jest of God* (1966), *The Fire-Dwellers* (1969), *A Bird in the House* (linked short stories, 1970), *The Diviners* (1974).

See also *The Prophet's Camel Bell* (travel, 1963), *Heart of a Stranger* (articles and reviews, 1976), and *Dance on the Earth* (memoir, 1989).

Interviews: Cameron (I 96–115), Gibson (185–208), Twigg (161–7).

Powers, Lyall. *Alien Heart: The Life & Work of Margaret Laurence* (Winnipeg: University of Manitoba Press, 2003).

Sparrow, Fiona. *Into Africa with Margaret Laurence* (ECW, 1992).

Warwick, Susan. 'Margaret Laurence'. ABCMA 1 (1979), 47–101.

Woodcock, George, ed. *A Place to Stand On: Essays by and about Margaret Laurence* (Edmonton: NeWest, 1983).

Layton, Irving (1912–2006)

A Wild Peculiar Joy: Selected Poems, first published in 1982, is now available in an expanded edition (M&S, 2004). *The Collected Poems* (M&S, 1971) reprints his early volumes, of which the most significant was *A Red Carpet for the Sun* (1959). Subsequent volumes include *Lovers and Lesser Men* (1973), *The Pole Vaulter* (1974), *For My Brother Jesus* (1976), *The Covenant* (1977), *The Tightrope Dancer* (1978), *Europe and Other Bad News* (1981), *The Gucci Bag* (1983), *Fortunate Exile* (1987), *Final Reckoning: Poems 1982–1986* (1987), and *Fornalutx: Selected Poems 1928–1990* (1992).

See also: *Engagements: The Prose of Irving Layton* (ed. Seymour Mayne, 1972), *Taking Sides: The Collected Social and Political Writings* (ed. Howard Auster, 1977), *Waiting for the Messiah* (memoir, 1985), *Wild Gooseberries: The Selected Letters of Irving Layton* (ed. Francis Mansbridge, 1989).

Interviews: Allen and Carr (1–6), Meyer and O'Riordan 1984 (11–24).

Cameron, Elspeth. *Irving Layton: A Portrait* (Stoddart, 1985). Controversial biography.

Francis, Wynne. 'Irving Layton'. CWTW Poetry 5 (1985), 143–234.

Mansbridge, Francis. 'Irving Layton'. ABCMA 8 (1994), 13–334.

Mayne, Seymour, ed. *Irving Layton: The Poet and His Critics* (McGraw-Hill Ryerson, 1978).

Leacock, Stephen (1869–1944)

Literary Lapses (1910), *Nonsense Novels* (1911), *Sunshine Sketches of a Little Town* (1912; ed. Carl Spadoni, Peterborough, ON: Broadway, 2002), *Arcadian Adventures of the Idle Rich* (1914), *Further Foolishness* (1916), *Frenzied Fiction* (1918), *My Discovery of England* (1922), *Winnowed Wisdom* (1926), *My Remarkable Uncle* (1942), *Last Leaves* (1945), *The Boy I Left Behind Me* (1946).

See also *On the Front Line of Life: Stephen Leacock, Memories and Reflections, 1935–44* (ed. Alan Bowker, 2004). Well-edited anthology of late essays.

Curry, Ralph. 'Stephen Leacock'. CWTW Fiction 3 (1988), 163–212.

Lynch, Gerald. *Stephen Leacock: Humour and Humanity* (MQUP, 1988).

Spadoni, Carl. *A Bibliography of Stephen Leacock* (ECW, 1998).

Lee, Dennis (1939–)

Nightwatch: New and Selected Poems 1968–1996 (M&S, 1996) reprints selections from earlier volumes, and includes recent poems. *Un* followed in 2003.

Also well-known for his children's verse, including *Alligator Pie* (1974) and *So Cool* (2004). See also *Body Music* (essays, 1998).

Interviews: Bowling (123–38), Pearce (45–59), Twigg (168–73).

MacPherson, Mary. 'Dennis Lee.' ABCMA 8 (1994), 335–467.

Mulhallen, Karen, et al., eds. *Tasks of Passion: Dennis Lee at Mid-Career* (Descant, 1982).

Middlebro', Tom. 'Dennis Lee'. CWTW Poetry 9 (1985), 189–228.

LePan, Douglas (1918–98)

Weathering It: Complete Poems 1948–1987 (M&S, 1987) is now the standard text for his verse. Subsequent volumes are *Far Voyages* (1990) and *Macalister, or Dying in the Dark* (1995). *Towards the Open: Georgian Bay Poems* (1998) consists almost entirely of reprinted material.

See also *The Deserter* (novel, 1964) and *Bright Glass of Memory* (political and literary memoirs, 1979).

Kertzer, J. M. 'The Wounded Eye: The Poetry of Douglas LePan'. *Studies in Canadian Literature 6.1* (1981), 5–23.

Robbins, Wendy. 'Douglas LePan'. DLB 88 (1989), 184–88.

Levine, Norman (1923–2005)

Short stories: *One Way Ticket* (1961), *I Don't Want to Know Anyone Too Well* (1971), and *Thin Ice* (1979); recent selections, generally including one or more original stories, are *Champagne Barn* and *Why Do You Live So Far Away?* (both 1984), *By a Frozen River* (2000), and *The Ability to Forget* (2003).

Has also published two novels, *The Angled Road* (1952), *From a Seaside Town* (1970), two volumes of poetry, and his controversial *Canada Made Me* (travel memoir, 1959). See also 'Norman Levine, 1924– ', *Contemporary Authors Autobiography Series 23* (Detroit: Gale Research, 1996), 165–80.

Interview: Twigg (174–77).

Canadian Notes & Queries 60 (2001). Special Levine issue.

Mathews, Lawrence. 'Norman Levine'. CWTW Fiction 8 (1989), 83–128.

Sweet, Frederick. 'Norman Levine'. PCL 4 (1982), 29–36.

Livesay, Dorothy (1909–96)

Collected Poems: The Two Seasons (1972) is an extensive collection of her earlier poetry. Later work includes *Ice Age* (1975), *The Phases of Love* (1983), *Feeling the Worlds: New Poems* (1984), *The Self-Completing Tree: Selected Poems* (1986), *Archive for Our Times* (ed. Dean J. Irvine, 1998).

See also *Right Hand, Left Hand* (memoir, ed. David Arnason and Kim Todd, 1977), *Beginnings* (memoir, 1988, expanded from *A Winnipeg Childhood,*

1973), and *Journey with My Selves: A Memoir 1909–1963* (1991).

Interviews: Meyer and O'Riordan 1984 (73–84), Twigg (178–83).

Darny, Lindsay, et al., eds. *A Public and Private Voice: Essays on the Life and Work of Dorothy Livesay* (Waterloo, ON: University of Waterloo Press, 1986).

Ricketts, Alan. 'Dorothy Livesay', ABCMA 4 (1983), 129–203.

Stevens, Peter. *Dorothy Livesay: Patterns in a Poetic Life* (ECW 1992). Concise biography.

Lochhead, Douglas (1922–)

The Full Furnace: Collected Poems (McGraw-Hill Ryerson 1975) presents his early work. His best verse, however, appeared later, in *High Marsh Road* and *A & E* (both 1980), *The Panic Field* (1984), *Upper Cape Poems* and *Dykelands* (both 1989), *Black Festival* (1991), *Homage to Henry Alline* (1992), *Breakfast at Mel's* and *All Things Do Continue* (both 1997), *Cape Enragé* (2000), *Weathers: Poems New & Selected* (2002), *Midgic* (2003).

Fancy, Margaret, 'To Remember a Landscape: A Checklist of the Works of Douglas Lochhead.' Thomas, Peter, ed. *The Red Jeep and Other Landscapes: A Collection in Honour of Douglas Lochhead* (Sackville, NB: Centre for Canadian Studies, Mount Allison University, 1987), 91–108.

Sanger, Peter. *As the Eye of Lyncaeus: A Celebration of Douglas Lochhead* (n.p.: Anchorage, 1990.

Lowry, Malcolm (1909–57)

Under the Volcano (1947), *Hear Us O Lord from Heaven Thy Dwelling Place* (short stories, 1961), *Dark as the Grave Wherein My Friend Is Laid* (1968), *October Ferry to Gabriola* (1970), *La Mordida* (ed. Patrick A. McCarthy, 1996).

See also *Sursum Corda: The Collected Letters of Malcolm Lowry* (ed. Sherrill Grace, 2 vols., UTP, 1996) and *The Collected Poetry of Malcolm Lowry* (ed. K. D. Scherf, 1992).

Bowker, Gordon. *Pursued by Furies: A Life of Malcolm Lowry* (London: HarperCollins, 1993).

McCulloch, Thomas (1776–1843)

The Letters of Mephibosheth Stepsure (1862), rpt. as *The Stepsure Letters* (1960) and *The Mephibosheth Stepsure Letters* (ed. Gwendolyn Davies, CEECT, 1990).

Mathews, Robin. '*The Stepsure Letters*: Puritanism and the Novel of the Land'. *Studies in Canadian Literature* 7 (1982), 127–38.

Whitelaw, Marjorie. *Thomas McCulloch, His Life and Times* (Halifax: Nova Scotia Museum, 1985).

MacEwen, Gwendolyn (1941–87)

The Poetry of Gwendolyn MacEwen (Exile) consists of two vols., both edited by Margaret Atwood and Barry Cameron: *The Early Years* (1993) and *The Later Years* (1994). However, vol. 2 prints only selections from *The T. E. Lawrence Poems* (1982), which needs to be read complete.

Fiction: *Julian the Magician* (1963), *King of Egypt, King of Dreams* (1971), *Noman* (short stories, 1972), and *Noman's Land* (linked short stories, 1985).

Interviews: Meyer and O'Riordan 1984 (97–106), Pearce (63–73).

Sullivan, Rosemary. *Shadow Maker: The Life of Gwendolyn MacEwen* (HarperCollins, 1995).

Mackenzie, Alexander (1764–1820)

Voyages from Montreal on the River St. Laurence through the Continent of North America to the Frozen and Pacific Oceans in the Years 1789 and 1793 (1801). *Journals and Letters of Alexander Mackenzie* (ed. W. Kaye Lamb, 1970).

Gough Barry. *First Across the Continent: Sir Alexander Mackenzie* (M&S, 1997).

McLulich, T. D. 'Alexander Mackenzie'. PCL 5 (1986), 17–24.

McLachlan, Alexander (1818–96)

The Emigrant and Other Poems (1861; ed. D. M. R. Bentley, CPP, 1991), *Poems and Songs* (1974).

Waterston, Elizabeth. 'Alexander McLachlan'. DLB 99 (1990), 242–43.

MacLennan, Hugh (1907–90)

Barometer Rising (1941), *Two Solitudes* (1945), *The Precipice* (1948), *Each Man's Son* (1951), *The Watch That Ends the Night* (1959), *Return of the Sphinx* (1967), *Voices in Time* (1980).

Non-Fiction: *Cross-Country* (1949), *Thirty and Three* (ed. Dorothy Duncan, 1956), *Scotchman's Return* (1960), *Seven Rivers of Canada* (1961), *The Other Side of Hugh MacLennan* (ed. Elspeth Cameron, 1978).

Interviews: Cameron (I 130–48), Twigg (184–90).

Cameron, Elspeth. *Hugh MacLennan: A Writer's Life* (UTP, 1981).

——. 'Hugh MacLennan'. ABCMA 1 (1979), 103–53.

——, ed. *Hugh MacLennan 1982* (Canadian Studies, University College, University of Toronto, 1982).

Hoy, Helen. 'Hugh MacLennan'. CWTW Fiction 5 (1990), 149–212.

MacLeod, Alistair (1936–)

Island: The Collected Stories (M&S, 2000) reprints *The Lost Salt Gift of Blood* (1976) and *As Birds Bring Forth the Sun* (1986), and includes two uncollected stories.

A novel, *No Great Mischief*, appeared in 1999. *To Every Thing There Is a Season: A Cape Breton Christmas Story*, published separately in 2004, originally appeared in *As Birds Bring Forth the Sun*.

Interviews: Kruk (159–71), Meyer and O'Riordan 1992 (65–73).

Guilford, Irene, ed. *Alistair MacLeod: Essays on His Works* (Guernica, 2001).

McLuhan, Marshall (1911–80)

Essential McLuhan (ed. Eric McLuhan and Frank Zingrone, Concord, ON: Anansi, 1995) provides an excellent introduction, selecting from a broad range of work including *The Mechanical Bride* (1951), *The Gutenberg Galaxy* (1962), and *Understanding Media* (1964; ed. W. Terrence Gordon, 2003).

See also *The Interior Landscape: The Literary Criticism of Marshall McLuhan 1943–62* (ed. Eugene MacNamara, 1969), *Letters of Marshall McLuhan* (ed. Matie Molinaro et al., 1987), and *Understanding Me: Letters and Interviews* (ed. Stephanie McLuhan and David Staines, 2003).

Gordon, W. Terrence. *Marshall McLuhan: Escape into Understanding* (Anansi, 1997). Biography.

Rosenthal, Raymond, ed. *McLuhan Pro and Con* (New York: Funk & Wagnalls, 1968). Varied collection of articles.

The Writings of Marshall McLuhan (Fort Lauderdale, FL: Wade Brook Press, 1975, slightly expanded in 1977). Bibliography. No author given.

Macpherson, Jay (1931–)

Poems Twice Told (OUP, 1982) reprints *The Boatman* (1957, expanded 1968) and *Welcoming Disaster* (1974).

The Four Ages of Man: The Classical Myths (1962; rpt. in Frye and Macpherson, *Biblical and Classical Myths: The Mythological Framework of Western Culture*, 2004), *The Spirit of Solitude: Conventions and Continuities in Late Romance* (1982).

Atwood, Margaret. 'Jay Macpherson: *Poems Twice Told*'. *Second Words*, 407–11.

Keith, W. J. 'Jay Macpherson's *Welcoming Disaster*: A Reconsideration'. *Canadian Poetry* 36 (Spring/Summer 1995), 32–43.

Reaney, James. 'The Third Eye: Jay Macpherson's *The Boatman*. *Canadian Literature* 3 (Winter 1960), 23–34.

Mair, Charles (1838–1927)

Tecumseh: A Drama and Canadian Poems (Champlain Society, 1926) reprints *Dreamland and Other Poems* (1868), *Tecumseh* (1886), 'The American Bison', *Through the Mackenzie Basin* (1908), and 'Memoirs and Reminiscences'.

Shrive, Norman. *Charles Mair: Literary Nationalist* (UTP, 1965).

——. *The Voice of the Burdash: Charles Mair and the Divided Mind in Canadian Literature* (CPP, 1995).

Mandel, Eli (1922–92)

The Other Harmony: The Collected Poetry of Eli Mandel (2 vols., ed. Andrew Stubbs and Judy Chapman, Regina: Canada Plains Research Centre, University of Regina, 2000) is now the standard text.

Critical writings include *Irving Layton* (1969), *Another Time* (1970), and *The Family Romance* (1986). He also edited *Contexts of Modern Criticism* (1971).

Interview: Meyer and O'Riordan 1984 (107–23).

Cooley, Dennis. 'Eli Mandel'. CWTW Poetry 10 (1992), 189–277.

Jewinski, Ed, and Andrew Stubbs, eds. *The Politics of Art: Eli Mandel's Poetry and Criticism* (Amsterdam - Atlanta GA: Rodopi, 1992). An academic collection, but contains bibliographical check-list.

Metcalf, John (1938–)

Standing Stones: The Best Stories of John Metcalf (Thomas Allen, 2004) reprints *Private Parts: A Memoir, Girl in Gingham, Polly Ongle,* and a selection of short stories. His earlier stories are found in *The Lady Who Sold Furniture* (1970) and *The Teeth of My Father* (1975), the later in *Adult Entertainment* (1986). His novels are *Going Down Slow* (1972) and *General Ludd* (1980); a novella, *Forde Abroad*, appeared in 2003.

His critical writing includes *Kicking Against the Pricks* (1982), *What Is a Canadian Literature?* (1988), and *Freedom from Culture* (1994). See also his literary memoir, *An Aesthetic Underground* (2003).

Keith, W. J. 'Criticism in Practice: John Metcalf's Private Part'. *An Independent Stance* (Erin, ON: Porcupine's Quill, 1991), 107–27.

Lecker, Robert. 'John Metcalf: Unburdening the Mystery.' *On the Line* (Downsview ON: ECW 1982), 59–97.

Rollins, Douglas. 'John Metcalf'. CWTW Fiction 7 (1985), 155–211.

Mistry, Rohinton (1952–)

Tales from Firozsha Baag (short stories, 1987), *Such a Long Journey* (1991), *A Fine Balance* (1995), *Family Matters* (2002).

Leckie, Barbara. 'Rohinton Mistry,' CWTW Fiction 11 (1996), 215–66.

Morey, Peter. *Rohinton Mistry* (Manchester, UK: Manchester University Press, 2004). Provides valuable religious, social, and political background.

Mitchell, W. O. (William Ormond, 1914–98)

Fiction: *Who Has Seen the Wind* (1947) [NB: Most editions prior to 1997 were textually incomplete]), *Jake and the Kid* (short stories, 1961), *The Kite* (1962),

The Vanishing Point (1973), *How I Spent My Summer Holidays* (1981), *Since Daisy Creek* (1984), *Ladybug, Ladybug ...* (1988), *According to Jake and the Kid* (short stories, 1989), *Roses Are Difficult Here* (1990), *For Art's Sake* (1992), *The Black Bonspiel of Wullie MacCrimmon* (novella, 1993).

See also *Dramatic W. O. Mitchell* (1992), which prints texts of his plays, and *An Evening with W. O. Mitchell* (ed. Barbara and Ormond Mitchell, 1997), which presents his more popular 'performance pieces', some not previously published.

Interviews: Cameron (II 48–63), Twigg (202–07).

Latham, Sheila. 'W. O. Mitchell'. ABCMA 3 (1981), 323–64.

Latham, Sheila and David, eds. *Magic Lies: The Art of W.O. Mitchell* (UTP, 1997).

Mitchell, Barbara and Ormond. *W. O.: The [Early] Life of W. O. Mitchell* (M&S, 1999); *Mitchell: The [Later] Life of W. O. Mitchell* (M&S, 2005).

Moodie, Susanna (1803–85)

Roughing It in the Bush (1852; ed. Carl Ballstadt, CEECT, 1988 [NB: early reprints were often abridged]), *Life in the Clearings* (1853).

See also *Susanna Moodie: Letters of a Lifetime* (ed. Ballstadt et al., 1985), *Letters of Love and Duty: The Correspondence of Susanna and John Moodie* (ed. Ballstadt et al., 1993).

Peterman, Michael. *Susanna Moodie: A Life* (ECW, 1999). Concise biography.

Moore, Brian (1921–99)

Selected novels: *Judith Hearne* (1955, also published as *The Lonely Passion of Judith Hearne*), *The Feast of Lupercal* (1957), *The Luck of Ginger Coffey* (1960), *An Answer from Limbo* (1962), *The Emperor of Ice Cream* (1965), *I Am Mary Dunne* (1968), *The Revolution Script* (1971), *The Doctor's Wife* (1976), *The Mangan Inheritance* (1979), *Black Robe* (1985), *The Colour of Blood* (1987), *Lies of Silence* (1990).

Interviews: Cameron (II 64–86), Meyer and O'Riordan 1984 (169–83).

Craig, Patricia. *Brian Moore: A Biography* (London: Bloomsbury, 2002).

O'Donogue, Jo. *Brian Moore: A Critical Study* (Dublin: Gill & Macmillan, 1991).

Mowat, Farley (1921–)

The World of Farley Mowat (ed. Peter Davison, M&S, 1980) contains a representative selection from his writings. His numerous books include *The People of the Deer* (1952, rev. 1975), *The Desperate People* (1959, rev. 1975), *Never Cry Wolf* (1963), *Westviking* (1965), *A Whale for the Killing* (1972), *Sea of Slaughter* (1984), *The New Founde Land* (1989), *No Man's River* (2004), and the *Top of the World* trilogy: *Ordeal by Fire* (1960), *The Polar Passion* (1967), *Tundra* (1973), etc., etc.

See also *The Snow Walker* (short stories, 1975), *Born Naked* (autobiography, 1993), and *My Father's Son* (war memoir, 1999)

Interview: Twigg (208–14).

King, James. *Farley: The Life of Farley Mowat* (HarperFlamingo, 2002).

Munro, Alice (1931–)

Selected Stories (M&S, 1998) reprints stories from *Dance of the Happy Shades* (1968), *Something I've Been Meaning to Tell You* (1974), *Who Do You Think You Are?* (1978), *The Moons of Jupiter* (1982), and *The Progress of Love* (1986). *No Love Lost* (M&S 2003) reprints from *Who Do You Think You Are?, The Moons of Jupiter, Friend of My Youth* (1990), *Open Secrets* (1994), and *The Love of a Good Woman* (1998). *Hateship, Friendship, Courtship, Loveship, Marriage* followed in 2001, *Runaway* in 2004, and *The View from Castle Rock* in 2006. *Lives of Girls and Women* (which can be regarded either as a novel or as linked short stories) appeared in 1971.

Interviews: Gibson (241–64), Hancock (187–224), Twigg (215–19).

MacKendrick, Louis K., ed. *Probable Fictions: Alice Munro's Narrative Acts* (ECW, 1983).

Munro, Sheila. *Lives of Mothers & Daughters: Growing Up with Alice Munro* (M&S, 2001). Memoir/biography by Munro's daughter, more revealing than much literary criticsm.

Thacker, Robert. *Alice Munro: Writing Her Lives* (M&S, 2005). Detailed biography.

——. 'Alice Munro'. ABCMA 5 (1984), 354–414.

Newlove, John (1938–2003)

Apology for Absence: Selected Poems 1962–1992 (Erin, ON: Porcupine's Quill, 1993) is the standard text, and includes previously uncollected poems.

Interviews: Pearce (113–27), Meyer and O'Riordan 1992 (82–89).

Barbour, Douglas. 'John Newlove'. CWTW Poetry 10 (1992), 281–336.

Bowering, George. 'The Poetry of John Newlove'. *A Way with Words* (Ottawa: Oberon, 1982), 121–34.

Lecker, Robert, and David O'Rourke. 'John Newlove. ABCMA 6 (1985), 67–128.

Niven, Frederick John (1878–1944)

The Flying Years (1931), *Mine Inheritance* (1940), *The Transplanted* (1944).

New, W. H. 'Frederick John Niven'. DLB 92 (1990), 271–75.

Nowlan, Alden (1933–83)

An Exchange of Gifts: Poems New and Selected (ed. Robert Gibbs, Irwin, 1985) provides the best introduction to the whole range of his work. *Early Poems* (ed. Gibbs, Fredericton, NB: Fiddlehead, 1983) is an almost complete edition of his verse up to 1962.

See also *Various Persons Named Kevin O'Brien* (fictional memoir, 1973), *The Wanton Troopers* (novel, 1988).

Keith, W. J. 'The Poetry of Alden Nowlan: A Critical Reassessment'. *Canadian Poetry* 53 (Fall/Winter 2003), 9–32.

Toner, Patrick. *If I Could Turn and Meet Myself: The Life of Alden Nowlan* (Fredericton, NB: Goose Lane, 2000).

O'Hagan, Howard (1902–82)

Novels: *Tay John* (1939), *The School-Marm Tree* (1977).

See also *Wilderness Men* (non-fiction, 1958) and *The Woman Who Got On at Jasper Station* (short stories, 1963), both rpt. together as *Trees Are Lonely Company* (1993).

Fee, Margery, ed. *Silence Made Visible: Howard O'Hagan and 'Tay John'* (ECW, 1992). Contains fugitive pieces by O'Hagan, an interview, articles, and Richard Arnold's 'Howard O'Hagan: An Annotated Bibliography'.

Tanner, Ella. *'Tay John' and the Cyclical Quest* (ECW, 1990).

Ondaatje, Michael (1943–)

Poetry: *The Cinnamon Peeler: Selected Poems* (M&S, 1989) offers a good selection from his shorter poems. See also *The Man with Seven Toes* (1969), *The Collected Works of Billy the Kid* (1970), and the later *Handwriting* (1998).

Fiction: *Coming Through Slaughter* (1976), *In the Skin of a Lion* (1987), *The English Patient* (1992), *Anil's Ghost* (2000).

See also *Leonard Cohen* (1969) and *Running in the Family* (fictional memoir, 1982).

Interviews: Bowling (31–43), Daurio (115–21), Pearce (131–44).

Brady, Judith. 'Michael Ondaatje'. ABCMA 6 (1985), 129–205.

Solecki, Sam, *Ragas of Longing: The Poetry of Michael Ondaatje* (UTP, 2003). Detailed critical study.

——, ed. *Spider Blues: Essays on Michael Ondaatje* (Montréal: Véhicule, 1985).

Ormsby, Eric (1941–)

Bavarian Shrine and Other Poems (1990), *Coastlines* (1992), *For a Modest God: New and Selected Poems* (1997), *Araby* (2001), *Daybreak at the Straits* (2004).

See also *Facsimiles of Time: Essays on Poetry and Translation* (2001).

Interview: Bowling (196–212).

Canadian Notes & Queries 68 (2005). Special Ormsby issue.

O'Meara, David. 'Lustrous as the Pleiades: Splendour and Decorum in the Poetry of Eric Ormsby'. *Canadian Notes & Queries 65* (2004), 28–32.

Ostenso, Martha (1900–63)

Wild Geese (1925), now believed to have been written in collaboration with her mentor and later husband, David Durkin. Other novels include *The Young May Moon* (1929).

Atherton, Stanley S. 'Martha Ostenso'. CWTW Fiction 4 (1991), 211–53.

Outram, Richard (1930–2005)

Selected Poems 1960–1980 (Exile, 1984) and *Dove Legend* (Erin, ON: Porcupine's Quill, 2001) provide a good introduction to his shorter individual poems. His other volumes are *Man in Love* (1985), *Hiram and Jenny* (1988), *Mogul Recollected* (1993), and *Benedict Abroad* (1998).

Canadian Notes & Queries 63 (2003). Special Outram issue.

Sanger, Peter. *'Her kindled shadow ...': An Introduction to the Work of Richard Outram* (Antigonish, NS: Antigonish Review, 2001). Thorough critical study.

Page, P. K. (1916–)

The Hidden Room: Collected Poems (2 vols. Erin, ON: Porcupine's Quill, 1997) is the most complete edition of her poems, though *Hologram: A Book of Glosas* (1994) deserves to be read as a separate volume. *Planet Earth: Poems Selected and New* (ed. Eric Ormsby, 2002) incorporates *Alphabetical* (1998). *Hand Luggage: A Memoir in Verse* was published by Porcupine's Quill in 2006.

See also *A Kind of Fiction* (short stories, 2001), *The Sun and the Moon, and Other Fictions* (romance and short stories,1973), and *Brazilian Journal* (travel, 1987).

Interviews: Bowling (11–30), Pearce (147–57).

Orange, John. 'P. K. Page'. ABCMA 6 (1985), 207–85.

Smith, A. J. M. 'The Poetry of P. K. Page'. *Towards a View of Canadian Letters* (Vancouver: University of British Columbia Press, 1973), 146–55.

Sullivan, Rosemary. 'A Size Larger than Seeing: The Poetry of P. K. Page'. *Canadian Literature* 79 (Winter 1978), 32–42.

Parker, Gilbert (1860–1932)

Pierre and His People (short stories, 1892), *The Seats of the Mighty* (1896), etc., etc.

Adams, John Coldwell. *Seated with the Mighty* (Ottawa: Borealis, 1979). Biography.

Waterston, Elizabeth. 'Gilbert Parker.' CWTW Fiction 2 (1987), 107–56.

Pollock, Sharon (1936–)

Published plays include *Walsh* (1973, rev. 1989) and *Blood Relations and Other Plays* (rev. ed., 2002).

Gilbert, Reid. 'Sharon Pollock', PCL 6 (1986), 113–20. Admirably balanced discussion.

Pratt, E. J. (Edwin Jay, 1882–1964)

The Collected Works of E. J. Pratt (gen. eds. Sandra Djwa, R. G. Moyles, and, later, Zailig Pollock, UTP) includes *The Complete Poems* (2 vols., ed. Moyles and Djwa, 1989), supplemented with corrections in a hypertext edition (www.trentu.ca/pratt).

Other volumes of *The Collected Works* include *E. J. Pratt on His Life and Poetry* (ed. Susan Gingell, 1983), *Pursuits Amateur and Academic* (ed. Gingell, 1995), and *Selected Poems* (ed. Djwa, W. J. Keith, and Pollock, 2000).

Djwa, Sandra, *E. J. Pratt: The Evolutionary Vision* (Copp Clark, 1974).

Laakso, Lily. 'Descriptive Bibliography'. *The Complete Poems* 2, 373–497.

Pitt, David G. *E. J. Pratt: The Truant Years 1882–1927* (UTP, 1984) and *E. J. Pratt: The Master Years 1927–1964* (UTP, 1987). Full biography.

Purdy, Al (1918–2000)

Beyond Remembering: The Collected Poems of Al Purdy (ed. Purdy and Sam Solecki, Madeira Park: Harbour Publishing, 2000) includes all the poems Purdy wished to preserve.

See also *A Splinter in the Heart* (novel, 1992), *Reaching for the Beaufort Sea: An Autobiography* (1993), *Starting from Ameliasburg: The Collected Prose of Al Purdy* (ed. Solecki, 1995), and *Yours, Al: The Collected Letters of Al Purdy* (ed. Solecki, 2004).

Interviews: Meyer and O'Riordan 1984 (135–45), Twigg (225–30).

Essays on Canadian Writing 49 (Summer 1993). Special Purdy issue.

Micros, Marianne. 'Al Purdy'. ABCMA 2 (1980), 221–77.

Rogers, Linda, ed. *Al Purdy: Essays on His Works* (Guernica, 2003).

Solecki, Sam. *The Last Canadian Poet: An Essay on Al Purdy* (UTP, 1999).

Solway, David. 'Standard Average Canadian'. *Director's Cut* (Erin ON: Porcupine's Quill, 2003), 87–100.

Raddall, Thomas Head (1903–94)

Novels: *His Majesty's Yankees* (1942), *Roger Sudden* (1944), *Pride's Fancy* (1946), *The Nymph and the Lamp* (1950), *The Governor's Lady* (1960), *Hangman's Beach* (1966).

Short stories: *The Pied Piper of Dipper Creek* (1939), *Tambour* (1945), *The Wedding Gift* (1947), *A Muster of Arms* (1954), *At the Tide's Turn* (selected stories, 1959).

See also *In My Time* (autobiography, 1976).

Interview: Cameron (II 99–113).

Young, Alan R. 'Thomas H. Raddall'. CWTW Fiction 5 (1990), 215–57.

——. 'Thomas H. Raddall'. ABCMA 7 (1987), 403–77.

——. *Thomas Head Raddall: A Bibliography* (Kingston, ON: Loyal Colonies Press, 1982).

Reaney, James (1926–)

Poems (ed. Germaine Warkentin, Erin, ON: Press Porcepic, 1972) collects his non-dramatic verse. *Souwesto Home* appeared in 2005.

Drama: *The Killdeer and Other Plays* (1962) also includes *Night-Blooming Cereus, The Sun and the Moon,* and *One-Man Mask; Masks of Childhood* (1972) contains *The Easter Egg, Three Desks,* and a revised version of *The Killdeer.* Other plays include *Colours in the Dark* (1969), *Listen to the Wind* (1972), *The Donnellys* (1 vol ed. 1983) consisting of *Sticks and Stones* (1974), *The St. Nicholas Hotel* (1976), and *Handcuffs* (1977), *Baldoon* (with C. H. Gervais, 1976), and *Wacousta!* (1979).

Interview: Meyer and O'Riordan 1984 (57–70).

Dragland, Stan, ed. *Approaches to the Work of James Reaney* (ECW, 1983). Uneven collection, but includes interview.

Parker, Gerald D. *How to Play: The Theatre of James Reaney* (ECW, 1991).

Richardson, John (1796–1852)

Selected fiction: *Wacousta* (1832; ed. Douglas Cronk, CEECT, 1987 [NB: earlier reprints were often corrupt]), *The Canadian Brothers* (1840; ed. David Stephens, CEECT, 1992).

See also *Tecumseh* (play, 1828), *Major John Richardson: A Selection of Reviews and Criticism* (ed. Carl Ballstadt, 1982), and *John Richardson's Short Stories* (ed. David Beasley, 1985).

Beasley, David. *The Canadian Don Quixote* (Erin, ON: Porcupine's Quill, 1977). Biography.

Duffy, Dennis. 'John Richardson'. CWTW Fiction 1 (1983), 107–46.

Morley, F. E. *A Bibliographical Study of Major John Richardson* (Bibliographical Society of Canada, 1973).

Richler, Mordecai (1931–2000)

The Acrobats (1954), *Son of a Smaller Hero* (1955), *A Choice of Enemies* (1957), *The Apprenticeship of Duddy Kravitz* (1959), *The Incomparable Atuk* (1963), *Cocksure* (1968), *The Street* (short stories, 1969), *St. Urbain's Horseman* (1971), *Joshua Then and Now* (1980), *Solomon Gursky Was Here* (1989; best read in later editions containing family-tree), *Barney's Version* (1997).

Journalistic non-fiction includes *Hunting Tigers Under Glass* (1968), *Shovelling Trouble* (1972), *Notes on an Endangered Species* (1974), *Home Sweet Home*

(1984), *Oh! Canada! Oh Quebec!* (1992), *This Year in Jerusalem* (1994), *Belling the Cat* (1998).

Interviews: Cameron (II 114–27), Daurio (141–52), Gibson (269–99).

Darling, Michael, 'Mordecai Richler'. ABCMA 1 (1979), 155–211.

——, ed. *Perspectives on Mordecai Richler* (ECW, 1986).

McSweeney, Kerry. 'Mordecai Richler'. CWTW Fiction 6 (1985), 131–79.

Posner, Michael. *The Last Honest Man. Mordecai Richler: An Oral Biography* (M&S, 2004). Despite the absurd title, a highly revealing compilation.

Ringwood, Gwen Pharis (1910–1984)

Collected Plays (ed. Enid Delgatty Rutland, Ottawa: Borealis, 1982).

Anthony, Geraldine. *Gwen Pharis Ringwood* (Boston: Twayne, 1981).

Johnson, Chris. 'Gwen Pharis Ringwood'. DLB 88 (1989), 260–65.

Roberts, Charles G. D. (1860–1943)

The Collected Poems (ed. Desmond Pacey and Graham Adams, Wolfville, NS: Wombat, 1985) is now the standard edition.

Selected fiction: *The Heart of the Ancient Wood* (novel, 1900), *The Heart That Knows* (novel, 1906), For his animal stories, the best introduction is *Selected Animal Stories* (ed. Terry Whalen, Ottawa: Tecumseh, 2005).

Selections from his critical prose may be found in *Charles G. D. Roberts: Selected Poetry and Critical Prose* (ed. W. J. Keith, UTP, 1974).

Adams, John Coldwell. *Sir Charles God Damn: The Life of Sir Charles G. D. Roberts* (UTP 1986).

Clever, Glenn, ed. *The Charles G. D. Roberts Symposium* (Ottawa: University of Ottawa Press, 1984). Uneven collection, but contains John Coldwell Adams's 'A Preliminary Bibliography'.

Cogswell, Fred. 'Charles G. D. Roberts'. CWTW Poetry 2 (1983), 187–232.

Whalen, Terry. 'Charles G. D. Roberts'. CWTW Fiction 2 (1989), 159–214.

Rooke, Leon (1934–)

The most accessible collections of short stories are *Sing Me No Love Songs I'll Say You No Prayers* (New York: Ecco, 1984), *The Happiness of Others* (Erin, ON: Porcupine's Quill, 1991), and *Painting the Dog: The Best Stories of Leon Rooke* (Thomas Allen, 2001). There is little overlap.

Selected novels: *Fat Woman* (1980), *Shakespeare's Dog* (1983), *A Good Baby* (1989), *The Fall of Gravity* (2001), *The Beautiful Wife* (2005).

See also *Hot Poppies* (poems, 2005).

Interviews: Hancock (164–86), Meyer and O'Riordan 1992 (91–99), O'Brien (285–308).

Canadian Fiction Magazine 38 (1981). Special Rooke issue.

Gorjup, Branko, ed. *White Gloves of the Doorman: The Works of Leon Rooke* (Exile, 2004). Includes reviews, critical essays, two interviews and a full bibliography.

Ross, Sinclair (1908–96)

As For Me and My House (1941), *The Well* (1958), *The Lamp at Noon* (short stories, 1968), *Whir of Gold* (1970), *Sawbones Memorial* (1982), *The Race and Other Stories* (ed. Lorraine McMullen, 1982).

Latham, David. 'Sinclair Ross'. ABCMA 3 (1981), 365–95.

Ross, Morton L. 'Sinclair Ross'. CWTW Fiction 4 (1991), 257–98.

Stouck, David. *As For Sinclair Ross* (UTP, 2005). Biography.

——, ed. *Sinclair Ross's 'As For Me and My House': Five Decades of Criticism* (UTP, 1991). Comprehensive anthology of criticism – good, bad, and indifferent.

Ross, W. W. E. (William Wroughton Eustace, 1894–1966)

Shapes & Sounds (ed. Raymond Souster and John Robert Colombo, Don Mills, ON: Longmans, 1968) is the standard edition of his verse.

See also *A Literary Friendship: The Correspondence of Ralph Gustafson and W. W. E. Ross* (ed. Bruce Whiteman, 1984).

Precosky, Don. 'W. W. E. Ross'. CWTW Poetry 3 (1987), 163–88.

Ryga, George (1932–87)

Plays: Best known for *The Ecstasy of Rita Joe* (1970), his other plays all collected in *George Ryga: The Other Plays* (ed. James Hoffman, Vancouver: Talonbooks, 2004).

The Athabasca George Ryga (ed. E. David Gregory, 1990) includes stories and essays. *Summerland* (ed. Anne Kujundzic, 1992) includes short stories, essay, and radio dramas. His novels are collected in *The Prairie Novels* (ed. Hoffman, 2004).

Hoffman, James. *The Ecstasy of Resistance: A Biography of George Ryga* (ECW, 1995).

Salverson, Laura (1890–1970)

The Viking Heart (novel, 1923), *Confessions of an Immigrant's Daughter* (autobiography, 1939).

Hjartarson, Paul. 'Laura Goodman Salverson'. DLB 92 (316–19).

Sangster, Charles (1822–93)

The St. Lawrence and the Saguenay (1856), *Hesperus and Other Poems and Lyrics* (1860), *Norland Echoes* (ed. Frank M. Tierney, 1976), *The Angel Guest and*

Other Poems (ed. Tierney, 1978). See also 'The St. Lawrence and the Saguenay' (title poem only, ed. D. M. R. Bentley, CPP, 1990).

Latham, David. 'Charles Sangster'. PCL 5 (1986), 41–48.

Tierney, Frank M. *The Journeys of Charles Sangster: A Biographical and Critical Investigation* (Ottawa: Tecumseh, 2000).

Sarah, Robyn (1949–)

The Touchstone: Poems New and Selected (Concord, ON: Anansi, 1992) covers her earlier poems. Also *Questions About the Stars* (1998) and *A Day's Grace* (2003), and two volumes of short stories.

Scobie, Stephen (1943–)

The Spaces In Between: Selected Poems 1965–2001 (Edmonton: NeWest, 2003) reprints shorter poems. Not included are *McAlmon's Chinese Opera* (1980), *The Ballad of Isabel Gunn* (1987), 'The Dunino Elegies' from *Dunino* (1989), *Gospel* (1994), *Taking the Gate* (1996), and *And Forget My Name* (1999).

Scott, Duncan Campbell (1862–1947)

Poetry: *The Magic House* (1893), *Labour and the Angel* (1898), *New World Lyrics and Ballads* (1905), *Lundy's Lane* (1916), *Poems* (1926), *The Green Cloister* (1935).

Short stories: *In the Village of Viger* (1891), *The Witching of Elspie* (1923), *Uncollected Short Stories* (ed. Tracy Ware, CPP, 2001).

The Circle of Affection (1947) contains both poems and short stories.

See also *Duncan Campbell Scott: Addresses, Essays, and Reviews* (2 vols., ed. Leslie Ritchie, CPP, 2000), McDougall, R. L., ed. *The Poet and the Critic: A Literary Correspondence between D. C. Scott and E. K. Brown* (1983).

Dragland, S. L., ed. *Duncan Campbell Scott: A Book of Criticism* (Ottawa: Tecumseh, 1974).

——. *Floating Voice: Duncan Campbell Scott and the Literature of Treaty* (Concord, ON: Anansi, 1994).

Groening, Laura. 'Duncan Campbell Scott'. ABCMA 8 (1994), 469–576.

Johnston, Gordon. 'Duncan Campbell Scott'. CWTW Poetry 2 (1983), 235–89.

Scott, F. R. (Francis Reginald, 1899–1985)

Collected Poems (M&S 1984) is the standard text for his poetry. See also *A New Endeavour: Selected Political Essays, Letters and Addresses* (ed. Michiel Horn, 1986).

Djwa, Sandra. *The Politics of the Imagination: A Life of F. R. Scott* (M&S, 1987).

——. 'F. R. Scott'. CWTW 4 (1990), 173–227.

Djwa, Sandra, and R. St. J. Macdonald, eds. *On F. R. Scott: Essays on His Contribution to Law, Literature, and Politics* (MQUP, 1983).

Still, Robert. 'F. R. Scott'. ABCMA 4 (1983), 205–65.

Seton, Ernest Thompson (1860–1946)

Wild Animals I Have Known (1898), *Lives of the Hunted* (1901), *Animal Heroes* (1905), *Trail of an Artist-Naturalist* (autobiography, 1940), etc., etc.

Keller, Betty. *Black Wolf: The Life of Ernest Thompson Seton* (Vancouver: Douglas & McIntyre, 1984).

McMullen, Lorraine. 'Ernest Thompson Seton'. CWTW Fiction 2 (1989), 217–70.

Wadland, John. *Ernest Thompson Seton: Man and Nature in the Progressive Era* (New York: Arno, 1978).

Smart, Elizabeth (1913–86)

By Grand Central Station I Sat Down and Wept (1945), *The Assumption of the Rogues and Rascals* (1978), *The Collected Poems* (1992, incorporating *A Bonus*, 1977).

Non-Fiction Prose: *Necessary Secrets* (journals, ed. Alice Van Wart, 1984), *Autobiographies* (ed. Christina Burridge, 1987), *On the Side of the Angels* (journals, ed. Van Wart, 1994).

Interview: Meyer and O'Riordan 1984 (185–96).

Sullivan, Rosemary. *By Heart: Elizabeth Smart's Life* (Viking 1991).

Weir, Lorraine. 'Elizabeth Smart'. DLB 88 (1989), 296–99.

Smith, A. J. M. (Arthur James Marshall, 1902–80)

The best single edition of Smith's verse is *Poems New and Collected* (OUP, 1967). See also *News of the Phoenix* (1943), *A Sort of Ecstasy* (1954), *The Classic Shade: Selected Poems* (1978).

Selected Criticism: *Towards a View of Canadian Letters* (1973), *On Poetry and Poets* (1977).

Edited *The Book of Canadian Poetry* (1943) and *Masks of Poetry* (1962).

Canadian Poetry 11 (Fall/Winter 1982). Special Smith memorial issue.

Compton, Anne. *A. J. M. Smith: Canadian Metaphysical* (ECW, 1994). Thorough critical study.

Darling, Michael. 'A. J. M. Smith'. CWTW Poetry 4 (1990), 231–86.

——. *A. J. M. Smith: An Annotated Bibliography* (Montréal: Véhicule, 1981).

Solway, David (1941–)

Selected Poems (Montréal: Véhicule, 1982) provides a good anthology of his earlier verse. Other volumes include *Stones in Water* (1983), *Modern Marriage* (1987), *Bedrock* (1993), *Chess Pieces* (1999), *Saracen Island: The Poems of Andreas Karavis* (2000), *The Lover's Progress* (2001), *Franklin's Passage* (2003), *The Pallikari of Nesmine Rifat* (2004), *Reaching for Clear* (2006).

Translation: *Demilunes: Little Windows in Québec* (Victoria: Frog Hollow Press, 2005).

Prose: *The Anatomy of Arcadia* (travel diary, 1992), *Random Walks: Essays on Elective Criticism* (1997), *An Andreas Karavis Companion* (2000), *Director's Cut* (on contemporary Canadian poetry, 2003), and three volumes on education.

Starnino, Carmine, ed. *David Solway: Essays on His Works* (Guernica, 2001).

Souster, Raymond (1921–)

The Collected Poems (10 vols. to date, Ottawa: Oberon, 1980–2004) represents a mammoth reprinting of the poems he wishes to preserve.

Interview: Meyer and O'Riordan 1984 (87–96), Pearce (161–73).

Whiteman, Bruce. *Collected Poems of Raymond Souster: Bibliography* (Ottawa: Oberon, 1984).

——. 'Raymond Souster'. CWTW 5 (1985), 237–76.

Starnino, Carmine (1970–)

The New World (1997), *Credo* (2000), *With English Subtitles* (2004).

See also *A Lover's Quarrel* (2004). Challenging poetry criticism.

Stead, Robert (1880–1959)

The Homesteaders (1916), *Neighbours* (1922), *The Smoking Flax* (1924), *Grain* (1926), *Dry Water* (ed. Prem Varma, 1983), etc., etc.

Thompson, Eric. 'Robert Stead'. CWTW Fiction 3 (1988), 215–76.

Stegner, Wallace (1909–93)

Relevant here for *Wolf Willow: A History, a Story, and a Memory of the Last Plains Frontier* (1962).

Benson, Jackson J. *Wallace Stegner: His Life and Work* (New York: Viking, 1996).

Robinson, Forrest G. and Margaret G. *Wallace Stegner* (Boston: Twayne, 1977).

Swan, Mary (1953–)

The Deep: A Novella (2002), also published with short stories as *The Deep and Other Stories* (New York, 2003), *Emma's Hands* (short stories, 2003).

Thompson, David (1770–1857)

David Thompson's Narrative of his Explorations in North America 1784–1812 (ed. J. B. Tyrrell, Champlain Society, 1916; rev. ed., Richard Glover, 1962).

Jenish, D'Arcy. *Epic Wanderer: David Thompson and the Mapping of the Canadian West* (Doubleday, 2003).

Warkentin, Germaine. 'David Thompson'. PCL 1 (1980), 1–8.

Traill, Catharine Parr (1802–99)

The Backwoods of Canada (1836; ed. Michael A. Peterman, CEECT, 1997

[NB: 1966 NCL edition was highly abridged]), *The Canadian Crusoes* (1852; ed. Rupert Schieder, CEECT, 1986), *The Female Emigrant's Guide* (1852, rpt. as *The Canadian Settler's Guide*), *Canadian Wild Flowers* (1868).

See also *Forest and Other Gleanings: The Fugitive Writings of Catharine Parr Traill* (ed. Michael A. Peterman et al., 1994), *I Bless You in My Heart: Selected Correspondence* (ed. Carl Ballstadt et al., 1996).

Ballstadt, Carl. 'Catharine Parr Traill'. CWTW 1 (1983), 149–93.

Vassanji, M. G. (1950–)

The Gunny Sack (1989), *No New Land* (1991), *Uhuru Street* (short stories, 1992), *The Book of Secrets* (1994), *Amriika* (1999), *The In-Between World of Vikram Lall* (2003), *When She Was Queen* (short stories, 2005).

Interview: Daurio (200–209).

Kanaganayakam, Chelva. 'M. G. Vassanji'. *Configurations of Exile: South Asian Writers and Their World* (TSAR, 1995), 127–37. Primarily an interview.

Rhodes, Shane. 'M. G. Vassanji: An Interview'. *Studies in Canadian Literature* 22.2 (1997), 105–117.

Waddington, Miriam (1917–2004)

Collected Poems (OUP 1986) is the standard text for her verse. She also published *The Last Landscape* (1992).

See also *Summer at Lonely Beach* (short stories, 1982), *Apartment Seven: Selected Essays* (1989).

Interviews: Bowling (184–95), Pearce (177–87).

Ricou, Laurie. 'Miriam [Dworkin] Waddington'. ABCMA 6 (1985), 287–388.

——. 'Miriam Waddington'. DLB 68 (1988), 334–39.

Walker, George F. (1947–)

His numerous plays are best sampled in *Shared Anxiety: Selected Plays* (Coach House, 1994).

Interview: Wallace and Zimmerman (212–25).

Johnson, Chris. *Playing with Anxiety: Essays on George Walker* (Winnipeg: Blizzard, 1999).

Wallace, Bronwen (1945–89)

Marrying into the Family (published with Mary di Michele's *Bread and Chocolate*, 1980), *Signs of the Former Tenant* (1983), *Common Magic* (1985), *The Stubborn Particulars of Grace* (1987), *Keep That Candle Burning Bright* (1991). Short stories and essays have appeared posthumously.

Interview: Meyer and O'Riordan 1992 (100–107).

Open Letter, Seventh series (Winter 1991). Special Wallace memorial issue. Too feminist/political in emphasis but contains excellent critical article by J. M. Kertzer (71–87).

Watson, Sheila (1919–98)

The Double Hook (novel, 1959), *Deep Hollow Creek* (novel, 1992, but written in 1930s), *A Father's Kingdom: The Complete Short Stories* (2004). 'Sheila Watson: A Collection', a special issue of *Open Letter,* Third Series, No.1 (Winter 1974–5) prints several prose pieces as well as stories.

Interview: Meyer and O'Riordan 1984 (157–67).

Bowering, George, ed. *Sheila Watson and 'The Double Hook'* (Ottawa: Golden Dog, 1985).

Flahiff, F. T. *Always Someone to Kill the Doves: A Life of Sheila Watson* (Edmonton: NeWest, 2005).

Webb, Phyllis (1927–)

The Vision Tree: Selected Poems (Vancouver: Talonbooks 1982) is a good introduction to her work. Subsequent volumes include *Water and Light: Ghazals and Anti Ghazals* (1984), *Hanging Fire* (1990).

Her essays include *Talking* (1982) and *Nothing But Brush Strokes: Selected Prose* (1995).

Interview: Bowling (225–43).

Hulcoop, John F. 'Phyllis Webb'. DLB 53 (1986), 372–79.

Frey, Cecelia. ABCMA 6 (1985), 387–448.

Wiebe, Rudy (1934–)

Novels: *Peace Shall Destroy Many* (1962), *First and Vital Candle* (1966), *The Blue Mountains of China* (1970), *The Temptations of Big Bear* (1973), *The Scorched-Wood People* (1977), *The Mad Trapper* (1980), *My Lovely Enemy* (1983), *A Discovery of Strangers* (1994), *Sweeter Than All the World* (2001).

Short stories: *Where Is the Voice Coming From?* (1974), *Alberta: A Celebration* (1979), *The Angel of the Tar Sands* (1982), *River of Stone: Fictions and Memories* (1995).

Other works include *Playing Dead: A Contemplation Concerning the Arctic* (1989), *Far As the Eye Can See* (play, 1977), *Of This Earth* (memoir, 2006).

Interview: Cameron (II 146–60), O'Brien (71–100), Twigg (280–86).

Keith, W. J. *Epic Fiction: The Art of Rudy Wiebe* (Edmonton: University of Alberta Press, 1981).

——, ed. *A Voice in the Land: Essays by and about Rudy Wiebe* (Edmonton: NeWest, 1981). Contains interviews.

Wilkinson, Anne (1910–61)

Heresies: The Complete Poems of Anne Wilkinson (ed. Dean Irvine, Montréal: Véhicule, 2003) is now the standard text for her verse. See also *The Tightrope Walker: Autobiographical Writings of Anne Wilkinson* (ed. Joan Coldwell, 1992).

Smith, A. J. M. 'A Reading of Anne Wilkinson'. *Towards a View of Canadian Letters* (Vancouver: University of British Columbia Press, 1973), 134–41.

Stevens, Peter. 'Anne Wilkinson'. DLB 88 (1989), 339–42.

Wilson, Ethel (1888–1980)

Hetty Dorval (1947), *The Innocent Traveller* (1949), *The Equations of Love* (1952), *Swamp Angel* (1954; ed. Li-Ping Geng, Ottawa: Tecumseh, 2005), *Love and Salt Water* (1956), *Mrs. Golightly and Other Stories* (1961). See also *Ethel Wilson: Stories, Essays, Letters* (ed. David Stouck, 1982).

McComb, Bonnie Martyn. 'Ethel Wilson'. ABCMA 5 (1984). 415–80.

McMullen, Lorraine, ed. *The Ethel Wilson Symposium* (Ottawa: University of Ottawa Press, 1982).

Stouck, David. *Ethel Wilson: A Critical Biography* (UTP, 2003).

Index

NB: Volume One contains its own index.

W. J. Keith was born and raised in England. He came to Canada in 1958 where he taught at McMaster (1961–66), then later at the University of Toronto (1966–95). Since 1995 he has held the position of Professor Emeritus of English at University College, University of Toronto.

His published work includes *Epic Fiction: The Art of Rudy Wiebe,* University of Alberta Press, 1981. *A Sense of Style: Studies in the Art of Fiction in English-Speaking Canada,* ECW Press, 1989. *An Independent Stance: Essays on English-Canadian Criticism and Fiction,* PQL, 1991. *Literary Images of Ontario,* University of Toronto Press, 1992 and *Canadian Odyssey: A Reading of Hugh Hood's The New Age/Le nouveau siècle,* McGill-Queen's University Press, 2002. Mr Keith has also published poetry, most recently *In the Beginning and Other Poems,* St. Thomas Poetry Series, 1999.

W. J. Keith edited the *University of Toronto Quarterly* (1976–85), and was elected a Fellow of the Royal Society of Canada in 1979.